To Audrey.

For y... ...

health!

Michel!

Oct 1983.

W9-CRA-780

Bake uncovered 5-10 minutes depending on fillets thickness till 3/4 cooked. Remove from oven. Add Tofu. Sprinkle with scal...

Russ Redmond

GOLDEN DOOR COOKBOOK

GOLDEN DOOR COOKBOOK

THE GREENING OF AMERICAN CUISINE

By Deborah Szekely
with Chef Michel Stroot

Golden Door,® Escondido, California 92025, U.S.A.

Editor: Roberta Ridgely
Design & Photography: Vivian Blackstone Lorrance
Illustrations: Michel Stroot
Cover: Vegetables from the 'Golden Door' garden
        photographed by Vivian Blackstone Lorrance

CONTENTS

FOREWORD

Why have the 'Golden Door' (founded in 1959) and Rancho La Puerta (the grand old lady of spas, who first opened her puerta in 1940) never published a cookbook?

The answer lies in perfectionism, that quality which has been the very life breath of the sister spas. Yet perfectionism can have its drawbacks. Several cookbooks were completed but aborted before publication, because upon consideration I felt they were good but not sufficiently exceptional.

Eureka! At long last here is the Golden Door Cookbook, a cookbook so good and so different that I can present it with complete pride. My delight grew apace as I read each newly completed chapter. And I acquiesced to our guests' demands that we publish the book ourselves so that the Golden Door Cookbook can without delay become your way of life.

Deborah Szekely,
founder, The Golden Door (1958);
co-founder, Rancho La Puerta (1940)

In this book, you will find the essence of 40 years of kitchen lore, adapted and refined during the last seven years under the very special, loving care of our superb chef Michel Stroot.

Michel and I wish to thank Shirley Matson, who helped organize the recipes when the book was first begun; Elaine Zola and Jill Morgan, who tested and added their own individual dash to the recipes; and Roberta Ridgely, who edited them. To Vivian Blackstone Lorrance goes the credit for the photographs of our 'Golden Door' gardens and food, and for the design of the book.

Please read well the first three chapters. In a quintessential nutshell they will introduce you to the 'Golden Door' way of life. Once you have tried it, you will wish to lead no other. Once you have joyfully balanced energy food and food energy, you will be prideful of your hardier, heartier newfound self. And you will respond to the fresh excitement of each passing day.

— Deborah Szekely

THE ZEST AND THE SURPRISE OF GOLDEN DOOR COOKERY

For 42 years I have made my livelihood by talking about food—about what choices you must consider if you wish a long and healthy life, and about what your food must continue to mean to you if you would live that life with great joy. Now I am in the position of being able to say an unqualified, "I told you so!"

Today, even the commercial food industry and many elegant restaurants reflect the tremendous national acceptance of what most recently has been called "the American* cuisine," is otherwise being referred to as "the new California cuisine," a few years ago was promoted in this country as an import called "la nouvelle cuisine," and which as "the 'Golden Door' cuisine" predates all those other terms.

No less gratifying than the growing U.S. popularity of the kind of food selection and cooking methods that distinguish the 'Golden Door' table is the increasing substantiation by the medical profession of the theory that, in most case histories of killer diseases, one's own personal menu becomes Chapter I; and that the results of bad dietary habits can be reversible if you eat wisely (and also eat less).

It was through many, many years of studying food, its properties, its history, its psychology, that I came to realize the significance of the way in which our human ancestors passed their daily lives...hard, hard, dawn-to-dusk work ...climbing trees to investigate what grew on them...digging up a grub here...ferreting out a hidden egg there... hours of wading icy streams to catch a fish...centuries upon centuries of waking hours passed in pursuit of food. Man the seed-gatherer. Man the wanderer. Grouping together in this pursuit, making long treks from waterhole to waterhole. Gradually, these paths of migration became routes of travel, the caravan trails of antiquity. In time, primitive, back-breaking farming methods developed; some of the nomads settled down to the land. Even shortly before the Renaissance, voyager Marco Polo (like Renaissance explorer Christopher Columbus) mainly sought new sources for edibles.

Just as man's body was created for a life of continuous movement, it was also dependent upon natural foods with undiminished nutrients. And, powering the urge to move and the urge to eat was Nature's survival mechanism, the human appetite. It motivated man to survive in harsh, unfriendly environments, to pit himself against other creatures in the hunt. In time, it made him a social animal. Group protection of food sources was the basis of society.

I knew that neither man nor his needs had basically changed. He must move normally and eat naturally, and do so in a way to satisfy the appetite, that great motivational force which has perpetuated our species for tens of thousands of years.

This theory is the basis of the talks I have always shared with each week's 'Golden Door' guests. I have expounded to them upon the necessity for accepting one's appetite for what it is — a marvelous survival mechanism. I have entreated those who have been brainwashed into thinking that they no longer need express any interest in food, and I have urged them to understand that food is more than just fuel. The quality of food determines the quality of our life, so closely are they connected.

Unfortunately, technology has modified modern daily life so that our desire for food exceeds our activity. Therefore we must adjust that food/activity balance (see pages ix-xii).

We must neither deny food nor let it take over our lives. Look to food as only one of the satisfactions that come our way. If no big love dominates one's existence, learn to indulge enthusiasms, to cultivate small contentments and little loves. The key word here is "small" or "little." If you allow some intense enthusiasm to absorb your interest

*Quoted from the First Symposium on the American Cuisine, held in Louisville in 1982. The symposium's conclusion about what constitutes American cuisine: extensive use of fresh fruits, vegetables, and mushrooms; fish; locally grown and produced foods; fresh rather than frozen; light sauces only; baked rather than fried meats; traditional dishes with new methods and ingredients; and, borrowed from the Far East, stir-frying plus emphasis upon food's visual appeal.

FETE YOURSELF WITH FRESH, FRESH, FLAVOR-FULL FOODS IN FASCINATING NEW TASTE COMBINATIONS

and energy, causing you to skip meals or show little interest in them, it will lead to a serious fuel imbalance in your body.

To lose all interest in food is to cancel out existence.

Think of eating as a glorious daily adventure. Become sensually aware of food. Imagine that you are making a trip with me to a Saturday market. I love to travel, and I've hundreds of memories of Saturday marketplaces: the lively hustle-bustle, colors, fragrances, captivating displays everywhere, everything strange and alluring. Such markets are the source of food stuffs for perhaps the majority of the world's population.

For contrast, compare that scene with our sterile supermarkets and the maze you follow from shelf to shelf. D. D. Williams, who founded the first supermarket, said (we quote D. D. Williams, Jr.) he built in this plan so that foot traffic from entrance to cash register could be controlled exactly like a cattle run.

Strongly painted placards and other printed signs flash across your vision as you shop. Brightly colored bottles and boxes and cans compete for your attention. But they give a poor imitation of a marketplace alive with fresh, whole, aromatic foods. Think about this the next time you're in a supermarket. Then make a beeline for the fresh fruits and vegetables, the eggs, and the cheeses.

You know the kind of food I'm talking about. Vivid colors and scents and tastes!

Step into your backyard. Do you already have a salad growing there? All it takes is a few fresh herbs, some leaf lettuce, green onions, red radishes. These and other vegetables can flourish right beside your flowers. We do it very successfully at the 'Golden Door.' Working in that garden is one of the unexpected pleasures our guests appreciate and exclaim about.

Variety of life implies variety in food. Fortunately, tantalizing flavors satisfy appetite even though their quantity be small. When you eat dull food, more and more of it is required for satisfaction.

If you are following today's trend among enlightened Americans, you are a very interesting shopping statistic. You are purchasing more yogurt, crop products, chicken, fish, margarine, and low-fat milk. That's great, and I don't mind if you accord some of the credit to my influence.

You're buying fewer potatoes, probably because you intend to cut down on starches. Potatoes are widely misunderstood. The only problem with them is what topping you select to put on the nutritious, not-high-calorie spud.

The average adult American annually consumes 67.8 pounds of salad greens and related ingredients, plus 12.9 pints of salad dressing. Good news only in part. Too many of those pints of dressing are prefabricated. I hope you won't ever deaden your fresh, gleaming 'Golden Door' salads with bottled dressings. The latter are a trap for hidden sugar and salt, and contain too much poor-quality oil.

Oils . . . fats . . . our national undoing. We double the fats incorporated into the Oriental diet; consequently, despite a recent reduction of heart attacks in the U.S., we are not a truly heart-healthy nation.

To duplicate many delightful Continental recipes, the 'Golden Door' in this book has shared its technique of quickly cooking in a heavy pan, over a medium fire, with only a dab of oil. Once you become accustomed to the incomparable lightness of this food, you'll never again want to violate true flavor with heavy sauces.

Undoubtedly you have by now been thoroughly acquainted with the findings of the two-year cancer study circulated by the National Academy of Sciences. My dear friend Dr. Clifford Grobstein was the chairman of the academy's committee. He says, "The evidence is increasingly impressive that what we eat does affect our chances of getting cancer." Number One recommendation: Decrease your consumption of foods high in fat, whether saturated or unsaturated.

The most ironic fact about our country's current food-buying habits is that people are consciously decreasing their purchases of sugar, per se. But due to consumption of soft drinks and prepared foods, our sugar intake remains appalling. I know that the ubiquitous soft drink isn't always easy to avoid. We are often exposed to the unedifying example of well-rated hospitals pouring soft drinks for the patients' trays! And piling on potato chips and hamburgers and sugar- and fat-heavy pastries!

So-called "diet" soft drinks are in a sense even worse than the originals for which they are named. They are especially bad for dieters, since they are clogged with chemicals which the dieting body, in particular, retains.

Here we are, creatures who once lived in the sea as fishes. When we first crept onto land, we sealed off within ourselves a part of the sea, forever keeping a saline fluid in our bodies. A millennium later, it still resembles the fluid of eons ago. If we suffer trauma, a saline solution is immediately prescribed—not a soft-drink fix, not a cola with its 9.2 teaspoons of sugar in one 12-ounce can.

Thirst is as urgent and elemental as hunger. Because the human body is a fluid medium, we must constantly replenish whatever fluid we lose daily. Children in particular play hard, perspire freely, feel warm, and turn up frequently at the refrigerator door. No doubt our youngsters, sad to say, are in large part responsible for running up those scary, astronomical soft-drink consumption figures.

The figures are puzzling when one considers that fresh-fruit sales are on the rise. Do try to wean your children with some of the fresh-fruit concoctions in the Beverages section (pages 137-141). Better still, if the children are small enough that a project seems like play, let them learn to mix their own. Children love to putter in a kitchen. Boys as well as girls, they love to make magic by baking. Kids who become familiar with the splendid ingredients in the whole-grain Breads chapter (pages 109-119) will grow up to disdain junk food as old-fashioned and no-class.

The press has furnished you with remarkable input about the killer diseases directly or possibly related to the use of excess sugar and salt. (Did you know that many nutri-

tionists now suspect that these two culprits may also be inimical to a good night of restful sleep?) Some of the newest disclosures about salt have been unusually upsetting. Even cottage cheese (excepting the uncreamed variety) and tuna and canned crab and so-called low-sodium soy sauce* are loaded. But don't be alarmed by the occasional use of them in this book — if you are generally following a 'Golden Door' menu plan, all the other genuine low-sodium recipes will offset these few exceptions.

A bright prospect is the likelihood that future salt content of all canned and packaged food will be more clearly identified on the label.

As for additives, even a 1982 poll taken inside the food industry revealed the public's distrust of them. (According to Louis Harris & Associates, 80% of those polled worried about the safety of food with additives.)

To turn your back on the pleasures of food is anti-survival. To eat the wrong food is anti-survival. And, since Nature intended foods to spoil and then ultimately to re-enrich the earth from which they came, to fill food with preservatives is anti-survival.

You wouldn't have bought this book if you didn't plan to survive.

*Soy sauce and bourbon, half and half, make an effective substitute now being adopted. Remember it if you wish to cut down on salt. In any of this book's recipes calling for low-sodium soy sauce, half bourbon and half l.s. soy sauce will do nicely and be thoroughly acceptable to your taste buds.

THE PRIDE AND JOY OF EXERCISE

People are the only self-endangered species.

As adults, we often live as carelessly as we did as teenagers — careless then, dangerous to ourselves today. After hours of sitting in school, we at least rose up and turned to. Very often, much of the high-energy part of the day still lay ahead.

And now? Unless we are running a ranch from the back of a horse, or raising six small kids, most of us are chair-bound at some sort of work for around eight hours each day. During that time, as you sit with body compressed, for every breath you inhale, you exhale a bit less, till at day's end your body is truly heavier.

How do you handle that? Too many merely exchange the desk chair for the car seat for the sofa in front of the TV set. In addition to your accumulation of unexpelled air, there's also a burden of unresolved tensions; impatiences and annoyances which, though felt strongly at the time, received no appropriate release. (Remember, stress need not be negative. I call it a growth hormone. It becomes negative only if you do not resolve it.)

So what do you do? Say the hell with it? Fix a quick drink to make you feel less tired (since a drink is a sedative, this is a contradiction in terms)...to make the TV news hour easier to take...to make those sit-com programs seem less boring?

What you really need, of course, is to fit your real physical self into your present-day life.

Real people weren't designed to sit indefinitely — if Nature had intended that, she would have provided us with some sort of marvelous tail-like appendage.

Real people weren't meant to be ignored, even by themselves.

I suggest that, instead of vaguely recognizing your attachment to a real body which you sometimes confess you possibly should do something about, some day, you start now, in this manner:

Let your consciousness enter your body. Try it! Pull it in, all the way!

At first, this may be a difficult accomplishment. And it may be much like meeting a stranger. (Sadly, you and your body very likely have become total strangers.) You may have to engage in superficial small talk about nothing of consequence while you try to become comfortable with each other. But do keep some sort of dialogue going. The point is to reopen a Physiology IA acquaintance with your vital systems — your faithfully functioning heart, your obediently circulating blood, your often-neglected lungs.

At length, you will move along to acquiring a vocabulary and an ease of understanding. And then you can establish a thriving mutual relationship, instead of the old one-sided one to which you contributed so little.

Become your body's best friend. You'll find it well worth knowing well.

Practice your dialogue in the morning as you stretch, s-t-r-e-t-c-h awake. Then feel your body by cupping your hands to pat-pat yourself from head to toe. As you do so, send yourself silent messages of encouragement. For a few minutes, as you lie in bed, center all your attention upon — and within — your body. Stretch tense muscles, relax them; tense other muscles, relax again.

Recognize this incredible instrument, this sender and receiver of all your most-intimate messages, this communicator of every tension, every pain, every joy. You will learn to recognize many bodily messages, and to intuit others. Just as children perceptively tell their father, "We'd better watch out. Mom's rattling the pots and pans in the kitchen," or as a wife surmises the meaning when her husband absently but doggedly mows the same patch of lawn five or six times, so you will read your own body's tell-tale signs and portents.

Work together, plan together. Several times daily, review your personal schedule and interview your physical self. Analyze. Learn when you are most uptight, when you most need to be unwound, when you will be most gratified by strokes. Tune in on your inner rhythms, and match them to Nature's powerful pendulum swing.

Consider that basic law of thermodynamics: Every form of energy is converted to another form. Make it work and win for you. Not only analyze the type of exercise which best suits you, but learn to expend energy at precisely the right psychological moment in order to cash in on maximum benefits.

The energy forms, the playing pieces which you will manipulate, are simple basics: a bit of natural food with which to lift your blood sugar (your high-level energy thermostat); and two kinds of movement — spurts of exercise which burn carbohydrates, and more-sustained but less-intense activity periods which burn up carbohydrates and also diminish stored fat. In all, these exercise breaks need total only minutes (usually just 60) daily. On each particular day, see how the cards fall, shuffle your exercise segments, and play them off to full advantage: 20-20-20 minutes, 40-10-10, 10-10-40, whatever combination wins for you. (This very flexibility adds a plus, for your capillaries and arteries also need to vary the load they carry.)

What kind of exercise should you select? You have many options. But above all be guided by the statement attributed to that fantastic old gentleman, the late and very eminent cardiologist, Dr. Paul Dudley White: ''The only sports that improve physical fitness are those that encourage rhythmical, continuous, nonsensitive exertion involving leg muscles. You'll never get fit just using your arms. Each leg is an auxiliary of the heart. Each leg is worth half a heart in maintaining maximum circulation during the activity.''

Obviously, exercise comes more easily for most people in the morning. After hours in bed, it's normal to want to break away and move with the world pendulum. Surge forward with the morning rhythm as the day becomes alive, sap rises in plants, flowers unfold, and birds rediscover their songs. Feel that you can stretch out and touch the sky. Try to do so for 10 minutes, or 20, or 30. For me, morning exercise gives maximum afterglow. Afterward, anything can be done more quickly and efficiently, and with greater ease.

If, after your morning wake-up exercise, you rise only to sit for four hours, noon exercise is a must. As little as five minutes a day can do a lot. During sedentary work, your mind operates at one speed, your body at another. Exercise puts them back in sync. Can you jump rope by your desk? Or take a brownbag lunch to the park? If not, set off at a fast pace to a restaurant six blocks away.

If you're an executive, you're probably worse off than those in less responsible positions. Fortunately, the cocktail-laced executive luncheon is being badmouthed nationwide and looks to be on its way out. But your 8-12 and 1-5 are still horrendous. Deskbound with one-on-one appointments, the average exec sandwiches two phone calls between each interview, while the receptionist ushers in the next conferee. I implore you to stand up and stretch between sessions, and to walk to your outer office and personally greet your next appointment.

Whoever and wherever you are, if an afternoon is to be unusually demanding, you may want your magic super exercise break at noon in order to crank up the day again as if you're starting fresh. Maybe you can manage a noontime run in the park. If it's crucial to be thoroughly wide-awake at two or three, and at that hour you often lapse into drowsiness, ask your body how it feels about dropping in at the health club for a workout or at the Y for a swim. (How often a friend will ask if you feel like a walk, or a game of golf, or—. And your response is totally cerebral. But I want you to be very literal in this matter. Find out what your body feels like doing. True feelings seldom go wrong.)

About four in the afternoon, I advocate a break with vegetable juice and a tiny piece of cheese, a half cup of yogurt, or a banana with a smidgen of peanut butter — just a bit of something to elevate your blood sugar and serve as excuse for your pausing at whatever you're doing.

After the nibble, lean back in your chair, breathe deeply, and take your own pulse. By that, I don't mean for you to count to 60 seconds. Just hold your wrist for five or six beats. This holding of your own hand focuses upon all the movement that is speaking to you from within. Listen to your pulse. Then listen even more intently. Be swept away from your external physical surroundings into a more-vital physical milieu. When I hold my own wrist and bring my perception to bear upon my innermost functionings, I am certain that (to employ biofeedback terms) I go from Beta to Alpha.

Now, consider the remainder of your day. How are you going to feel about it? How long will it take you to unwind? Think with your head — and with your gut.

Ask yourself what you would like as a special treat.

It can't be just food and wine alone. There must be counter-movement. Perhaps you can postpone dinner to an hour later and set up tennis with a friend. For you have already adopted some kind of twilight exercise pattern as you learn to put balance into your days. (Dawn to dusk! That was the continuity of movement of our primitive ancestors, the seed-gatherers, the followers of the harvest. That is why it is so important to segment your 60 minutes of exercise and distribute them over the whole day in pallid imitation of man's natural dawn-to-dusk movement pattern. Our bodies are still fashioned to roam during daylight hours. Of course they are — we are the survivors of the early humans who kept up that continuous, often-laborious movement. Those who didn't move didn't make it, and are nobody's ancestors.)

Counter-movement, preferably in the fresh air, is the prescription for the splitting headache, the blahs, the blues, or any indication that you've been mistreating yourself. You know when you have done so and what the repercussions are. Headache, heartburn, indigestion, ulcers, colitis, hemorrhoids, you name it; it's all swallowed tension gone wrong. Quite naturally, there are times when you feel like throttling some offending or offensive person. Being civilized, you do not — but that primal urge to throttle brings constriction to your own throat. The frustration goes on, you are bugged, you are stymied, till injury is added to this persistent insult to your body. For whether smouldering resentment or bottled-up fury, this is negative tension and it must go somewhere. Remember that energy can be neither created nor destroyed. It can only be transformed.

When you and your body learn to unwind hostile tension in a sensible and systematic way, you then can wind yourself up with creative energy.

The only alternative is to continue to punish yourself to such a point that one day when you give your body a message, your body will reply "I cannot." This is a dreadful but a just retribution. The mills of justice grind slowly, but they grind exceedingly fine.

How tragic and how needless, when there is plenty of room for your body in your life and for exercise in your life-style. And you will find no simpler method than that of squirreling away minutes each day. You will learn to do it so smoothly, so unobtrusively, that there can be no sense of time lost. You will feel pride in exuberant energy gained. So long corked down, the real you will leap out

— Wow! — like a jack-in-the-box, from your captivity in your daily series of boxes. The smaller the cubbyholes in which you are compressed, the more urgent your need to break out. After all, the maximum punishment has always been confinement in the very smallest space, whether in the Iron Maiden or in solitary confinement.

To recap: befriend your cardiovascular-pulmonary system, and three times a week adjust your daily breakdown of 60 energetic minutes to accommodate at least half an hour of moderately intense activity such as a really brisk walk, a run, a jog, or continuous lap swimming. After approximately 30 minutes, carbohydrates will not be able to fuel this activity, and you will be drawing upon stored fat. Shorter stretches of less-intense exercise will draw only upon the stored carbohydrates in your liver and muscles. The latter is what I call huffy-puffy exercise, and it's important too. Just feel the force of that oxygen surge, pushing its way through arteries and capillaries, opening them up to flexibility and youth.

As you prescribe for yourself that wonderful antidote, natural, free-swinging, happy movement, visualize and thrill to what goes on within. You are reuniting body and mind to perform harmoniously at the same level. Soon you will be reaching up and out, you will involuntarily stand and walk more proudly.

Now you will be open to constant discovery, eager for new challenges. This is living for life.

THE GOLDEN DOOR RECIPES AND YOU

Our 'Golden Door' chef creates many elaborate presentations to dazzle our guests, but to offset any complicated recipes we have included a like number of instructions for vegetables, salads, and desserts to be put together in mere moments. The Menus section (pages 145-153) suggests how some of the recipes might be grouped. Whatever time you spend on a meal, always add an extra touch of eye appeal to each individual course. Be guided by thinking of each plate as if it were a still-life painting.

This book provides you with essential instructions for creating meals as tempting and delectable as they are wholesome. Never hesitate to make them appear even more appealing. Joy is not fattening. Make your dinner very enticing for those you care for — or decorate your dinner tray with at least one flower if you dine alone.

Introduce each course separately, on a pretty dish. Aesthetics aside, the latter point is tremendously important, for it also does away with the communal serving dish. I am adamant on this one point: no family-style serving, ever. Plates should always be prepared in the kitchen, with due regard to the size of the individual being served and the size that individual might prefer to be.

For the dieter, another hard-and-fast rule about plate sizes: dinner plates for the salad course, bread-and-butter plates for the entree, demitasse spoons for a dessert fluffed up in a champagne glass.

Of course the food you are serving is fresh, fresh, fresh. I recommend it be purchased on that very day, both to guarantee freshness and because food assembled with spontaneous pleasure elicits a like response when it is served. Buy only the precise quantity you need. Portions are easy to estimate. Again, remember they should be smaller for those who would like to be smaller. Never over-buy. Once you have eliminated waste, you will find yourself becoming more and more demanding about food quality. And you will carefully read labeling on that occasional container of packaged food.

You have many favorite dishes, and it isn't expected that you turn your back on them and all at once espouse a totally new set of recipes. There is deep emotional satisfaction implicit in favorite foods or combinations thereof. The important thing is that you be aware of the plan behind the first three weeks of 'Golden Door' menus. You'll note that seafood is eaten three or four times a week. Chicken appears frequently. Then there are meals relying on tofu, legumes, cheese, eggs. At lunch and dinner you must have some form of complete protein—but not in the quantity once thought necessary.

There is no beef in any of our recipes. When the 'Golden Door' was very new and we were experimenting with our first Men's Weeks, our male guests felt they had to have steaks. There has been much nutritional and ecological education since then, and most American males have modernized beyond their old-time steak-and-potatoes routine.

The low-calorie sauces to dress certain dishes, the soup stocks to augment flavors, and the promise of a dinner sweet are meal accessories not to be ignored. After all, this cookbook was designed to make you live more exuberantly as well as to make you trim and healthy.

Recipes are divided among those entrees which must be served immediately, and those requiring two-stage cooking. There are desserts which can be prepared in the morning, and others which go together easily in the few minutes between courses. (Be careful to observe dessert-refrigeration limitations. When egg whites beaten up with air are the basis of a dessert, they are apt to fall if refrigerated too long.) All in all, this cookbook should permit you to eat enjoyable food prepared in the time you want to give to it.

You can't take your cookbook with you to a party but you can emulate the 'Golden Door' philosophy the next time you are invited for cocktails. Before you leave for the event, begin to spoil your appetite. Drink a large glass of water. Eat a slice of melon or a serving of strawberries. As you drive, nibble on carrot sticks. When you arrive, ask for a glass of soda water with a sliver of lime. Only afterward do you order an alcoholic drink, and that on the rocks. Toy with it. Avoid peanuts, salted nuts, and chips. These only make you thirsty — before you know it, you may down your drink hastily and have a second one pressed upon you by your convivial party-giving friends.

Wherever you are — partying, shopping, poring over a menu, taking potluck as a dinner guest — let me provide you with a simple though magic phrase that can transform, enhance, and probably prolong your life. It's a phrase you knew as a child: Stop, Look, and Listen. You learned it in kindergarten so you could safely cross streets and remain whole of body and limb. Now use it to get safely through the rest of your life.

Whenever and wherever you encounter food, first of all STOP. Relate the food, both its content and quality, to yourself. How much of it will be required to satisfy both your physical and psychological hunger? (In medicine there is a strong theory that aging is related to the decline of the immune system. Experiments indicate that a limited diet of high-quality nutrients make a big difference in maintaining an effective immune system, and hence less illness and more life.) And how does this particular food match your own measurements: small, medium, or large?

We've all heard the doctor's old joke that the best prescription for a long life is to choose long-lived parents. Similarly, if you would be a long-lived thin person capable of eating large portions, you must be sure to pick tall parents for yourself. If you're the offspring of small parents, and are offered a heaping dish, you will have to stop and ponder the situation.

If you're over 40, better develop a passion for the ethnic food prepared so well by the world's smaller peoples — Chinese, Japanese, Vietnamese, Indian. That will mean not much starch and very little sugar or fat. Very little meat, lots of fish. Many exotic seasonings but, basically, vegetables and whole grains, with mostly legumes for protein.

Now, LOOK at the food. As long as you're just looking at it, you still have options. Whether it will give you an after-taste of pleasure or guilt is still your choice.

Look very, very closely at your food. Can you visualize the energy it represents on your dish? Nature prepared us for times of feast or famine, times when there would be an abundance of nuts and grains and fruits for us to eat so that we might store energy for the months when snow covered the ground and we slept in caves. Understand this process. Realize that there still can be times when you will want to store energy, and other times when you will need extra satisfaction because the day has been decidedly difficult. Offsetting those off days are others filled with enough verve and excitement to cause your body to draw upon energy stores. Joyously balance your diet with energy output and food input.

Look at yourself in your plate, at your today and your tomorrow.

Now, LISTEN. With your mind and all your senses. What is the food telling you — that it's "life enhancing" or "life diminishing"? Particularly listen for those words when you're grocery shopping. They can make you drop that bag of potato chips and head for the fresh-produce section.

In order to hear what your food is trying to tell you, it's doubly important to remember the rule of not eating while reading or watching TV, or when at the movies. Give each meal your full attention in order to respond to food's true nutritive and psychological worth.

As explained in Jane Brody's *Nutrition Book,* once the human animal ceases to be an infant, there remains no natural instinct that distinguishes between what's nourishing and what isn't. That's another reason why it's so crucial to Stop, Look, and Listen.

It has been very difficult to separate the food and the movement material in this introduction, and keep it all concise and independently set forth. Everything in this life is constantly in motion, the earth and heaven around us, the neutrons within. Human appetite and our kinetic body were created simultaneously and indivisibly (and at the same time the body was equipped to handle it all).

Following such a regimen as I've outlined in this book would solve both nutritive and caloric problems, and would help you avoid that most insidious type of weight gain: the increase of only a pound a year, which when accumulated between the ages of 25 and 50 can make you overweight in the period of your later life which should find you in your most creative, most rewarding years.

A MESSAGE FROM MICHEL

The cooking utensils you will require for 'Golden Door' cuisine are extremely practical ones. Most of them are so sturdy they will last a lifetime.

The only special technique you will need to learn is the art of cooking with little or no oil, over a medium-low fire. You will find this easy to do if you have heavy pots, pans, and skillets (with lids) that do not burn easily. Stainless steel, which leaves no residue on food, is ideal. It should never have to be replaced. The stainless-steel pots and pans you need are those with heavy bottoms, to prevent burning.

Incidentally, Italy is now exporting cooking ware which is stainless steel inside, aluminum outside — a combination which works very well, and one I recommend to you.

Silverstone is fine for cooking but must be watched carefully. Although more durable than its predecessor, Teflon, in time its coating will wear off.

In the 'Golden Door' kitchen we also use cast-iron a good deal. A heavy cast-iron skillet is a great kitchen standby. But cast-iron takes special care: after washing, you must dry it especially well and then rub with a few drops of oil to prevent rust.*

What about Le Creuset and other heavy cooking ware with baked-on enamel coating? They must be handled gingerly. If the pan ever chips inside, it is done for. Eventually you may have dangerous enamel chips in your food.

Among other (preferably stainless-steel or porcelain, never aluminum) kitchen necessities:

> mixing bowls, varying sizes
> measuring cups (glass will do)
> measuring spoons
> spoons, varying sizes, slotted and unslotted
> wire whisks in varying sizes
> strainers, varying sizes
> grater
> spatulas, in several sizes
> omelette and crepe pans (to be used only for this purpose*)
> tongs
> tea caddy (to hold bouquet garni)

My preference is a whisk with a wooden handle that will not burn the cook.

My 'Golden Door' kitchen is outfitted with carbon-steel knives but because they rust very easily they should be used only by a professional who knows how to care for them properly. For the home kitchen, a high-quality stainless steel such as that marketed by Sabatier and Cuisinart is a better choice.

A good sharp knife is no luxury. For some reason, non-professional American cooks have a hang-up about keeping any sharp knives about. Many an otherwise perfectly outfitted kitchen will yield nothing but a dull blade.

For the nonprofessional cook, an 8-inch long chopping knife is one of the handiest kitchen accessories.

A food processor of course will take over some of your chopping and slicing chores, and perform countless other services such as making dough and grating cheese. In my opinion Cuisinart was the leader among food processors. That name has now been sold to a Japanese company. But the original producer of Cuisinart—Robot-Coupe—now makes a fine processor called Robot-Coupe. Whatever make you choose, be sure that it is not a belt-driven model; replacing the belt can require dismantling the whole machine.

For soups and dressings and other liquids with a thinner consistency than a puree, I like to process with a blender. I believe the commercial-size Osterizer is by far the best.

Quite expensive but very useful is the Champion juicer, also a leader in its line.

Not indispensable but worth a dieter's notice is a new 1½-cup fat separator called Gravy-Strain. It is a running mate of Souper-Strain, which performs the same service for soups. Both save the time of clarifying.

Essential to your kitchen inventory are reliable oven-baking dishes. To my mind, clay dishes with a glazed finish are the best because the glaze makes the dish stronger as well as easier to clean. These need not be hard-to-find imported clay dishes. I see that the ones I am using now were made in Bennington, Vermont. However, ovenproof glass dishes are quite satisfactory.

No kitchen is complete without a spatula. Wooden ones are the chef's first choice. However, for mixtures which require scraping the sides of a blender receptacle, only a rubber spatula will do the job. Rubber spatulas absorb odors, should be used only when absolutely necessary, and should be replaced often.

Have on hand aluminum foil with which to seal the stainless-steel lid to its cooking pot: after light sauteing and the placing of the lid on the pot, many 'Golden Door' dishes are virtually steamed.

Other excellent choices for your kitchen are cannisters with tight-fitting lids; a scale to measure ounces; a timer; and above all, a clock, placed where you can see it at all times.

The clock will remind you never to overcook, and to keep your meal's delightful freshness by serving immediately. You are not covering your food with butter, margarine, or a rich sauce; consequently, fish, chicken, and even vegetables if set aside in the cooking vessel after removal from the fire will continue to cook and become very overdone or dry.

*After washing and drying, place paper toweling between before stacking.

MICHEL'S ACKNOWLEDGEMENTS

The 'Golden Door' has renowned Japanese gardens of great beauty. And only a few minutes' walk from the kitchen, on a gradually sloping hillside, is the well-tended vegetable garden. This is the source of many of our wonderfully fresh salads and other vegetable dishes. Our orchards provide an ever-abundant supply of fresh citrus and other seasonal fruits. One hundred hens give birth each day to fertile eggs. Just outside my kitchen window is the delightful herb patch which is so important for enhancing the natural flavors of the 'Golden Door' cuisine.

This heavenly environment has been my inspiration for seven happy years. So too have the guests themselves. And above all there is Deborah Szekely, who created this setting and then entrusted me with the feeding of her cherished guests.

In such an atmosphere, creativity comes from the heart, and food is prepared with loving care.

Guests at the 'Golden Door' usually make do with a little over 100 calories for the morning meal. Departing guests are urged to distribute their caloric wealth mainly between luncheon and dinner and to slight the first meal of the day.

Hibernating animals awaken hungry from their long winter's nap. But Nature arranged for the human body to sleep through only a portion of each night. After a few hours of bed rest, the body has no pressing need for much food. Nevertheless, there are certain people for whom a sizeable breakfast has always represented a significant starting point for each day. It is very difficult to woo them away from their attachment to the cereal bowl and the electric toaster.

Some of the 'Golden Door' morning-meal suggestions are familiar, some are not. All are important and satisfying substitutes for sweet rolls and for pre-packaged cereals with their concealed sugar and for cholesterol-saturated fried meats and the daily egg. Each morning, tune-up with a true high instead of suspect hype.

The wonderful recipe called GRO-GRAINS® invites comparison with the granola cereal you can buy in prepackaged form: the U.S. Department of Agriculture estimates that most of these products contain sugar in excess of 20% of their dry weight. Some tested at 32%—a particularly shocking example of hidden sugar in packaged foods, since granola is associated in the public mind with what is termed "health food." This GRO-GRAINS® recipe is delicious with only 2 tablespoons of honey, plus what natural sugar is contained in 1 tablespoon of sun-dried raisins.

We lead off our recipe section with Bran Breakfast because every breakfast, every day, should contain at least some amount of that friendly fibre.

Bran Breakfast

8 tablespoons	miller's bran, unprocessed
4 tablespoons	raw wheat germ
4 tablespoons	raw sunflower seeds
4 teaspoons	sun-dried raisins ground cinnamon, to taste

Combine all ingredients and mix well.

Note: Top with ½ cup unfiltered apple juice or other juice of your choice — i.e., apricot, pear, grapefruit — or ½ cup low-fat milk or low-fat yogurt.

SERVES 4. CALORIES PER SERVING: 103

PREPARATION TIME: 5 MINUTES

Muesli

⅔ cup	rolled oats (old-fashioned variety)
6	sun-dried black Mission figs, chopped
¼ teaspoon	ground cinnamon
⅔ cup	water
½	apple, medium size, with skin
1	banana, sliced
1 cup	plain, low-fat yogurt
8	almonds or hazelnuts, freshly chopped

Combine oats, figs, and cinnamon; cover with water and soak overnight.

Before serving, grate apple and stir into oat mixture. Divide in 4 portions; trim each with banana slices.

Top with ¼ cup yogurt sprinkled with nuts.

Note: Other sun-dried fruits, such as apricots, dates, or prunes may be substituted for figs.

SERVES 4. CALORIES PER SERVING: 205

PREPARE NIGHT BEFORE

Bran-Nut Muffins

¾ cup	miller's bran, unprocessed
½ cup	whole-wheat pastry flour
¼ cup	sun-dried raisins or dates, chopped
¼ cup	walnuts or almonds, freshly chopped
½ teaspoon	baking soda
¾ teaspoon	ground cinnamon
¾ teaspoon	grated nutmeg
1	egg, beaten
¼ cup	honey or blackstrap molasses (or combination)
1 tablespoon	sesame-seed or safflower oil
½ teaspoon	vanilla extract
6 tablespoons	plain, low-fat yogurt

Preheat oven to 375°.

Blend dry ingredients in mixing bowl. Mix together remaining ingredients, and pour over dry mixture. Stir until just blended.

Spoon into muffin pans lined with muffin papers, about 1 heaping tablespoon per muffin.

Bake 12-15 minutes.

MAKES 10 MUFFINS. CALORIES PER MUFFIN: 110
PREPARATION TIME: 25 MINUTES

Breakfast Gro-Grains®

3 tablespoons	peanuts, raw
4½ tablespoons	rolled oats (old-fashioned variety)
1 tablespoon	wheat germ, raw
1 tablespoon	sunflower seeds, raw
2 teaspoons	pumpkin seeds, raw
2 teaspoons	sesame seeds, raw
2 teaspoons	almonds, freshly sliced, chopped, or slivered
¼ teaspoon	ground cinnamon
⅛ teaspoon	grated nutmeg
2 teaspoons	unsweetened coconut, grated
2 tablespoons	honey
2 teaspoons	sesame-seed or safflower oil
¼ teaspoon	vanilla extract
2 tablespoons	sun-dried apricots, chopped
1 teaspoon	grated orange rind

Preheat oven to 250°.

Roast peanuts on baking sheet till golden brown, 45 minutes to 1 hour.

Cool, chop coarsely, and combine with oats, wheat germ, seeds, almonds, cinnamon, nutmeg, and coconut.

Preheat oven to 325°.

Heat honey with oil and vanilla till syrupy. Drizzle over Gro-grains mixture and toss to mix thoroughly, using fork. Spread on baking sheet and bake 15 minutes to ½ hour; stir every 5 or 10 minutes till golden brown. Remove from oven and stir in apricots and orange rind. Cool.

To maintain crisp, crunchy texture, store in freezer. If softer texture is desired, refrigerate.

MAKES 1½ CUPS (SERVE ¼-CUP PORTIONS).
PREPARATION TIME: 1 HOUR 15 MINUTES
CALORIES: 65 PER TABLESPOON

Brunch with Deborah: Huevos Rancheros

2 tablespoons	sesame-seed or safflower oil
3	onions, medium size, sliced
1	bell pepper (optional), chopped
1 tablespoon	dried whole oregano
1 tablespoon	dried sweet basil
1 teaspoon	vegetable seasoning
1 28-ounce can	whole tomatoes, chopped, or 4 large fresh tomatoes, peeled and chopped coarsely
½ teaspoon	black pepper, freshly ground
4	eggs
8 tablespoons	Monterey jack cheese, freshly grated, or 4 thin mozzarella cheese slices

In heavy pan, heat oil. Gently saute onions over low fire till light golden brown; stir with wooden spatula. Add bell pepper, and season with oregano, basil, and vegetable seasoning. Cook 2-3 minutes. Add tomatoes and pepper. Simmer 10-15 minutes, till sauce is somewhat thick.

With spoon, make 4 pockets in mixture, and drop in eggs. Cover eggs with cheese. Cook, covered, 10 minutes for soft eggs, 15 minutes for eggs more done. Serve immediately.

SERVES 4. CALORIES PER SERVING: 244
PREPARATION TIME: 30-35 MINUTES

Papaya and Cottage Cheese

2	papayas, ripe
1 cup	low-fat cottage cheese
4 teaspoons	miller's bran, unprocessed
4 teaspoons	sunflower seeds, raw
garnish:	strawberries and fresh mint sprigs

Halve papayas, scrape out seeds. Fill each half with ¼ cup low-fat cottage cheese. Sprinkle top with bran and sunflower seeds. Garnish and serve.

SERVES 4. CALORIES PER SERVING: 103
PREPARATION TIME: 10 MINUTES

Yogurt for Breakfast

2 cups	plain, low-fat yogurt
1 cup	strawberry slices
4 tablespoons	sunflower seeds, raw

Combine yogurt and strawberries. Top with sunflower seeds, and serve.

SERVES 4. CALORIES PER SERVING: 135
PREPARATION TIME: 5 MINUTES

Pear and Peanut Butter

4	Bartlett pears, ripe and juicy
8 teaspoons	pure fresh peanut butter (from health food store, or made in your own food processor)
garnish:	4 lemon wedges and 4 mint sprigs

Wash and halve pears. Scoop out seeds. Fill each half with 1 teaspoon peanut butter. Garnish and serve.

SERVES 4. CALORIES PER SERVING: 150
PREPARATION TIME: 5 MINUTES

Broiled Grapefruit

2 grapefruit, halved and seeded
honey, to taste

Broil grapefruit halves until tops begin to brown slightly. Sprinkle with honey. Serve hot.

You may serve this with 1 hard-cooked egg.

SERVES 4. CALORIES PER SERVING: 50

PREPARATION TIME: 10 MINUTES

Apple-and-Raisin Energy Snack

2	apples (crisp), grated with skin
6 tablespoons	fresh orange juice
2 tablespoons	sun-dried raisins, chopped
4 tablespoons	almonds, slivered
1 teaspoon	ground cinnamon
garnish:	orange slices and strawberries

Mix ingredients together. Garnish and serve at once.

SERVES 4. CALORIES PER SERVING: 112

PREPARATION TIME: 10 MINUTES

Grilled Cheese on Tecate Bread

4 slices	Tecate Bread (page 109)
6 ounces	Monterey jack cheese, freshly grated
8	thin tomato slices
garnish:	fruit (strawberries, apple slices, orange wedges) to decorate plate

Put bread on cookie sheet. Broil, toasting lightly on both sides. Spread cheese over toast and cover with thin tomato slices. Broil till cheese melts and tomato sizzles.

SERVES 4. CALORIES PER SERVING: 255

PREPARATION TIME: 10 MINUTES

LET'S TALK ABOUT THESE RECIPES

BRAN, SEEDS, SUN-DRIED FRUITS, UNFILTERED APPLE JUICE, ET AL: Undoubtedly you realize that all these items are best found in a top health-food store. Bran is beginning to appear again in the supermarkets, put up by companies trying to cash in on the big natural-fibre windfall. Instead, go to a health-food store and request unprocessed miller's bran.

Health-food stores are now plentiful enough that you can pick and choose. When purchasing seeds and grains in bulk, select a store that orders them in a realistic quantity and moves them quickly, or you will be noticing fluttering little wings in your cupboard. No 10- or 20-pound sacks for you. Buy only a one-month supply.

Neither should you trust the sulphur-treated dried fruits in the big chain markets. Insist on genuine sun-dried fruit. To impress yourself with the difference, on the one hand think of heavenly sunshine; on the other, consider that sulphur fumes were important stage effects in Dante's Inferno.

Another dandy use for sun-dried fruits: Chop them into cooked cereals during the last few minutes on the stove. A natural sweetener.

CINNAMON: Visit the genuine Aisles of Spice by buying your spices in the most extravagant fancy-food stores. The purchase price will be returned to you at least twofold in terms of exciting scents and flavors. In small, class food stores and kitchen shops, ground cinnamon comes in three varieties, ranging from the sweetest to the spiciest. Familiarize yourself with all three. Determine which is your favorite, and when.

HONEY: Often featured in 'Golden Door' recipes, honey is a beautiful, completely natural food. We recommend honey gathered from wild sage or other mountain blossoms; it adds luscious flavor beyond mere sweetness.

You may have heard the argument that honey contains more calories then refined sugar. Because honey is sweeter, you can use about 25% less in a recipe regularly calling for refined sugar. That more or less balances out the 28% more calories attributed to honey. Besides, refined sugar steals potassium.

Honey is mostly fructose. Hence it is more easily digested than most granulated or syrup sweeteners. It is the one food so pure, it cannot spoil. Intact honey has been unearthed in ancient tombs. Please don't throw it away if it crystallizes in the jar. Simply place the jar in warm water.

Of course you know the trick of accurately pouring honey by first oiling the measuring spoon, or rinsing it in water.

NUTS: Purchase nuts that are still in the healthy home environment of their own shells — not ripped out and put on display in little plastic bags.

OIL: Note that only cold-pressed oil — sesame seed or safflower — is to be used in most of this book's cooking recipes.

The cold-press process is important because it does not remove so many valuable minerals from the oil.

Because sesame oil is such a favorite in Chinese and Japanese cuisine for the flavor it imparts, it is often added to cooked Oriental dishes just before serving. Any oil or fat loses nutrients if overheated, and sesame oil should not be heated above 350°. It performs extremely satisfactorily in the 'Golden Door' system of quick cooking, in a small amount of oil, over medium heat. Safflower oil can withstand slightly more heat then sesame oil.

If you do not already rely upon these oils, so light in flavor and consistency, you will be surprised by the pleasurable dimensions they can add to many of your own familiar recipes.

RAISINS: A quick way to chop raisins is to freeze them beforehand. Chop a half-cup of them at a time into your blender, after having lightly coated its jar and blades with oil.

Plumped-up raisins can be an especially rich source of

natural sweetening and flavoring if, instead of soaking them in hot water, you let them stand in fresh fruit juice. Always a handy, wholesome sweetener, raisins are fantastic after four hours to overnight in a combination of grated lemon peel, vanilla extract, and lemon juice to cover.

VEGETABLE SEASONING: The 'Golden Door' always uses a substitute for regular table salt — an all-vegetable seasoning like Vegit, or better still, mix your own.

Golden Door Herb Seasoning

4 tablespoons	dried whole thyme
2 tablespoons	dried tarragon
2 tablespoons	dried rosemary
2 tablespoons	sea salt
1 teaspoon	lemon pepper
1 teaspoon	curry powder
½ teaspoon	celery seed
4 tablespoons	dried sweet basil
1 tablespoon	dried lemon peel
2 teaspoons	fennel seeds
1 gram	saffron (optional)
1 teaspoon	ground coriander
2 teaspoons	juniper berries

Put all ingredients into a coffee grinder (or food processor or blender). Blend till fine.

Yield: about ¾ cup. Store in refrigerator.

Use sparingly.

WHOLE-WHEAT FLOUR: Again, buy only a one-month supply. When measuring whole-wheat flour, scoop it up with a measuring cup, level it off with a spatula. Do not shake down.

EGGS, SOUFFLES AND QUICHES

The prized 'Golden Door' chicken yard is always doubly admired by guests: first, because of the fine-looking, well-feathered fowl strutting about there; later, because of the excellent, superfresh fertile eggs the hens produce.

It may not be easy for you to obtain fertile eggs. But do make a point of buying truly fresh ones. Nearly every carton is labeled "fresh," of course — like "gourmet," the word is often loosely applied. A fresh egg will float when submerged (in its shell) in water. When you carefully break the shell but not the yolk, the fresh yolk will be well-rounded and protruberant, rather than flattish. Week by week, you can judge the age of an egg by the diameter of its yolk (something like counting the age rings on a tree).

Like most standard recipes, those of the 'Golden Door' require the "Large" egg. A dozen U..S-graded "Large" eggs must weigh at least 24 ounces. If measured by the spoonful, a "Large" egg should equal 3 tablespoons plus ¼ teaspoon. It is the equivalent of 1½ "Small" eggs. A dozen "Small" eggs must weigh at least 18 ounces.

Egg dishes such as fluffly omelettes and frothy souffles are a marvelously smooth source of protein, pleasant to eat and simple to digest. And they are great calorie-savers. Unless your physician has warned you of a cholesterol problem, there is no reason why you shouldn't enjoy them several times a week if you are following the 'Golden Door' diet, which is otherwise low in cholesterol.

Breakfast Eggs

At the 'Golden Door,' eggs are cooked in pretty oven-proof Japanese cups, without the use of fat or oil.

To cook one egg:

Heat 1 inch of water in saucepan. Place cup in water. Break 1 egg into cup. Cover cup with lid or saucer, and cover saucepan with lid. Steam gently 15 minutes for soft-cooked egg, 20 minutes or more for hard-cooked egg.

SERVES 1. CALORIES PER EGG: 80

PREPARATION TIME: 15-20 MINUTES

Eggs with Mushrooms, Scallions, and Cheese

Heat 1 inch of water in saucepan. Place a cup in water. Break 1 egg into it. Add 1 large raw mushroom, sliced; 1 teaspoon scallion, chopped; and 1 tablespoon Monterey jack or Swiss cheese, freshly grated. Steam, covered, 15-20 minutes.

SERVES 1. CALORIES PER SERVING: 110

PREPARATION TIME: 20 MINUTES

Cheese Omelette

1	egg
1	egg white
2 teaspoons	fresh parsley, chopped
1 ounce	Monterey jack, Jarlsberg, Swiss, or similar cheese, freshly grated
½ teaspoon	sesame-seed or safflower oil
garnish:	lettuce, sliced tomatoes, fresh parsley, grated carrot, or other fresh vegetable

Preheat oven to 400°.

With wire whisk or fork, beat egg and egg white in bowl.

Use well-seasoned omelette pan. Add oil and heat, tilting pan to coat evenly with oil. Pour in egg mixture, and cook 1-2 minutes over medium fire. Remove from fire. Spread grated cheese and chopped parsley in omelette center. Using a spatula, lift omelette (begin near handle), and fold in half.

Place omelette in oven about 1 minute, to melt cheese.

Tilt pan, and roll out omelette onto heated plate. Garnish and serve.

SERVES 1. CALORIES PER SERVING: 215

PREPARATION TIME: 10 MINUTES

Asparagus Omelette

16	fresh asparagus stalks (peeled at bottom), washed
4	eggs
4	egg whites
8 teaspoons	fresh parsley, chopped
2 teaspoons	sesame-seed or safflower oil
4 ounces	Monterey jack cheese (optional)
1 cup	alfalfa sprouts
	vegetable seasoning, to taste
	black pepper, freshly ground, to taste
garnish:	lettuce and fresh garden vegetables

Steam asparagus 3 to 4 minutes. Make sure stalks are firm.

Preheat oven to 400°.

Make 1 omelette at a time, following directions as for **Cheese Omelette** (page 7). Spread ¼ of asparagus and ¼ of cheese in omelette; top with ¼ cup alfalfa sprouts. Fold omelette in half. Bake 1 minute or broil briefly.

Tilt omelette, and roll out onto heated plate. Garnish and serve.

SERVES 4. CALORIES PER SERVING: 250

PREPARATION TIME: 20 MINUTES

Curried Crab Omelette

1 teaspoon	sesame-seed or safflower oil
1 tablespoon	scallions (white part), minced
1 teaspoon	curry powder
1 6-ounce can	crab meat (or ¾ cup), reserving juice
2 tablespoons	scallions, chopped
4	eggs
4	egg whites
8 teaspoons	fresh parsley, chopped
2 teaspoons	sesame-seed or safflower oil
garnish:	4 thin pineapple slices, 4 apple wedges, 4 banana slices, fresh mint, and shredded lettuce

Heat 1 teaspoon of oil gently. Add white scallions. With wooden spatula, stir in curry powder to make a paste. Add flaked, cooked crab meat and its juice. Stir well till mixture starts to bubble. Add scallions.

Preheat oven to 400°.

Make 1 omelette at a time, following directions as for **Cheese Omelette** (page 7). Spread ¼ of crab mixture in omelette center. Fold omelette in half. Place it under broiler about 1 minute.

Tilt omelette, and roll out onto heated plate. Garnish and serve.

SERVES 4. CALORIES PER SERVING: 168

PREPARATION TIME: 15 MINUTES

Omelette Chinoise

2 teaspoons	sesame-seed or safflower oil
1	onion, thinly sliced
1 teaspoon	garlic, minced
¼ cup	zucchini, Chinese cut (diagonal)
¼ cup	bell pepper, Chinese cut
¼ cup	celery, Chinese cut
½ cup	bean sprouts
2-3 tablespoons	scallions, chopped
1 tablespoon	soy sauce (low-sodium)
¼ cup	Vegetable Stock (page 47) (optional)
4	eggs
4	egg whites
8 teaspoons	scallions, chopped
2 teaspoons	sesame-seed or safflower oil
garnish:	grated daikon and lettuce leaves

Heat oil, in a wok — or heavy pan. Add onion and garlic. Stir quickly. Add zucchini, bell pepper, and celery. Toss until vegetables stick a bit. Add bean sprouts and scallions. Sprinkle with soy sauce. If vegetables stick, add **Vegetable Stock** and stop cooking. This whole process should take only 3-4 minutes. Vegetables should still be crispy.

Preheat oven to 400°.

Make 1 omelette at a time, following directions as for **Cheese Omelette** (page 7). Spread inside of omelette with ¼ cup of vegetable mixture (lift out with slotted spoon). Fold omelette in half. Bake briefly — 1 minute or so. Roll onto heated plate, garnish, and serve.

SERVES 4. CALORIES PER SERVING: 150

PREPARATION TIME: 30 MINUTES

Mushroom Omelette

2 cups	fresh mushrooms, sliced black pepper, freshly ground vegetable seasoning, to taste
1 tablespoon	fresh lemon juice
¼ cup	water
4	eggs
4	egg whites
4 teaspoons	fresh parsley, chopped
2 teaspoons	sesame-seed or safflower oil
garnish:	lettuce leaves, grapefruit wedges, strawberries, orange slices, parsley sprigs

Place mushrooms, pepper and vegetable seasoning to taste, lemon juice, and water in stainless-steel pan. Cover, and steam 4-5 minutes.

Preheat oven to 400°.

Make 1 omelette at a time, following directions as for **Cheese Omelette** (page 7). With slotted spoon, lift out ¼ of mushroom mixture and place in center of omelette. Fold in half. Bake 1 minute. Roll out onto heated plate. Garnish and serve.

SERVES 4. CALORIES PER SERVING: 122

PREPARATION TIME: 15 MINUTES

Tomato-and-Basil Omelette

4	eggs
4	egg whites
4 teaspoons	fresh parsley, chopped
4 teaspoons	chives, chopped
2 teaspoons	sesame-seed or safflower oil
12-16	tomato slices
	black pepper, freshly ground, to taste
4	sweet basil leaves, coarsely chopped, or 1 teaspoon dried sweet basil
garnish:	Chinese pea pods or other fresh vegetables

Preheat oven to 400°.

Make 1 omelette at a time, following directions as for **Cheese Omelette** (page 7). Spread 3 or 4 tomato slices in middle. Grind pepper on tomatoes; sprinkle with parsley, chives, and sweet basil. Fold omelette in half, and bake up to 1 minute.

Roll out onto heated plate. Garnish and serve.

No fresh basil? Substitute chopped scallions or fresh tarragon leaves.

SERVES 4. CALORIES PER SERVING: 128
PREPARATION TIME: 15 MINUTES

Other Omelette Suggestions

Top with **Ignacio's Salsa** (page 23).

Fill each omelette with 2 tablespoons baby shrimp.

Fill each with low-fat cottage cheese and diced tomato.

Fill with raw sunflower seeds and fresh sliced strawberries.

With diced, cooked chicken; grated raw zucchini; coriander seeds; topped with yogurt.

Sun-dried raisins; freshly roasted peanuts; sliced cucumbers; coriander seeds.

Sprouts, avocado slices, and freshly grated Monterey jack cheese.

Browned onion rings, grated raw zucchini, and 1 teaspoon paprika.

Steamed corn (cut off the cob); sprinkled with freshly grated Monterey jack cheese; seasoned with ground cumin and chili powder.

Rapini, freshly grated mozzarella cheese, and **Tomato Sauce** (page 24).

Red and white cabbage, sweet and sour; topped with finely chopped, browned onion; sprinkled with caraway seed.

Apple slices and sun-dried raisins, seasoned with ground cinnamon, topped with yogurt.

Cooked banana slices; pineapple chunks browned in smidgen of sesame-seed oil over low flame; seasoned with grated nutmeg, ground cinnamon, and ground ginger.

Cheese Blintzes

½ cup	unbleached white flour
⅛ teaspoon	grated nutmeg
1	egg
1	egg white
½ cup	low-fat milk
¼ cup	water
½ teaspoon	sesame-seed or safflower oil
2 cups	low-fat cottage cheese
1 teaspoon	fructose
1	apple, small, peeled and grated
¼ teaspoon	grated nutmeg
¼ teaspoon	ground cinnamon
¼ teaspoon	vanilla extract
1	lemon rind, grated
1 tablespoon	fresh lemon juice

Put flour and ⅛ teaspoon nutmeg in mixing bowl. Make a well in center. Add egg, egg white. Use wire whisk to break up eggs; gradually stir in about 2-3 tablespoons of flour. Add milk and water gradually, and whisk till well blended. Let batter stand 1 hour before making blintzes. Preheat oven to 325°.

In 6-inch crepe pan or iron skillet, place drop of oil to coat pan. Heat. Pour in batter for 1 blintz, and quickly tilt pan to coat evenly. Cook over medium fire about 30 seconds, till crepe is bubbling and lightly browned. Turn over and cook briefly on reverse side. Turn onto plate. Repeat process with remaining batter (makes 10-12 crepes).

For filling, mix together cottage cheese, fructose, apple, nutmeg, cinnamon, vanilla, lemon rind, and lemon juice. Divide cheese filling and fill each crepe. Roll crepe, and place on platter. Before serving, heat in oven. Top with **Strawberry Strawberries** (page 126).

MAKES 10-12 BLINTZES. CALORIES PER BLINTZ: 84

PREPARE BATTER 1 HOUR AHEAD

COOKING TIME: 30 MINUTES

Zucchini-Spinach Frittata

3 cups	zucchini, grated
1 tablespoon	vegetable seasoning
¾ cup	fresh spinach, cooked, squeezed, and chopped
1 teaspoon	dried sweet basil
1 tablespoon	Parmesan or Romano cheese, freshly grated
½ teaspoon	black pepper, freshly ground
2 tablespoons	chives or green onions, chopped coarsely
4	eggs
2	egg whites
¼ cup	low-fat milk
2 teaspoons	garlic, minced
1	onion, medium, diced
1 teaspoon	dried whole thyme
2 teaspoons	olive oil
1 cup	raw mushrooms, thickly sliced
½ cup	artichoke hearts, thickly sliced
3 ounces	mozzarella cheese, sliced

Preheat oven to 350°.

In large bowl, grate zucchini and add vegetable seasoning. Mix well. Let stand about ½ hour in colander. Combine with chopped spinach. Add basil, cheese, pepper, and chives. Mix well.

In separate bowl, beat eggs, egg whites, and milk. Combine with zucchini mixture.

In 9-inch skillet, gently saute garlic, onion, and thyme in oil till they start to soften. Add mushrooms; stir with wooden spoon till they start to soften. Add artichokes, and heat well.

Transfer mixture to casserole.

Pour spinach/zucchini mixture over onion mixture. Let bubble a few seconds. Cover with sliced cheese. Bake 45-50 minutes, till knife comes out clean when tested.

Remove from oven and let sit 10 minutes before serving. Serve with **Tomato Sauce** (page 24).

MAKES 8 SMALL PORTIONS. CALORIES PER PORTION: 111

MAKES 4 LARGE PORTIONS. CALORIES PER PORTION: 222

PREPARATION TIME: 1 HOUR 35 MINUTES

Broccoli Souffle

10 ounces	broccoli tops, cut in chunks
1½ cups	water
1 cup	broccoli broth (reserved)
2½ tablespoons	corn-oil margarine
3½ tablespoons	unbleached white flour
½ teaspoon	dried sweet basil
	grated nutmeg, to taste
¼ teaspoon	white pepper
¼ teaspoon	vegetable seasoning
4 tablespoons	Parmesan or Romano cheese, grated
3	egg yolks
2 teaspoons	low-fat milk
5	egg whites, room temperature
	sea salt
	cream of tartar

In covered saucepan, gently cook broccoli tops, covered with water, till tender (about 15 minutes). Drain broccoli. Reserve 1 cup broth. Chop broccoli finely, or use food processor.

Over a low fire, melt margarine and add flour with wire whisk to make a paste (roux). Pour broccoli broth into roux and whisk vigorously till mixture becomes a thick sauce and bubbles. Add basil, nutmeg, pepper, vegetable seasoning, 3 tablespoons grated cheese, and chopped broccoli. Cook 3-4 minutes. Remove from fire, and transfer mixture to bowl. Stir occasionally to cool. When cooled, beat egg yolks with 2 teaspoons milk, and stir into mixture.

This step can be prepared several hours in advance.
Preheat oven to 350°.

Beat egg whites with pinch of salt and pinch of cream of tartar until stiff. Fold ¼ of whites into broccoli mixture. Gently fold in remainder. Pour mixture into 4 lightly oiled, 1¾-cup souffle dishes. Sprinkle each with remainder of cheese.

Place souffle dishes on baking tray. Bake 20 minutes. Reduce heat to 325°, and bake 15 minutes more. Serve immediately.

MAKES 4 SOUFFLES. CALORIES PER SERVING: 233

PREPARATION TIME: 35 MINUTES

BAKING TIME: 30-35 MINUTES

Spinach Souffle

Using basic **Broccoli Souffle** recipe at left, substitute 1½ pounds of fresh spinach for the broccoli. In heavy covered pan over low fire, steam spinach in ¼ cup water. Drain spinach, reserving 1 cup of spinach broth. Then chop spinach — do not puree.

Proceed as with recipe for **Broccoli Souffle**.

MAKES 4 SOUFFLES. CALORIES PER SERVING: 223

PREPARATION TIME: 30 MINUTES

BAKING TIME: 30-35 MINUTES

Asparagus Souffle

Using basic **Broccoli Souffle** recipe at left, substitute 10 ounces of asparagus for the broccoli. Do not use fibrous lower stems of asparagus spears, but reserve these for other uses, such as **Potassium Broth** (page 143).

Boil asparagus in 1½ cups water till tender. Chop finely. Proceed as with recipe for **Broccoli Souffle**.

MAKES 4 SOUFFLES. CALORIES PER SERVING: 228

PREPARATION TIME: 30 MINUTES

BAKING TIME: 30-35 MINUTES

Mushroom Souffle

2 tablespoons	corn-oil margarine
1 tablespoon	shallots, or white bulb of green onion, chopped
6 ounces	fresh mushrooms, chopped in food processor
½ teaspoon	dried whole thyme
¼ teaspoon	white pepper
2 teaspoons	vegetable seasoning
3½ tablespoons	unbleached white flour
1¼ cups	low-fat milk
4 tablespoons	Parmesan or Romano cheese, freshly grated
	grated nutmeg, to taste
	cayenne pepper, to taste
3	egg yolks
2 teaspoons	low-fat milk
5	egg whites, room temperature
	sea salt
	cream of tartar

Heat margarine, and gently saute shallots. Stir in mushrooms, and season with thyme, pepper, and vegetable seasoning. Cook mushrooms several minutes till they are soft and water starts to evaporate. Add flour to make a paste (roux). Add milk, and whisk vigorously till sauce thickens. Add 3 tablespoons cheese, and season with nutmeg and cayenne pepper to taste. Bubble about 5 minutes over medium fire. Remove from fire. Cool to room temperature.

Stir in egg yolks beaten with 2 teaspoons milk.

This step can be prepared several hours in advance.

Preheat oven to 350°.

Beat egg whites with pinch of salt and pinch of cream of tartar till stiff but still smooth. Fold ¼ of this mixture into cooked mushrooms. Then gently fold in remainder. Pour mixture into 4 lightly oiled 1½-cup souffle dishes; sprinkle each with remainder of cheese.

Place souffle dishes on baking tray. Bake 20 minutes. Reduce heat to 325°, and bake 15 minutes more. Serve immediately.

MAKES 4 SOUFFLES. CALORIES PER SERVING: 249

PREPARATION TIME: 30 MINUTES

BAKING TIME: 35 MINUTES

Shrimp Souffle

3 tablespoons	corn-oil margarine
1 tablespoon	shallots, or white bulb of green onion, chopped
3½ tablespoons	unbleached white flour
4 tablespoons	tomato puree
1½ cups	low-fat milk, scalded
1 cup	bay shrimp, cooked, chopped
1 tablespoon	fresh lemon juice
	cayenne pepper, to taste
	vegetable seasoning, to taste
3	egg yolks
1 tablespoon	low-fat milk
5	egg whites, room temperature
	sea salt
	cream of tartar
1 tablespoon	Parmesan or Romano cheese, freshly grated

In heavy skillet, melt margarine over medium fire. Gently saute shallots 3-4 minutes. Add flour, whisking in to form a paste (roux). Mix in tomato puree with a wire whisk, and add scalded milk to make a veloute sauce; whisk vigorously, and add bay shrimp. Add lemon juice plus cayenne pepper and vegetable seasoning to taste. Cook 8-10 minutes; stir occasionally. Pour into mixing bowl and cool; stir once in a while with wooden spatula. Stir in yolks beaten with 1 tablespoon milk.

This step can be prepared several hours in advance.

Preheat oven to 350°.

Beat egg whites with a pinch of salt and pinch of cream of tartar till stiff, but still smooth. Fold ¼ of this mixture into souffle mixture. Then gently fold in remainder. Pour mixture into 4 lightly oiled 1½-cup souffle dishes; sprinkle each with cheese.

Place souffle dishes on baking tray. Bake 15 minutes. Reduce heat to 325°, and bake 15 minutes more. Serve immediately.

MAKES 4 SOUFFLES. CALORIES PER SERVING: 266

PREPARATION TIME: 30 MINUTES

BAKING TIME: 30 MINUTES

Salmon-and-Broccoli Quiche

2 tablespoons	olive oil
1	onion, small, finely chopped
1 teaspoon	dried whole thyme
2 tablespoons	fresh parsley, chopped
1 7-ounce can	sockeye salmon (reserve juice)
1 cup	small broccoli flowerets, par-steamed
1 tablespoon	fresh lemon juice
	cayenne pepper, to taste
1	prebaked Whole-Wheat Pastry Crust (page 111)
2	eggs
2	egg whites
½ cup	low-fat milk, scalded
2 tablespoons	Parmesan or Romano cheese, freshly grated
	paprika, to taste
garnish:	fresh parsley and lemon wedges

Preheat oven to 350°.

Heat oil in heavy skillet. Gently saute onion till glazed. Add thyme, and stir with wooden spatula. Put onion in mixing bowl, and add chopped parsley.

Add salmon (with juice) in flaky, small pieces; also add broccoli. Mix by hand. Add lemon juice and dash of cayenne pepper. Put mixture in prebaked **Whole-Wheat Pastry Crust.**

Beat together eggs, egg whites, and milk. Strain over salmon-and-broccoli mixture. Cover with cheese, and sprinkle evenly with paprika. Bake about 50 minutes, till done. Garnish and serve.

Note: Spinach or zucchini may be substituted for broccoli.

MAKES 8 SMALL PORTIONS. CALORIES PER PORTION: 179

MAKES 4 LARGE PORTIONS. CALORIES PER PORTION: 358

PREPARATION TIME: 20 MINUTES

BAKING TIME: 50 MINUTES

Zucchini-and-Spinach Quiche

2 teaspoons	olive oil
2 teaspoons	garlic, minced
½	onion, chopped
1½ cup	zucchini, sliced
2 teaspoons	dried sweet basil
2 teaspoons	vegetable seasoning
1	prebaked Whole-Wheat Pastry Crust (page 111)
¾ cup	fresh spinach, cooked, chopped, and well-drained
½ teaspoon	grated nutmeg
2	eggs
2	egg whites
⅔ cup	low-fat milk, scalded
1 tablespoon	Parmesan or Romano cheese, freshly grated
3 ounces	mozzarella cheese, freshly grated

Preheat oven to 350°.

Heat oil in heavy skillet over medium fire. Gently saute garlic and onion till onion begins to soften. Add zucchini, sprinkle with basil and vegetable seasoning. Stir with wooden spatula, and saute 3-4 minutes. Cover. Simmer till zucchini begins to soften.

Pour contents into prebaked **Whole-Wheat Pastry Crust.** Cover with chopped spinach, and sprinkle with nutmeg. Beat together eggs, egg whites, and milk. Strain over zucchini and spinach. Sprinkle grated cheese over top. Bake about 50 minutes, till done.

MAKES 8 SMALL PORTIONS. CALORIES PER PORTION: 181

MAKES 4 LARGE PORTIONS. CALORIES PER PORTION: 361

PREPARATION TIME: 20 MINUTES

BAKING TIME: 50 MINUTES

Onion-Tomato Pie

2 teaspoons	olive oil
2	onions, medium size, thinly sliced
1 teaspoon	dried whole thyme
1 teaspoon	vegetable seasoning
1 prebaked	Whole-Wheat Pastry Crust (page 111)
6	thin tomato slices
1 tablespoon	Parmesan or Romano cheese, freshly grated
¼ teaspoon	grated nutmeg
2	eggs
2	egg whites
⅔ cup	low-fat milk, scalded
3 ounces	Jarlsberg or mozzarella cheese, freshly grated
garnish:	parsley sprigs

Preheat oven to 350°.

Heat oil in heavy skillet. Saute onions over medium fire until glazed. Sprinkle thyme and vegetable seasoning over onions, and mix with wooden spatula. Cover and simmer 5 minutes to soften onions. Pour contents into prebaked **Whole-Wheat Pastry Crust.**

Cover with tomato slices; sprinkle with Parmesan cheese and nutmeg. Beat eggs and scalded milk together; strain over the top. Top with Jarlsberg cheese. Bake 50 minutes, until pie is brown and knife comes out clean. Garnish and serve.

MAKES 8 SMALL PORTIONS. CALORIES PER PORTION: 183

MAKES 4 LARGE PORTIONS. CALORIES PER PORTION: 367

PREPARATION TIME: 20 MINUTES

BAKING TIME: 50 MINUTES

LET'S TALK ABOUT THESE RECIPES

OMELETTES: For the dieter cutting both calories and cholesterol, the classic 'Golden Door' omelette is prepared with 1 whole egg plus 1 egg white, per serving.

SHRIMPS: For years it was customary to overcook shrimp. Latest cooking instructions require fewer minutes at boiling point. One method for very tender shrimp calls for boiling water to be poured over shelled, raw shrimps to cover; the pan is then covered, and the shrimps are allowed to stand without additional heating — for 5 minutes.

SOUFFLES: When beating souffle eggs with a wire whisk, it is recommended that they be placed in a metal bowl (not aluminum). As with all souffles, those of the 'Golden Door' must be handled most carefully, must not be shaken, and must not be jarred by the oven door opening during the cooking process. Check the souffle only at the very end of the oven period, and then look quickly as you apply the finger test. Souffle should spring to the touch. If if doesn't, gently close the oven door and bide your time till you test again.

SOY SAUCE: For Chinese and other dishes requiring soy sauce, the 'Golden Door' employs only the low-sodium variety, such as that marketed by Kikoman. But if you wish to be very careful about salt, you will further cut sodium by using bourbon and soy sauce, half and half.

DRESSINGS, DIPS AND SAUCES

Dressings and sauces dictate whether many a course is a high- or low-calorie dish. For decades, the 'Golden Door' has been demonstrating that haute cuisine can be low-calorie without diminishing either its elegance or savory appeal. Indeed, when in the 1970's the French introduced la nouvelle cuisine, New York Times food columnist Marian Burros (her latest book is Keep It Simple) pointed out that it was not very nouvelle at such a place as the 'Golden Door,' where "that kind of cooking has been going on for years."

Recognizing that a salad with a proper dressing can be a dieter's delight, many people have mistakenly resorted to the unsatisfactory bottled diet dressings. These concoctions usually make up in excessive salt for what they lack in calories. They also are boobytrapped with synthetic flavorings and artificial preservatives.

A proper diet dressing tastes as fresh as the salad it complements. A cook's rule of thumb for our choice 'Golden Door' recipes: a dressing containing lemon juice must be prepared the day it is served; so too should dressing made with fresh herbs, if you would savor their zesty seasoning. Those with a base of mustard/vinegar, yogurt, or vegetables may be refrigerated for a limited time.

Too Spartan for most genuine lovers of good food, unadorned meals devoid of sauces and dressings have been the ruin of many a diet plan.

Gravies, sauces, hors d'oeuvres complete with dips are the glamorous accessories, the fuss and furbelows, among foodstuffs. For many years they also were caloric culprits because traditional Continental cookery dictated dependence upon rich butter and/or heavy cream.

Today, innovative chefs have bypassed those offending products, yet found ways to imitate every triumph of the chef saucier. Don't dismiss the sauce section as an interesting novelty that you may look into sometime. Regard it as a means of safeguarding a sensible diet by adding low-calorie magic to daily dining.

Lemon Dressing

4 tablespoons	sesame-seed or safflower oil
3 tablespoons	fresh lemon juice
2 tablespoons	fresh parsley
½ teaspoon	vegetable seasoning
¼ teaspoon	black pepper, freshly ground,
2 to 3 tablespoons	Parmesan or Romano cheese, freshly grated

In blender, place all ingredients except cheese. Blend till parsley is finely chopped. Add cheese when tossing salad.

Note: To preserve fresh lemon flavor, prepare this dressing just before serving.

MAKES ¾ CUP OF DRESSING. CALORIES PER TABLESPOON: 96

PREPARATION TIME: 5 MINUTES

Mustard Vinaigrette Dressing

1 tablespoon	Dijon mustard
1 teaspoon	black pepper, freshly ground
5½ tablespoons	apple-cider vinegar
6½ tablespoons	sesame-seed or safflower oil
1 tablespoon	water

Mix together all ingredients in an 8-ounce (Dijon mustard size) jar. Before using, close lid tightly, and shake vigorously.

A strong dressing, it should be used sparingly. Excellent with **Green Bean-Tomato Salad** (page 31), **Crudites** (page 43), and other salads.

Note: Keeps well under refrigeration.

CALORIES PER TABLESPOON: 59

PREPARATION TIME: 5 MINUTES

Onion-Basil Sauce

1 tablespoon	sesame-seed or safflower oil
2	onions, large, finely chopped
1 teaspoon	vegetable seasoning
2 teaspoons	dried sweet basil (or 1 tablespoon fresh basil)
2 ounces	Neufchatel low-fat cream cheese
¼ cup	half-and-half cream
½ teaspoon	black pepper, freshly ground
1 tablespoon	arrowroot, dissolved in 2 tablespoons water
¾ cup	Chicken Broth (page 48), heated

In tightly covered, heavy skillet, cook onions — with oil and vegetable seasoning — 1 hour, over very low fire. Do not lift lid.

Stir, and add basil. Cover again, and cook 20 minutes more. Add cheese, and whip vigorously with whisk till smooth. Add half and half, pepper, arrowroot dissolved in water, and **Chicken Broth.** Let bubble. Whisk, and serve.

Excellent with plain chicken, fish, or salmon pate.

SERVES 4. CALORIES PER SERVING: 126

PREPARATION TIME: 1 HOUR 20 MINUTES

Mustard Dressing with Shallots

2 tablespoons	shallots, coarsely chopped
2 tablespoons	water
1 recipe	Mustard Vinaigrette Dressing (page 17)

Combine in blender until smooth.

This is also a strong dressing to be used sparingly. It goes well with such ingredients as tomatoes, watercress, and bean sprouts, and keeps well under refrigeration.

Use about 2 teaspoons per individual serving.

CALORIES PER TABLESPOON: 59

PREPARATION TIME: 3 MINUTES

Blue Cheese Dressing

¾ cup	plain, low-fat yogurt
½ teaspoon	garlic, minced
1 teaspoon	black pepper, freshly ground
1½ ounce	Danish blue cheese, crumbled

Put in blender all ingredients except cheese, blending till smooth. Add cheese, and blend briefly on pulse cycle, making sure cheese stays crumbly.

Use as dressing or dip.

Makes 1 cup.

CALORIES PER TABLESPOON: 18

PREPARATION TIME: 3 MINUTES

Vegetarian Dressing Delight

1	celery stalk, finely chopped
1	tomato, medium size, peeled and quartered
¼ cup	chives, chopped
¼ cup	fresh parsley, chopped
¼ cup	onion, chopped
1 cup	water
4 tablespoons	cider vinegar
2 teaspoons	vegetable seasoning

In saucepan, bring all ingredients to boil. Simmer 5 minutes. Puree in blender. Makes 2 cups.

Chill before serving.

Serve on green salads and all raw salads.

CALORIES PER TABLESPOON: 2

PREPARATION TIME: 10 MINUTES

Buttermilk Dressing

1 cup	buttermilk
1 tablespoon	Dijon mustard
2 tablespoons	scallions, minced
¼ cup	cucumber, grated
¼ teaspoon	dill weed
2 teaspoons	fresh parsley, chopped
¼ teaspoon	black pepper, freshly ground
2 teaspoons	fresh lemon juice

Mix all ingredients in jar, and shake to blend. Chill in freezer 10 minutes.

CALORIES PER TABLESPOON: 7

PREPARATION TIME: 5 MINUTES

Sauce Raifort

½ cup	plain, low-fat yogurt
2 tablespoons	creamed horseradish
1 tablespoon	Dijon mustard
	cayenne pepper, to taste
garnish:	radishes, thinly sliced; or scallions, chopped

With a wire whisk, mix all ingredients well till smooth. Top with radish or scallion.

Excellent with plain baked or broiled fish. May also be used as a dip.

CALORIES PER TABLESPOON: 10

PREPARATION TIME: 5 MINUTES

500-Island Dressing

1 cup	Mayonette Sauce (page 20)
2	ripe tomatoes, peeled and chopped
3 tablespoons	pimiento or red bell pepper, chopped
3 tablespoons	chives or scallions, chopped
2 tablespoons	cornichons (optional), chopped
	cayenne pepper, to taste
1 tablespoon	cilantro (optional)

In mixing bowl, mix all ingredients with spatula. (To keep dressing chunky, do not use blender.)

If you have fresh cilantro, it will lend zest to the sauce.

Ideal for shrimp salad or other seafood dishes.

CALORIES PER TABLESPOON: 24

PREPARATION TIME: 10 MINUTES

Raspberry Dressing
(FOR FRUIT SALADS)

½ cup	plain, low-fat yogurt
¼ cup	raspberries
2 teaspoons	honey

Place all ingredients in blender. Mix until just blended (over-blending raspberry seeds will make sauce tart).

Makes about ¾ cup.

Note: A delicious dressing for fruit salad can be made with any contrasting fruit (such as bananas, strawberries, peaches, mangoes, etc.).

CALORIES PER TABLESPOON: 12

PREPARATION TIME: 3 MINUTES

Mayonnaise

2 teaspoons	Dijon mustard
1	egg yolk
2	shallots, chunked (about 4 teaspoons)
1 teaspoon	black pepper, freshly ground
2 tablespoons	apple-cider vinegar or fresh lemon juice
½ cup	sesame-seed or safflower oil

Put all ingredients except oil in blender. Blend until smooth, and slowly add oil to thicken.

CALORIES PER TABLESPOON: 67
PREPARATION TIME: 5 MINUTES

Hummus

2 cups	chick-peas (or garbanzo beans), cooked
1-2	garlic cloves, minced
2 tablespoons	tahini-sesame butter
½ teaspoon	olive oil
	juice of 1 lemon
3 teaspoons	soy sauce (low sodium)
½ cup	water
½ teaspoon	white pepper
garnish:	fresh parsley

Soak chick-peas overnight. Drain, and put into heavy pan, covering with a few inches of water. Simmer, covered, 1½-2 hours, or till tender.

Drain and cool.

In food processor, combine all ingredients till smooth. Serve garnished in a bowl.

This is a spicy spread to be served as a dip with crackers or bread, or as a stuffing for vegetables.

MAKES 48 TABLESPOONS. CALORIES PER TABLESPOON: 21

PREPARATION TIME: 2 HOURS

Mayonette Sauce

1 cup	Mayonnaise (at left)
½ cup	plain, low-fat yogurt

Combine in blender until smooth.

CALORIES PER TABLESPOON: 58
PREPARATION TIME: 3 MINUTES

Vincent Sauce

1 cup	Mayonette Sauce (above)
1 cup	fresh herb mixture: parsley, chives or scallions, mint, sweet basil, and tarragon
1 tablespoon	fresh lemon juice

In blender, mix all ingredients until they are well combined, but herbs are still leafy. Serve immediately.

Excellent for cold salmon and other seafood, or **Crudites** (page 43).

CALORIES PER TABLESPOON: 34
PREPARATION TIME: 3 MINUTES

Tarragon Sauce

recipe **Mayonnaise** (upper left)

Follow instructions of original recipe, but eliminate apple-cider vinegar (or lemon juice). Instead, substitute:

⅓ cup	fresh tarragon leaves (or 3 tablespoons dried tarragon in tarragon vinegar)
⅓ cup	fresh parsley

CALORIES PER TABLESPOON: 37
PREPARATION TIME: 3 MINUTES

Mock Bearnaise Sauce

½ cup	plain, low-fat yogurt
2 tablespoons	shallots, chopped fine
2 tablespoons	dried tarragon
¼ cup	dry white wine
3 tablespoons	tarragon vinegar
1 teaspoon	black pepper, freshly ground
2 teaspoons	Dijon mustard
1	hard-cooked egg, chopped
3 tablespoons	fresh parsley, minced
3 tablespoons	fresh tarragon (optional), chopped

Put yogurt in blender. In small saucepan combine shallots, tarragon, white wine, vinegar, and pepper. Simmer till reduced by about half. Cool. Strain mixture over mustard and egg.

Add mustard and egg to yogurt. Blend till smooth. Add parsley and fresh tarragon, and blend briefly.

A welcome accompaniment to broiled fish, seafood, and meat.

CALORIES PER TABLESPOON: 9
PREPARATION TIME: 10 MINUTES

Sauce Celeriac

½ cup	plain, low-fat yogurt
½ cup	celery root (or celery), finely grated
2 tablespoons	fresh lemon juice
1 tablespoon	Dijon mustard
	cayenne pepper, to taste

Grate celery root into lemon juice.

Put all ingredients in blender and combine briefly, to keep celery somewhat chunky.

A fine dip, or sauce for broiled chicken or fish.

CALORIES PER TABLESPOON: 7
PREPARATION TIME: 10 MINUTES

Sauce Madras (Curry)

1 cup	Mayonette Sauce (page 20)
1 teaspoon	sesame-seed or safflower oil
1 tablespoon	shallots, chopped fine
1-2 teaspoons	curry powder, to taste
	cayenne pepper
½	ripe banana

In small skillet, lightly saute oil and shallots till they are glazed. Add curry powder; mix with wooden spatula to make a paste. Take care not to burn the curry powder. In blender, combine curry mixture, banana and **Mayonette** until smooth. Add dash of cayenne pepper. Use this sauce to coat broccoli, cauliflower, or cabbage. Nice with seafood.

CALORIES PER TABLESPOON: 62
PREPARATION TIME: 5 MINUTES

Curry Sauce

½ cup	plain, low-fat yogurt
1 teaspoon	sesame-seed or safflower oil
1 tablespoon	shallot or white scallion, chopped
2-3 teaspoons	curry powder
½	banana

Put yogurt in blender. In skillet, heat oil and add shallot and curry powder; stir with wooden spatula. Cook 3-4 minutes, to make a paste. Add mixture to yogurt. Blend in banana, and puree till smooth.

Good with broiled sea bass or red snapper. Or use as dip.

CALORIES PER TABLESPOON: 13
PREPARATION TIME: 10 MINUTES

Yogurt-Dill Sauce

½ cup	plain, low-fat yogurt
1 tablespoon	shallot or white scallion, chopped fine
1 tablespoon	rice vinegar
1 tablespoon	dill weed
1 tablespoon	fresh parsley, chopped
	cayenne pepper, to taste

Put yogurt, shallot, and vinegar into blender; blend till smooth. Add dill weed and parsley, and blend quickly with the pulse cycle. Season with dash of cayenne pepper.

This is especially good over fish or chicken, or cucumber or cabbage salad.

CALORIES PER TABLESPOON: 8

PREPARATION TIME: 3 MINUTES

Ponzu (Oriental) Dip

4 ounces	tofu (bean curd)
⅓ cup	Chicken Broth (page 48)
1 tablespoon	miso paste
2 tablespoons	Mirin (sweet Sake)
1 tablespoon	soy sauce (low-sodium)
1	lemon zest (½″ wide, 2″ long)
2 teaspoons	fresh ginger, minced
1 teaspoon	garlic, minced

Combine all ingredients in blender. Blend at high speed, till smooth. Use with **Yakitori** (page 86), broiled chicken, or shrimp on skewers.

CALORIES PER TABLESPOON: 10

PREPARATION TIME: 5 MINUTES

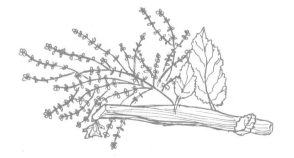

Guacamole Surprise

1 pound	fresh asparagus
½ cup	water
1 tablespoon	fresh lemon juice
2 tablespoons	onion, finely chopped
1	ripe tomato, chopped
1 teaspoon	vegetable seasoning
¼ teaspoon	ground cumin
¼ teaspoon	chili powder
½ teaspoon	garlic, minced
½ cup	plain, low-fat yogurt
1	envelope unflavored gelatin
¼ cup	lukewarm water

Wash asparagus, and trim off tough ends. Cut spears into 1″ pieces. Steam in ½ cup water about 4 minutes. Drain and cool.

Put asparagus and other ingredients — except gelatin and lukewarm water — into blender and combine.

Dissolve gelatin in lukewarm water, softening it 5 minutes before adding to pureed asparagus. Puree "guacamole" till smooth.

Chill till firm. Use as dip or salad dressing.

Makes about 2 cups.

CALORIES PER TABLESPOON: 7

PREPARATION TIME: 20 MINUTES

Spinach Sauce

1	recipe Sauce Michel (page 23)
¾ cup	spinach, cooked

Combine briefly in blender. Sauce should have coarse texture. Heat to a simmer.

Serve immediately as cream sauce for fish, poultry, and vegetables.

CALORIES PER TABLESPOON: 8

PREPARATION TIME: 10 MINUTES

Ignacio's Salsa

4	tomatoes, medium size, peeled and finely chopped
¼ cup	scallions, chopped fine
1-2 teaspoons	dried (hot!) chili flakes
1 tablespoon	fresh cilantro, chopped
½ teaspoon	dried whole oregano
½ teaspoon	sea salt
½ teaspoon	black pepper, freshly ground

Combine all ingredients 1 day in advance, and store in refrigerator. (Will keep several days.)

Serve with fish, beans, egg dishes, cottage cheese, salads, etc.

Makes about 2 cups.

CALORIES PER TABLESPOON: 5

PREPARATION TIME: 10 MINUTES

Sauce Michel

1	onion
1	small celery stalk
	water to cover
½ cup	broth (reserved)
3 ounces	Neufchatel low-fat cream cheese
1 tablespoon	arrowroot
2 teaspoons	fresh lemon juice
	grated nutmeg, to taste
	cayenne pepper, to taste

Place onion and celery in saucepan, with water to cover. Simmer gently, covered, about 45 minutes, till tender. Drain. Reserve ½ cup of broth.

In blender or food processor puree onion, celery, broth, cream cheese, arrowroot, lemon juice, and dash of nutmeg and cayenne pepper.

Reheat and serve immediately as cream sauce for fish, poultry, vegetables.

CALORIES PER TABLESPOON: 9

PREPARATION TIME: 1 HOUR

Tomato Pimiento Andalusia

½ cup	plain, low-fat yogurt
⅓ to ½ cup	tomatoes (preferably plum), peeled and chopped
¼ cup	pimiento, diced
¼ cup	scallions, finely diced
1 teaspoon	garlic, minced
1 teaspoon	dried whole oregano
	cayenne pepper, to taste

With a wire whisk, whip yogurt till smooth. Add other ingredients; fold together with spatula.

CALORIES PER TABLESPOON: 6

PREPARATION TIME: 5 MINUTES

Mushroom Cream Sauce

2 cups	fresh mushrooms, sliced
1 tablespoon	fresh lemon juice
¼ cup	water
1 teaspoon	vegetable seasoning
½ teaspoon	black pepper, freshly ground
1	recipe Sauce Michel (lower left)
¼ cup	scallions, chopped

In covered saucepan, steam mushrooms 5 minutes with lemon juice, water, vegetable seasoning, and pepper.

Drain. Add mushrooms to **Sauce Michel.** Heat to a simmer. Add scallions.

Serve immediately as cream sauce for chicken breasts and other white meat (such as veal) and for white fish (such as sea bass).

CALORIES PER TABLESPOON: 6

PREPARATION TIME: 10 MINUTES

Tomato Concassee

2 teaspoons	olive oil
2 teaspoons	garlic, minced
1 tablespoon	shallots, minced
1 tablespoon	dried sweet basil
1	bay leaf
5	tomatoes, large, peeled and diced (or 1 18-ounce can whole plum tomatoes)
1 teaspoon	black pepper, freshly ground

Gently saute garlic and shallots in oil. Add basil, bay leaf, tomatoes, and pepper. Cover, and simmer 5 minutes. Simmer uncovered 10-15 additional minutes.

Concassee means "diced small."

This sauce stores (it can be frozen) and reheats well. It becomes an excellent base for **San Francisco Cioppino** (page 74); **Ignacio's Salsa** (page 23); **Tomato Sauce** (below); and **Eggplant Florentine** (page 66).

CALORIES PER TABLESPOON: 8
PREPARATION TIME: 30 MINUTES

Tomato Sauce

1 recipe	Tomato Concassee (above)
1 cup	tomato puree
¼ cup	water
2 tablespoons	fresh parsley, chopped
2 tablespoons	Parmesan cheese, freshly grated

To simmering **Tomato Concassee**, add tomato puree and water. Simmer uncovered 20 minutes, till sauce has thick consistency. Sprinkle with parsley and cheese, and mix. Admirable with spaghetti, squash, or broiled fish or chicken.

CALORIES PER TABLESPOON: 8
PREPARATION TIME: 20 MINUTES

Tomato-Cilantro Sauce

2 cups	fresh tomatoes, peeled and chopped
2	garlic cloves, chopped
1 tablespoon	fresh cilantro, chopped, or ¼ teaspoon ground coriander
2 teaspoons	fresh parsley, chopped
1 tablespoon	olive oil
	vegetable seasoning, to taste
¼ teaspoon	black pepper, freshly ground

Mix all ingredients in a pot, and heat over low fire. Makes 2 cups.

Serve hot over fish, chicken, or vegetarian entree.

MAKES 32 TABLESPOONS. CALORIES PER TABLESPOON: 12
PREPARATION TIME: 35 MINUTES

Ginger Dressing

¼ cup	sesame-seed or safflower oil
¼ cup	rice vinegar
1	lemon zest (½" wide, 2½" long)
1 teaspoon	garlic, minced
1½ teaspoons	fresh ginger root, coarsely chopped
2 tablespoons	raw sesame seeds, freshly toasted
2 tablespoons	scallions, chopped
garnish:	radishes, thinly sliced

Place oil, vinegar, lemon zest, garlic, and ginger root in blender; blend until smooth.

Use 1 tablespoon per individual serving. After tossing salad and dressing well, add sesame seeds and scallions; top with radishes, for color.

CALORIES PER SERVING: 39
PREPARATION TIME: 5 MINUTES

LET'S TALK ABOUT THESE RECIPES

ARROWROOT: The finely ground tuberous rootstocks of the arrowroot make a nutritious starch. As a thickening agent, it is a fine substitute for white flour. It does not brown, and is particularly indicated for thickening fruit and other clear sauces.

CELERY ROOT (CELERIAC): This turnip-rooted celery is cultivated for its base, which should be examined carefully before purchase. Avoid celeriac which has sprouting or very large roots, or a soft spot on top.

The medium-sized celeriac is preferable to the very large specimens.

Another use for celeriac is to peel it, chop into bite-size pieces, and cook in boiling water or soup stock to cover. Drain and serve as a potato substitute.

CHILES: Members of the capsicum family have a wide range, from the merely provocative to the downright rambunctious. A good selection of colorful shiny chiles has become a decorative asset to many U.S. supermarkets, but most Anglo shoppers shy away for fear of selecting a fiery variety. A simple rule for the novice to remember is that the smaller the variety, the hotter. This is not strictly true, but usually holds till you find yourself in a market in Mexico, where the chile section is likely to be bewildering in its bounty.

If you do not have access to fresh chiles, or are unsure about them, you can always fall back on the canned jalapeno chile — very mild and well-mannered if you dispose of all the seeds, fairly hot if you do not.

CILANTRO (MEXICAN OR CHINESE PARSLEY): This leaf of the coriander plant has been widely used in Mexico and the Far East for centuries. It has become an important Mexican export to the U.S., for Americans are learning that cilantro is a sometimes superior stand-in for parsley.

More tender than parsley, cilantro is also a bit more lively in flavor; therefore, when substituting, you will require less.

CORNICHONS: Tiny French gherkins, quite sour because they are made from certain young cucumbers which are picked green before being pickled in vinegar and spices.

DIJON MUSTARD: The choice of most European chefs, who regard it as France's premier mustard, probably because it contains verjuice, a tangy juice from large grapes which are not yet ripe.

GINGER ROOT: This gnarled-looking tuber from Fiji has along its sides new little sprouts which should not be discarded, since they have a more delicate flavor than the main root.

To store, place in a small container with a tight-fitting lid, and cover with Sherry. Will keep for up to three months. When you use the stored ginger, don't throw away the Sherry. Cook fish in it (worth the three-month wait!).

LEMON JUICE: Lemon juice can be used interchangeably with vinegar in any recipe. Lemons are nutritive, whereas vinegar is almost without food value. In addition, lemons have the amazing ability to coax more flavor out of the recipe ingredients.

LEMON ZEST: this is the yellow part of the lemon skin. It may be shaved off with a sharp knife or removed with a lemon zester, purchasable at kitchen shops.

MAYONNAISE: The unusual 'Golden Door' low-calorie mayonnaise relies on shallots and egg yolks for thickness.

MISO: This Japanese import is coming to be regarded as the world's most protean protein. There seems to be no part of a meal to which miso can't be added with some stunning effect.

Miso is the result of marriage between soybeans and rice (or, sometimes, barley). After fermentation with bacterium Aspergillus oryzar, miso keeps well. The Japanese have been known to store it for years in wooden vats.

OLIVE OIL: Various foreign brands, especially the very light varieties, can impart an exquisite flavor to salads. If you are on a maintenance diet, there's no reason why you can't substitute olive oil for at least half the required oil in a dressing.

SOYBEAN CURD (TOFU): Twice as protein-rich as milk, tofu excels milk on every count except content of Vitamin A, Riboflavin, and Vitamin C. Don't be misled by comparison figures showing ounce-for-ounce calorie similarity. Soybean curd is so light that a 4-ounce serving is always sufficient, as against an 8-ounce glass of milk.

For 2,000 years, Orientals relied upon tofu as a diet staple second only to rice. In this country, it is predicted that tofu may soon rival the popularity of yogurt.

Tofu is perishable. The 16-ounce plastic container in which it is sold should be refrigerated at once. If not all the tofu is used at one time, add water to the remainder in the container — and use up within three days.

Better still, make your own tofu. Just follow instructions which are now being widely circulated in the press.

TOASTED SESAME SEEDS: Spread on cookie sheet, and place in 325° oven till brown. Watch carefully, and turn several times.

Once you have mastered the concept of low-calorie salad dressings, you will want to introduce them to some of your favorite salad combinations. And you'll be interested to adopt Deborah's Great Instant Salad method. When a busy executive herself prepares salad for guests, it must be special.

Of course you always wash and dry your salad greens first of all. Next, mix the dressing ingredients in a salad bowl. Over and into the bowl, chop and dice your salad ingredients in the order of their resiliency, the tender ones last. In other words, you might begin with onions, green pepper, celery, cucumber, sprouts, then end with tomato and avocado. Toss after each addition, so that all ingredients will have opportunity to marinate thoroughly without diminishing their crispness and freshness. If your guests are old friends, do not spare the onions. Sweet Spanish will be fine, Bermuda even better. Low-sodium onions wake up taste buds and make salt unnecessary. Top with a few walnuts — permissible for those on a maintenance diet — which have been browning in a bit of butter. (Remember the edict for butter sauteing: do not add the food till heating butter has foamed up and then ebbed a little.)

Serve on chilled plates with frosty forks. (There is no other way.) Your guests will ask, "How did you get so much wonderful flavor into this salad?"

A variation of the above idea will require three stainless-steel bowls. Let sliced tomatoes absorb the flavor of oregano (bowl number one) while you chop cucumbers into yogurt (bowl two), then grate carrots into oil and lemon juice accented with a knife tip of Dijon mustard (the last bowl). Place three lettuce cups on each salad plate and serve from your bowls.

We take it for granted that you will never desecrate fresh, fragrant salad vegetables with commercially bottled dressings. And you will always use the best oils and the best vinegars.

On to other important salad advice. Nearly every 'Golden Door' salad recipe for four can become a main-dish luncheon salad for two, by the addition of cheese, legumes, or sliced hard-cooked eggs, or tuna or other seafood.

Leaf Salad

greens:	4 varieties (romaine, spinach, Boston lettuce, watercress, etc.), to make 4 portions
1 tablespoon	Parmesan or Romano cheese, freshly grated
2 tablespoons	pumpkin seeds, sliced almonds, or raw sesame seeds, freshly toasted
3 tablespoons	Lemon Dressing (page 17)
garnish:	bean sprouts

Wash and dry greens. Cut, tear, or shred them. Place in large bowl. Add cheese and seeds or nuts. Toss with **Lemon Dressing.**
Garnish and serve.

SERVES 4. CALORIES PER SERVING: 99

PREPARATION TIME: 10 MINUTES

Spinach Salad Mimosa

	fresh spinach leaves for 4 servings
3 tablespoons	Lemon Dressing (page 17)
2	eggs, hard-cooked, chopped
2 tablespoons	Parmesan or Romano cheese, freshly grated; or raw sesame seeds, freshly toasted

Wash, trim, and dry spinach. Tear leaves by hand.
Pour **Lemon Dressing** over spinach, and toss well. Add cheese and 1 chopped egg. Toss again.
Spoon onto plates, and top with remaining chopped egg.

SERVES 4. CALORIES PER SERVING: 130

PREPARATION TIME: 10 MINUTES

Celery Victor

2 bunches	celery, firm, compact, as white as possible
¼ cup	Mustard Vinaigrette Dressing (page 17)
	red lettuce leaves to line 4 plates
12	chives (optional)
garnish:	½ egg, hard-cooked, coarsely chopped; 12 cherry tomatoes

Remove tough outer celery stalks. Cut tops, leaving celery hearts approximately 2″ wide by 6″ long. Trim root ends. With sharp knife or potato peeler, remove coarse celery strings from hearts. Cut each heart in ½.

Place celery hearts in stainless-steel pan; cover with water. Bring to gentle boil over medium fire. Poach 15 minutes, till tender.

Remove from water, drain, and cool. Refrigerate 2 hours or more.

At serving time, pour **Mustard Vinaigrette Dressing** into shallow pan. Dredge celery in dressing; coat well.

Place each celery heart half on lettuce bed. Make another lengthwise cut through heart. (For more festive look, lay 3 long fresh chives down center of each celery heart.) Garnish and serve.

SERVES 4. CALORIES PER SERVING: 99

PREPARATION TIME: 1 HOUR

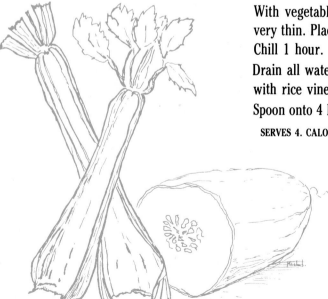

Romaine-and-Blue-Cheese Salad

	romaine lettuce for 4 servings
3 tablespoons	Blue Cheese Dressing (page 18)
garnish:	bean sprouts or tomato wedges

Wash, dry, and tear lettuce. Place in large bowl. Add **Blue Cheese Dressing** and toss well.

Spoon onto 4 plates. Garnish and serve.

SERVES 4. CALORIES PER SERVING: 32

PREPARATION TIME: 10 MINUTES

Cucumber Salad Nippon

1	European cucumber, large
¼ teaspoon	sea salt
2 tablespoons	rice vinegar
1 tablespoon	chives, chopped
	lettuce leaves to line 4 plates
garnish:	crab meat or bay shrimp (cooked), or grated daikon (optional)

With vegetable slicer or knife, peel and slice cucumber very thin. Place slices in colander. Sprinkle with sea salt. Chill 1 hour.

Drain all water from cucumbers. Place in bowl and mix with rice vinegar and chives.

Spoon onto 4 lettuce beds. Garnish (if desired) and serve.

SERVES 4. CALORIES PER SERVING: 13 (WITHOUT SEAFOOD GARNISH)

PREPARATION TIME: 1 HOUR

Two-Cabbage Slaw

½ head green cabbage, medium size, shredded
½ head red cabbage, medium size, shredded
2 carrots, peeled and grated
¾ cup Mayonette Sauce (page 20)
2 tablespoons cider vinegar
½ teaspoon celery seeds
1 tablespoon sugar

Combine cabbage and carrots.

In separate bowl, gradually whisk vinegar into **Mayonette Sauce**. Add celery seeds and sugar; mix well. Pour over cabbage, and marinate 2 hours.

SERVES 4. CALORIES PER SERVING: 161

PREPARATION TIME: 15 MINUTES

Lifeline Salad

4 cups of any of following, or a combination of: celery, broccoli, turnips, cauliflower, carrots, asparagus, jicama, radishes, bell pepper, and zucchini
4 ounces feta cheese, chopped
½ cup chives, parsley, or scallions, chopped
2 tablespoons tarragon vinegar lettuce leaves to line 4 plates

Wash, trim, peel vegetables; slice. Combine with cheese, chives, and vinegar. Spoon onto 4 lettuce beds and serve.

SERVES 4. CALORIES PER SERVING: 187

PREPARATION TIME: 15-20 MINUTES

Leek Salad

4 leeks, large
lettuce to line 4 plates
2-3 tablespoons Mustard Vinaigrette Dressing (page 17)
garnish: 4 parsley or watercress sprigs; 4 radishes or tomato wedges

Trim leeks and wash well. Leave about 1″ of green on white end; discard remainder. Halve leeks lengthwise, but not all the way through to tip end.

Place in saucepan. Half-fill with water. Simmer gently, covered, 20-30 minutes, till tender.

Chill leeks in cooking liquid, so they remain moist and tender.

At serving time, pour **Mustard Vinaigrette** dressing into shallow pan. Dredge leeks in dressing; coat well. Drain chilled leeks well. Spoon onto 4 lettuce beds, garnish, and serve.

SERVES 4. CALORIES PER SERVING: 44

PREPARATION TIME: 10 MINUTES

COOKING TIME: 30 MINUTES

Watercress Salad

2½ to 3 tablespoons Mustard Vinaigrette Dressing (page 17)
1 tomato, peeled and diced
2 teaspoons scallions (white part), chopped
watercress, fresh, trimmed, for 4 servings
1 cup bean sprouts

Combine in large bowl tomato, dressing, and scallions. Marinate 1 hour in refrigerator.

Just before serving, toss with watercress and bean sprouts.

SERVES 4. CALORIES PER SERVING: 62

PREPARE 1 HOUR AHEAD

PREPARATION TIME: 10 MINUTES

Hearts of Palm Vinaigrette

	Boston lettuce leaves to line 4 plates
8-12	hearts of palm, depending on size
4 tablespoons	Mustard Dressing with Shallots (page 18)

Place 2 or 3 hearts of palm on each lettuce bed. Pour over **Mustard Dressing with Shallots,** and serve.

SERVES 4. CALORIES PER SERVING: 100

PREPARATION TIME: 10 MINUTES

Grated-Beet Salad

3 cups	beets, raw
3-4 tablespoons	apple cider vinegar
3-4 tablespoons	olive oil
2 tablespoons	fresh parsley, chopped lettuce leaves to line 4 plates
garnish:	parsley sprigs, thin radish and cucumber slices

Peel and grate beets in fine vegetable shredder or food processor. Sprinkle with vinegar and olive oil; toss well with fork.

Spoon onto 4 lettuce beds. Garnish and serve.

SERVES 4. CALORIES PER SERVING: 66

PREPARATION TIME: 10 MINUTES

Greek Salad

1 head	romaine lettuce, large
12	tiny Greek olives
2 ounces	feta cheese, crumbled
1	Bermuda onion, small, sliced thin
1	bell pepper, small, sliced thin
2 tablespoons	olive oil
2 tablespoons	red-wine vinegar
1	garlic clove, small, crushed
	black pepper, freshly ground, to taste
	Golden Door Herb Seasoning (page 5), to taste

Toss lettuce leaves, olives, onion, and green pepper. Top with cheese.

In separate bowl, gradually whisk oil into vinegar, garlic, and seasonings.

Pour over salad ingredients, and serve.

SERVES 4. CALORIES PER SERVING: 180

PREPARATION TIME: 15 MINUTES

Apple-Mushroom Salad

1	apple, small; washed, cored, and sliced with skin
½ pound	fresh mushrooms, sliced
2 tablespoons	fresh lemon juice
2 teaspoons	sesame-seed or safflower oil
2 tablespoons	fresh parsley, chopped
¼ teaspoon	vegetable seasoning watercress or alfalfa sprouts to line 4 plates

Combine apple, mushrooms, lemon juice, oil, parsley, and vegetable seasoning. Spoon onto 4 beds of watercress or sprouts, and serve.

SERVES 4. CALORIES PER SERVING: 52

PREPARATION TIME: 10 MINUTES

Green Bean-Tomato Salad

¾ pound	green beans, French cut (at angle)
1	tomato, peeled and diced
3 tablespoons	Mustard Vinaigrette Dressing (page 17)
2 teaspoons	shallots, minced
1	garlic clove (minced) black pepper, freshly ground, to taste
1 teaspoon	dried whole oregano
4 ounces	Chinese pea pods (optional), washed, trimmed, and sliced lengthwise
garnish:	scallions or chives, chopped

Blanch green beans in boiling water 3-4 minutes. They should still be crisp when removed from fire. Drain, cool with ice cubes. Refrigerate.

Place tomato in large bowl. Add **Mustard Vinaigrette Dressing,** shallot, garlic, pepper, and oregano. Mix well. Marinate in refrigerator 3-4 hours.

Toss pea pods (if desired) and beans with tomato mixture. Garnish and serve.

SERVES 4. CALORIES PER SERVING: 87

PREPARATION TIME: 10 MINUTES

Sprout Salad

	Boston and romaine lettuce leaves, to line 4 plates
4	fresh mushrooms, sliced thin
1 cup	alfalfa sprouts
1 cup	bean sprouts
2 tablespoons	sunflower seeds, raw
4 tablespoons	Lemon Dressing (page 17)

Combine lettuce leaves with mushroom slices. Arrange 4 lettuce beds. Top each with ¼ cup of each sprout variety. Sprinkle on sunflower seeds and **Lemon Dressing.**

SERVES 4. CALORIES PER SERVING: 144

PREPARATION TIME: 10 MINUTES

Mushroom Salad Warm or Cold

1½ tablespoons	sun-dried white raisins
1 tablespoon	shallots or scallions, minced
1 teaspoon	garlic, minced
2 tablespoons	olive oil
1 pound	fresh mushrooms,
1 teaspoon	dried whole thyme, or ½ teaspoon fresh thyme
1 teaspoon	vegetable seasoning
½ teaspoon	black pepper, freshly ground
¼ cup	dry white wine
1 cup	tomato, peeled, seeded, and diced
1 tablespoon	fresh lemon juice
¼ cup	fresh parsley, chopped
garnish:	lettuce leaves or watercress

Pre-soak raisins in warm water to cover, till plump. In heavy skillet, gently saute shallots and garlic in 1 tablespoon olive oil till they start to soften. Add mushrooms, thyme, vegetable seasoning, and pepper; stir with wooden spatula. Quickly add wine, tomato, raisins (drained), and lemon juice. Remove from fire as soon as mixture comes to a boil.

Sprinkle with parsley and remainder of olive oil. Garnish and serve, warm or cold.

SERVES 4. CALORIES PER SERVING: 127

PREPARATION TIME: 15 MINUTES

Tabbouleh Salad

½ cup	bulgar wheat, medium (purchase at health-food store)
1¼ cups	water
¾ cup	fresh parsley, finely chopped
½ cup	scallions, finely sliced
1	tomato, peeled and finely chopped
6	radishes, finely chopped
1 tablespoon	fresh mint leaves, minced
3 tablespoons	fresh lemon juice
3 tablespoons	olive oil
1 teaspoon	garlic, minced
	cayenne pepper
	lettuce leaves to line 4 plates
garnish:	cucumber and radish slices and bell pepper rings

Pre-soak bulgar wheat, up to 4 hours; it should be slightly crunchy. Strain, and press out excess water.

With fork, gradually fold in parsley, scallions, tomato, radishes, and mint leaves. Add lemon juice, olive oil, garlic, and dash of cayenne pepper. Mix well; fold several times with spatula.

Spoon onto 4 lettuce beds. Garnish and serve.

MAKES 8 SMALL PORTIONS. CALORIES PER PORTION: 108

MAKES 4 LARGE PORTIONS. CALORIES PER PORTION: 215

PREPARATION TIME: 15 MINUTES

COOKING TIME: 4 HOURS

Jerusalem Salad

6	Jerusalem artichokes, grated
2	carrots, grated
3	celery stalks, chopped fine
⅓ cup	fresh parsley, chopped fine
¼ cup	Mayonette Sauce (page 20)

Mix all ingredients and serve.

SERVES 4. CALORIES PER SERVING: 170

PREPARATION TIME: 15 MINUTES

Dilled Cucumber Salad

3 cups	cucumber, peeled and diced (about 1 European cucumber, or 1½ regular)
2 tablespoons	radishes, sliced (5 or 6 radishes)
½ cup	plain, low-fat yogurt
2 tablespoons	tarragon vinegar
¼ teaspoon	ground cardamom
¼ teaspoon	dill weed

Place cucumbers and radishes in bowl. In another bowl, combine yogurt, vinegar, cardamom, and dill weed; mix well, and pour over cucumbers. Refrigerate at least 1 hour before serving.

This can be served with **Parsley-Carrot Salad** (page 37); **Green Bean-Tomato Salad** (page 31); or **Grated Beet Salad** (page 30).

SERVES 4. CALORIES PER SERVING: 38

PREPARATION TIME: 1 HOUR

California-Style Salad

	mixed greens (romaine, Boston lettuce, watercress, spinach, etc.), to make 4 portions
4 tablespoons	Lemon Dressing (page 17)
3 tablespoons	sesame seeds, freshly toasted
12	grapefruit wedges, large
1	avocado, ripe, thinly sliced
1	Bermuda onion, thinly sliced and marinated in vinegar
garnish:	parsley sprigs

Toss salad greens with **Lemon Dressing** and sesame seeds. Place in 4 chilled bowls. On each salad, place 3 grapefruit wedges alternated with 3 avocado slices; top with 2 or 3 onion rings.

Garnish and serve.

SERVES 4. CALORIES PER SERVING: 223
PREPARATION TIME: 15 MINUTES

Cottage Cheese for Fruit Plates

2 cups	low-fat cottage cheese
1	apple, crisp, grated with skin
1 teaspoon	ground cinnamon
2 tablespoons	sunflower seeds, raw

With spatula, combine all ingredients in mixing bowl. Place a scoop of mixture on ½ melon, or serve with any fresh fruit.

SERVES 4. CALORIES PER SERVING: 97
PREPARATION TIME: 5 MINUTES

Celery Root-and-Apple Salad

1	celery root (about ¾ pound), washed and peeled
sprinkle	fresh lemon juice
1 tablespoon	Mayonnaise (page 20)
2 teaspoons	Dijon mustard
3 teaspoons	fresh lemon juice
¼ teaspoon	white pepper
1	green apple, crisp, or golden delicious; grated with skin
	butter lettuce leaves to line 4 plates
garnish:	parsley sprigs

Cut celery into thin strips or grate with food processor, or by hand. Immediately sprinkle with lemon juice to prevent from turning brown. Combine **Mayonnaise**, mustard, lemon juice, and pepper. Add to celery root. Toss well. Add apple and mix.

Spoon onto 4 lettuce beds. Garnish and serve.

Note: In summer months, try ½ cup jicama and ½ celery root, or substitute heart-of-celery julienne.

SERVES 4. CALORIES PER SERVING: 46
PREPARATION TIME: 20 MINUTES

Yogurt Salad

3 cups	plain, low-fat yogurt
1	cucumber, medium size, sliced thin
½ cup	thin radish slices
4	scallions, chopped fine black pepper, freshly ground, to taste Golden Door Herb Seasoning (page 5), to taste lettuce leaves to line 4 plates (optional)

Mix vegetables well with yogurt. Season. Serve either in chilled glasses or on lettuce beds.

SERVES 4. CALORIES PER SERVING: 126
PREPARATION TIME: 10 MINUTES

Green Salad with Onion and Orange

1	garlic clove, halved
3 cups	watercress sprigs, or small pieces curly endive, or romaine
2	onion slices, thin, sweet white or red, separated into rings; or 2 green onions, thinly sliced
1	orange, small; peeled, thinly sliced, and seeded
1 tablespoon	corn or olive oil
1 teaspoon	red-wine vinegar
1 teaspoon	red wine (or water)
pinch	dry mustard
	sea salt, to taste
	black pepper, freshly grated, to taste

Rub salad bowl with cut side of garlic. Add greens, onions, and orange. Mix.

Combine remaining ingredients in blender. Dribble over greens as you toss with fork. (Add more vinegar if desired.)

Serve at once.

SERVES 4. CALORIES PER SERVING: 47

PREPARATION TIME: 15 MINUTES

California Fruit "Club Sandwich"

	lettuce to line 4 plates
garnish:	grape cluster and watercress

RICOTTA FRUIT CREME FILLING:

1½ cups	ricotta cheese
¾ cup	low-fat cottage cheese
3½ tablespoons	honey
5 tablespoons	fresh lemon or lime juice
½ cup	fresh mango (or canned peach)
4	pineapple rings
4	melon slices, ½"
4	grapefruit slices, ¼"
4	orange slices, ¼"
4	thin kiwi slices
4	strawberries

Cover 4 plates with lettuce beds, and add garnish. Refrigerate. Prepare Ricotta Fruit Creme Filling:

In food processor, puree till smooth ricotta cheese, cottage cheese, honey, lemon juice, and mango. (Never prepare in advance, for it tends to become bitter.)

On each chilled, garnished plate, center pineapple ring with 2 tablespoons Riccota Fruit Creme in middle. Top with melon ring and 1 tablespoon Ricotta Fruit Creme. Continue to build in pyramid fashion with 1 grapefruit slice, 1 teaspoon Ricotta Fruit Creme, orange slice, kiwi slice. Top with strawberry. Hold layers together with toothpick.

Fill 4 separate side dishes with **Raspberry Dressing** (page 19).

Pour over "club sandwich" just before eating.

SERVES 4. CALORIES PER SERVING: 287

PREPARATION TIME: 30 MINUTES

Michel's Cold Shrimp-and-Fish Salad

1 pound	sea bass fillets (or ling cod, cabrilla, or other large white fish fillets), cut in diagonal slices 1" thick
1 cup	dry white wine
1 tablespoon	fresh lemon juice
1	bay leaf
1	fresh thyme sprig, or ½ teaspoon dried whole thyme
2	celery stalks, cut in 6 pieces
1 cup	bay shrimp, cooked
1 tablespoon	shallots (or white part of scallion)
1	egg yolk
1 tablespoon	fresh lemon juice
2 teaspoons	Dijon mustard
2 tablespoons	fish broth, reserved black pepper, freshly ground, to taste
3 tablespoons	sesame-seed or safflower oil cayenne pepper, to taste vegetable seasoning, to taste
4-6	parsley sprigs
2	hard-cooked eggs, chopped
¼ cup	pimiento, canned (or fresh, blanched), chopped lettuce leaves to line 4 plates
garnish:	shredded lettuce, lemon wedges, radish rosettes, alfalfa sprouts

Preheat oven to 375°.

In baking dish, place fish, white wine, 1 tablespoon lemon juice, bay leaf, thyme, and celery. Bake, covered, 20-25 minutes till done. (Test with fork. Fish should flake easily.) Put aside to cool completely. This step can be prepared several hours in advance.

With slotted spoon, lift fish from liquid, reserving 2 tablespoons fish broth. Place fish in bowl, and add shrimp.

Make dressing by placing in blender shallots, egg yolk, 1 tablespoon lemon juice, mustard, fish broth, and pepper. Blend well. Slowly add oil. Season with dash of cayenne pepper and vegetable seasoning, to taste. Add parsley and chopped hard-cooked eggs. Combine quickly, using pulse button; eggs should remain chunky.

Pour dressing over fish and shrimp. Mix well. Add pimiento, and mix with spatula.

Either marinate a few hours, or immediately spoon onto 4 lettuce beds.

Garnish and serve.

SERVES 4. CALORIES PER SERVING: 369
PREPARATION TIME: 1 HOUR

Honeydew-and-Crab-Meat Bali

4	grapefruit halves, large, hollowed (drain insides, and reserve ½ cup juice)
2 teaspoons	olive oil
1 tablespoon	shallots, minced (or white parts of scallions)
2 teaspoons	curry powder
2 cups	king crab meat
3 cups	honeydew melon balls (and their own juice)
4 tablespoons	coconut, grated, freshly toasted
2 tablespoons	scallions, chopped
garnish:	4 strawberries

In heavy skillet, heat oil and shallots. Add curry powder. With wooden spatula, mix to make paste. Add crab meat. Mix together quickly. Cook, covered, over very low fire 5 minutes.

In separate, preheated pan, quickly saute melon balls in their own juice, just enough to warm melon. Add ½ of toasted coconut.

Add mixture to crab meat. Mix well over fire.

Add grapefruit juice. Sprinkle with scallions or chives. Fill grapefruit halves, and top with remaining coconut. Garnish and serve.

SERVES 4. CALORIES PER SERVING: 226
PREPARATION TIME: 25 MINUTES

Crab-Stuffed Papaya

2	papayas, large (approximately 1 pound each), ripe; halved lengthwise and seeded
¾ pound	king crab meat, cooked, shredded
1½ teaspoons	curry powder
3 tablespoons	chives, finely chopped
2 tablespoons	sunflower seeds, raw
2 teaspoons	fresh lemon juice lettuce leaves to line 4 plates
garnish:	lemon wedges; fresh vegetables, such as string beans julienne or Chinese pea pods (cooked), or red peppers, cherry tomatoes, or shredded carrots

With small melon-ball scooper, remove most of papaya from shells, leaving only enough to give shells stability.

Place papaya balls in bowl. Add crab, curry powder, chives, sunflower seeds, and lemon juice. Spoon filling into papaya shells.

Place papaya shells on 4 lettuce beds. Garnish with whatever you have on hand — fresh vegetables with compatible flavor and color — and serve.

SERVES 4. CALORIES PER SERVING: 167
PREPARATION TIME: 15 MINUTES

Stuffed Artichoke with Crab Meat

4	fresh artichokes, large
1 tablespoon	fresh lemon juice
¾ cups	low-fat cottage cheese
3 tablespoons	chives or scallions, chopped
6 ounces	crab meat, flaked red lettuce leaves to line 4 plates
garnish:	watercress or fresh parsley, lemon wedges, and alfalfa sprouts

Remove small, tough outer rows of leaves surrounding artichoke bases. Cut off stems even with bases, so artichokes stand evenly. Cut down tops, leaving artichokes 2″ high.

Fill 8-10″ stainless-steel pan with lemon juice and water to 3″ depth. Bring to rapid boil. Add artichokes. Put heavy plate directly on top of artichokes to keep them submerged, or cover tightly. Reduce fire. Boil gently 30-35 minutes, till artichoke bases are tender when pierced with knife. Drain upside down.

When cool enough to handle, remove fuzzy chokes with small spoon; be careful not to damage hearts.

Chill artichokes thoroughly.

Stir together cottage cheese, chives, and crab meat. Fill artichokes with cottage-cheese mixture. Place them on 4 lettuce beds. Garnish and serve.

SERVES 4. CALORIES PER SERVING: 75
PREPARATION TIME: 1 HOUR 20 MINUTES

Tropical Turkey Salad

4 small heads	Bibb lettuce
1	apple, small, thinly sliced with skin
8	turkey slices, cooked (about 3-3½ ounces per serving)
garnish:	8 radishes, thinly sliced; 4 black olives, pitted and sliced; 1 bunch watercress; 4 lemon wedges
4 ounces	Mustard Vinaigrette Dressing (page 17)
½ cup	ripe mango (or pineapple or pear)
2 teaspoons	fresh lemon juice

Place lettuce in middle of each of 4 chilled salad plates. Surround lettuce with 4 apple slices and 2 turkey slices. Garnish.

In blender mix **Mustard Vinaigrette Dressing**, mango, and lemon juice. Serve this dressing on side—pour up to 1 tablespoon over each serving of turkey and apples.

SERVES 4. CALORIES PER SERVING: 214
PREPARATION TIME: 20 MINUTES

Parsley-Carrot Salad

3 cups	carrots, raw, finely grated
3 tablespoons	apple-cider vinegar
2 teaspoons	olive oil
2 tablespoons	fresh parsley, chopped lettuce leaves to line 4 plates
garnish:	parsley sprigs

Scrape, and finely grate carrots in fine vegetable shredder or food processor. Sprinkle with vinegar and olive oil; toss well with fork. Add parsley.

Spoon onto 4 lettuce beds. Garnish and serve.

SERVES 4. CALORIES PER SERVING: 57
PREPARATION TIME: 15 MINUTES

Belgian Endive Salad

8	butter lettuce leaves
4	endives, each weighing 2½ ounces
3 tablespoons	fresh lemon juice
2 tablespoons	olive oil
garnish:	4 tablespoons chives, chopped

On each plate, place 2 lettuce leaves parallel to each other; then place 2 long endive leaves across lettuce leaves.

Wash endives well, and shake dry.

Slice endives. Toss immediately with lemon juice, to prevent their turning brown (also sprinkle juice on endive leaves). This step should be prepared not more than ½ hour before serving.

Toss endives in olive oil, and spoon onto lettuce beds. Garnish and serve.

SERVES 4. CALORIES PER SERVING: 60
PREPARATION TIME: 15 MINUTES

Gold-and-Silver Salad

2	grapefruit, large, or enough to make 20 sections
2	oranges, medium size, or enough to make 8 slices lettuce leaves to line 4 plates
8	thin Bermuda onion slices (optional)
garnish:	4 strawberries and 4 mint sprigs

On each lettuce bed, place 2 orange slices on one side, and arrange 5 grapefruit sections fanning out from them. Add onion slices (if desired).

Garnish and serve.

SERVES 4. CALORIES PER SERVING: 93
PREPARATION TIME: 15 MINUTES

Tuna Salad

1 13-ounce can	solid white tuna in water, drained
½ cup	low-fat cottage cheese
2 tablespoons	shallots (or white part of scallions), minced
2 tablespoons	Mustard Vinaigrette Dressing (page 17)
2 tablespoons	celery, chopped
2 tablespoons	fresh parsley, chopped
1 tablespoon	fresh lemon juice
	salad greens to line 4 plates
garnish:	tomato wedges, lemon wedges, parsley sprigs, radish roses

Crumble tuna, and mix with cottage cheese. Combine shallots and **Mustard Vinaigrette Dressing**; add to tuna. Add celery, parsley, and lemon juice; mix well. Spoon onto 4 beds of greens. Garnish and serve.

SERVES 4. CALORIES PER SERVING: 144

PREPARATION TIME: 15 MINUTES

Tuna Mold

1 recipe	Tuna Salad (above)
garnish:	Crudites (see suggestions, page 43); lemon wedges, radish roses, and fresh parsley

Press **Tuna Salad** (without garnishes) into 3-cup mold. Refrigerate at least 1 hour.

Turn out of mold. Garnish and serve.

SERVES 4. CALORIES PER SERVING: 144

PREPARATION TIME: 15 MINUTES

Caesar Salad

	romaine lettuce to make 4 salad portions
5-6 tablespoons	Quick Caesar Dressing (below)
2 tablespoons	Parmesan cheese, freshly grated

Wash, drain, and dry tender romaine lettuce leaves. Tear into bite-size pieces. Toss well with **Quick Caesar Dressing**, following all instructions below. Sprinkle with Parmesan.

SERVES 4. CALORIES PER SERVING: 85

PREPARATION TIME: 5 MINUTES

Quick Caesar Dressing

7	anchovy fillets
1	egg, coddled (set in boiling water 30 seconds)
½ cup	sesame-seed, safflower, or olive oil
⅓ cup	fresh lime or lemon juice
2	garlic cloves, large, quartered
2 teaspoons	black pepper, freshly ground
2 teaspoons	Worcestershire sauce
2 tablespoons	Parmesan cheese, freshly grated
garnish:	alfalfa sprouts

Put all ingredients except cheese in blender, and blend until garlic is pureed and salad dressing is smooth. After tossing salad with dressing, add cheese. Top with alfalfa sprouts.

Makes 1⅓ cups.

CALORIES PER TABLESPOON: 56

PREPARATION TIME: 5 MINUTES

Garden Salad

¾ cup	carrots, diced, cooked al dente
¾ cup	broccoli flowerets, blanched
¾ cup	green beans, blanched
¾ cup	cauliflower flowerets, cooked
¼ cup	pimiento, chopped
¼ cup	scallions, chopped
1 tablespoon	fresh tarragon (or 1 teaspoon dried tarragon)
4-5 tablespoons	Mayonette Sauce (page 20)
	vegetable seasoning, to taste
	lettuce leaves to line 4 plates
garnish:	parsley sprigs and cherry tomatoes

In large bowl, combine all ingredients except lettuce. Spoon onto 4 lettuce beds. Garnish and serve.

SERVES 4. CALORIES PER SERVING: 98

PREPARATION TIME: 35 MINUTES

Winter Salad

1 head	Boston lettuce, small
1 head	romaine lettuce, small
2	tomatoes, large, quartered
½	cucumber, medium size, sliced thin
4	fresh mushrooms, large, sliced thin
¼ cup	chick-peas (or garbanzo beans), cooked
4 tablespoons	Mustard Vinaigrette Dressing (page 17)

Toss all ingredients and serve immediately.

SERVES 4. CALORIES PER SERVING: 100

PREPARATION TIME: 15 MINUTES

Shrimp-and-Cucumber Salad Sunomo (Sweet and Sour)

2	Japanese cucumbers (or 1 European cucumber), peeled, quartered lengthwise, sliced ¼″ thin; to make 2 cups
2 teaspoons	sea salt
¾ cup	small shrimp, cooked or canned
1 tablespoon	seaweed (or shredded seaweed sold in packages in Oriental food stores), presoaked, coarsely chopped
6 tablespoons	rice vinegar
3 tablespoons	Mirin (sweet Sake)
2 tablespoons	scallions, chopped
	lettuce leaves to line 4 plates
garnish:	daikon, grated (kept fresh in water with lemon juice), or red radishes, thinly sliced

Place cucumber slices in colander, and sprinkle with sea salt. Toss well. Refrigerate, covered, 2 or 3 hours.

Drain water from cucumbers. Place cucumbers in bowl, and add cooked shrimp, seaweed, rice vinegar, and Mirin. Toss salad. Let stand 30 minutes.

Before serving, add scallions. Spoon salad mixture onto 4 lettuce beds. Garnish and serve.

SERVES 4. CALORIES PER SERVING: 68

PREPARE 3 HOURS AHEAD

PREPARATION TIME: 10 MINUTES

Ceviche

1 pound	sea bass, ling cod, or red snapper, cut in thin strips
½ cup	fresh lime or lemon juice
1 teaspoon	garlic, minced
½ cup	scallions, finely chopped
	lettuce leaves to line 4 plates
4 tablespoons	fresh cilantro or parsley, chopped
	black pepper, freshly ground, to taste
2	tomatoes, peeled and diced
garnish:	fresh parsley sprigs and lemon wedges

Combine fish, lime juice, garlic, scallions, cilantro, and pepper. Marinate overnight. Drain well.

Season to taste by adding any of the above.

Add tomatoes. Spoon onto 4 lettuce beds. Garnish and serve.

SERVES 4. CALORIES PER SERVING: 149

CAN BE PREPARED DAY AHEAD

PREPARATION TIME: 20 MINUTES

Tossed Salad

1 head	romaine lettuce, medium size
½ cup	red cabbage, shredded fine
1	cucumber, medium size, sliced
1	tomato, medium size, cut into 4 wedges
½ cup	chick-peas (or garbanzo beans), cooked
½ cup	Vegetarian Dressing Delight (page 18)
garnish:	homemade whole-wheat croutons

Toss all ingredients. Garnish with croutons, and serve.

SERVES 4. CALORIES PER SERVING: 80

PREPARATION TIME: 15 MINUTES

Tomato Oregano

4	tomatoes, peeled
1 tablespoon	shallots, chopped
1 teaspoon	garlic, minced
1 teaspoon	dried whole oregano (or 4 fresh basil leaves)
3 tablespoons	Mustard Vinaigrette Dressing (page 17)
3 teaspoons	chives, chopped
	lettuce leaves to line 4 plates

Cut each tomato into 8 wedges. Put into salad bowl. Add shallots, garlic, and oregano (or basil leaves).

Spoon **Mustard Vinaigrette Dressing** over tomatoes. Mix well with other salad-bowl ingredients. Refrigerate 4 hours.

Spoon onto 4 lettuce beds, add chives, and serve.

SERVES 4. CALORIES PER SERVING: 77

PREPARATION TIME: 15 MINUTES

Chicken Salad Usu Zukuri

(COLD CHICKEN BREASTS WITH TOFU SAUCE)

1 teaspoon	sesame-seed or safflower oil
1	garlic clove, large, minced
2	chicken breasts (about 3½ ounces per serving); reserve 2 tablespoons pan juices from chicken
2 tablespoons	shallots, minced
2 teaspoons	soy sauce (low sodium)
2 tablespoons	fresh lemon juice
3 teaspoons	lemon zest, minced
2 tablespoons	fresh ginger root, minced
5 ounces	tofu
	lettuce leaves to line 4 plates
garnish:	radish slices, mung beans, cucumber slices (peeled), carrots julienne, chopped tomatoes

Preheat oven to 350°.

Heat oil in 6″ skillet. Gently saute garlic 1-2 minutes; stir frequently. Add chicken breasts, skin-side down. Sprinkle shallots around them. Cook chicken 2-3 minutes on each side till golden brown; shake pan if necessary to prevent chicken from sticking. Pour soy sauce and lemon juice over chicken. Add ginger and 2 teaspoons lemon zest. Turn breasts till completely immersed in sauce. Bake, covered, 25-30 minutes.

Remove pan from oven. Cool chicken breasts. This step can be prepared several hours in advance.

Prepare tofu sauce: Pour 2 tablespoons pan juices into blender. Add tofu and remaining lemon zest. Puree till smooth.

Peel and debone cooled chicken breasts. Starting at wide end, slash each breast half at an angle (not straight up and down) 4 or 5 times, cutting ¾ of way through.

Fan breasts out into gentle curves, and arrange on 4 lettuce beds. Pour tofu sauce over chicken. Garnish and serve.

Note: Dish gets its name from Japanese method of slicing foods at an angle (usu zukuri).

SERVES 4. CALORIES PER SERVING: 161
PREPARATION TIME: 1 HOUR

LET'S TALK ABOUT THESE RECIPES

ARTICHOKE: Sign of a fresh artichoke: leaves curled tightly inward. Rub fresh artichokes together, and they will squeak.

AVOCADO: To hasten the ripening of this beautiful nutritive fruit, place it in a brown paper bag. Do not refrigerate.

CHINESE PEA PODS (SNOW PEAS): These are not very very young versions of your common garden variety pea pod. Unlike regular pea pods, they have no parchment lining. To cook, drop into boiling water for 2 or 3 minutes.

COCONUT, TOASTED: Buy vacuum-packed and sealed coconut, not the dried type sold in a bag.

Toast in a 325° oven, in a small pan; watch carefully, and toss several times.

DAIKON (or DIKON, THE JAPANESE WHITE RADISH): A large white radish with a nice tang to it.

JICAMA: The Mexican potato, jicama looks like a turnip, tastes like a water chestnut (for which it can be used as an inexpensive substitute). Best of all, it slices into the ultimate dip chip (see Hors d'Oeuvres, pages 43-45).

LEEKS: Select medium-sized leeks, with fresh green tops, white root ends, and no soft spots.

Wash and rinse well, and crisp in refrigerator before cooking.

MANGO: Avoid too-green fruit which may never ripen, as well as mangoes which look black and shriveled. The mango should be smooth, its red color starting to develop. Ripen at room temperature for several days. The Mexican mango reaches its prime in June.

PAPAYA: Choose a medium-size fruit, one that is a ripe yellow over at least ⅓ of its skin.

SHALLOTS: An upper-class onion imparting a distinctive sweetish flavor quite unlike the sharpness of the green onion. Aside from use in salads, the shallot is a wonderful accompaniment, for instance, for veal.

SPROUTS: These days, it's possible even to find sprouts tucked into a take-out sandwich, but over 40 years ago we were considered very avant when we first made and served our own sprouts at Rancho La Puerta. It's simple enough to do, and I hope you'll try it regardless of the handy sprout containers sold in supermarkets.

If you buy ready-made bean sprouts, tips should not be dry and sprouts should be short (longer is older). If you serve your purchased bean sprouts raw, first chill in ice water for half an hour.

HORS D'OEUVRES

Hors d'oeuvres lend a sense of party-like fun to dinner. When served formally, they have considerable elegance. But underlying it all is the wonderful boost they give the dieter at the dinner hour by taking the edge off hunger, besides prolonging the pleasure of food involvement by allowing us extra chewing time.

Hors d'oeuvres, despite their elegant connotations, are a windfall for the man or woman who must hurry home after work to create a low-calorie meal, and perhaps even serve guests. These nibbles will work out into perfect timing for a dinner that requires only 30 minutes of preparation. The meal then can stretch into the requisite 40-minute period necessary to lift your blood sugar so that your body will send out happy signals meaning full and satisfied.

Upon arriving at home, set out hors d'oeuvres at once. They don't have to be fancy and time-consuming. Almost any fresh raw vegetable is hors d'oeuvre material if attractively arranged around a dip in a pretty bowl. That bowl may contain something as simple as yogurt flavored with curry powder; or feta cheese, buttermilk, and oregano whipped in a blender and then augmented with half a dozen Greek olives. The possibilities are endless.

The cook puts the main dish in the oven, and afterward is free to enjoy some hors d'oeuvre nibbles with family or guests. Next, back to the kitchen to turn out a quick salad. At the end of the salad course, the entree is popped out of the oven. Dessert has been prepared in advance.

Crudités for Hors d'Oeuvres

sliced carrots · Chinese pea pods
cherry tomatoes · jicama slices
sliced turnips · zucchini sticks
celery sticks · bell pepper rings
radish rosettes · cucumber slices
lettuce for serving tray

The above will make a tantalizing tray of crudités—a French term meaning "raw." They should be presented attractively on a bed of lettuce, and centered with a dip. **Vincent Sauce** (page 20) is particularly tasty with these raw vegetables. Dips made with **Yogurt Dill Sauce** (page 22) are also excellent.

PREPARATION TIME: 15 MINUTES

Seafood Hors d'Oeuvres

cold shrimp
small bite-size lobster pieces
crab claws
crab legs

These are tasty low-calorie foods by themselves. Do not diminish their value and taste by deep-frying or coating with batter or bread crumbs!

Serve on a bed of crushed ice with a cold dip: **Vincent Sauce** (page 20); **Sauce Madras** (page 21); **Sauce Raifort** (page 19); **Yogurt Dill Sauce** (page 22); or low-calorie dip of your choice.

PREPARATION TIME: 10 MINUTES

Stuffed Eggs

4	hard-cooked eggs
4 teaspoons	Mayonnaise (page 20)
2 teaspoons	Dijon mustard
2 teaspoons	fresh parsley, chopped
1 teaspoon	apple-cider vinegar
	cayenne pepper, to taste
1 tablespoon	caviar or salmon roe
garnish:	fresh parsley sprigs

Peel eggs, cut in half lengthwise. Remove yolks and press through sieve. Add **Mayonnaise,** mustard. chopped parsley, vinegar, and dash of cayenne pepper.

Mix well. Spoon into egg-white shells. Garnish and serve.

Not just an hors d'oeuvre but a lovely addition to any salad meal.

SERVES 4. CALORIES PER HALF EGG: 59

PREPARATION TIME: 15 MINUTES

Yogurt-Fruit Dip

½ cup	peaches, berries, apricot, mango, banana (or any fresh fruit of a definite flavor)
½ cup	plain, low-fat yogurt
	honey, to taste

Puree fruit in blender. Add yogurt, plus honey to taste.

CALORIES PER TABLESPOON: 11

PREPARATION TIME: 5 MINUTES

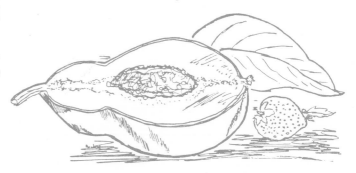

Eggplant "Caviar"

1	large eggplant
1 tablespoon	olive oil
2 tablespoons	black olives, chopped
2 tablespoons	capers, finely chopped
2 tablespoons	fresh parsley, chopped
1 teaspoon	Worcestershire sauce
2 teaspoons	apple-cider vinegar
¾ teaspoon	black pepper, freshly ground

Preheat oven to 350°.

In small baking dish bake eggplant 1 hour, till completely soft; turn. Cool, peel, and chop very finely. Add all other ingredients, and mix well with spatula.

Serve cold with jicama, carrot, or cucumber sticks, or on celery stalks.

MAKES 8 SMALL PORTIONS. CALORIES PER PORTION: 35

MAKES 4 LARGE PORTIONS. CALORIES PER PORTION: 70

PREPARATION TIME: 15 MINUTES

BAKING TIME: 1 HOUR

Mushroom Guacamole

2-3 tablespoons	fresh lemon juice
24	fresh mushrooms, washed, stems removed
1	ripe avocado
1	tomato, peeled, seeded, diced
1 teaspoon	scallions, minced
	vegetable seasoning or Tabasco sauce, to taste
	cayenne pepper, to taste
garnish:	fresh parsley, chopped

Mushrooms should be fresh, firm, unblemished. After removing stems, brush inside of mushrooms with lemon juice.

After removing seed and skin, mash avocado with potato masher till smooth. Add tomato, scallions, and 3 teaspoons lemon juice. Season with vegetable seasoning. Add dash of cayenne pepper.

Fill each mushroom cap with spoonful of avocado mixture. Garnish and serve.

SERVES 4. CALORIES PER SERVING: 115

PREPARATION TIME: 15 MINUTES

Stuffed Mushrooms Florentine

24 fresh mushrooms, medium size
¼ cup dry Vermouth or dry Sherry
1 tablespoon fresh lemon juice
vegetable seasoning, to taste
1 medium shallot, coarsely chopped
2 garlic cloves, coarsely chopped
1 teaspoon dried whole marjoram
¼ teaspoon black pepper, freshly ground
¾ teaspoon vegetable seasoning
1 cup fresh spinach, cooked, drained, and chopped
grated nutmeg, to taste
3 ounces Monterey jack cheese, freshly grated
paprika

Wash mushrooms well. Separate stems from caps. In shallow skillet, place mushroom caps upside down. Add Vermouth and lemon juice, and light sprinkle of vegetable seasoning. Cover, and steam 5 minutes.

In food processor, grate mushroom stems, shallots, and garlic. In small, heavy skillet, cook over medium fire with marjoram, pepper, and vegetable seasoning. Mix with wooden spatula. Cook till all moisture has evaporated.

Add spinach, dash of nutmeg, and cheese. Stir till cheese melts and is creamy.

Remove from heat. Fill each mushroom cap. Reheat caps in skillet in their own juice, and sprinkle with paprika before serving.

SERVES 4. CALORIES PER SERVING: 105
PREPARATION TIME: 25 MINUTES

Oysters Rockefeller

12 oysters, shucked
1½ cups fresh spinach, blanched and drained
grated nutmeg, to taste
2 ounces Monterey jack cheese
Pernod liqueur
Parmesan cheese, freshly grated

Preheat oven to 400°.

Loosen oyster meat from shells; rinse if necessary. Place them on bed of rock salt in baking dish.

In skillet, heat spinach with jack cheese and dash of nutmeg till cheese is melted and mixture is creamy.

Place drop of Pernod on each oyster; cover each oyster with spinach. Sprinkle Parmesan cheese on top.

Bake 10-15 minutes. Serve immediately.

SERVES 4. CALORIES PER SERVING: 93
PREPARATION TIME: 35 MINUTES

Fresh Fruit Kebob

8 strawberries
8 pineapple cubes, ¾"
8 melon balls, ¾"
8 watermelon or honeydew balls
8 grapes
8 strawberries

Following above order, arrange fruit on 8 6-inch bamboo skewers. Serve as appetizer, with **Yogurt Fruit Dip** (page 44).

SERVES 4. CALORIES PER SERVING: 15
PREPARATION TIME: 15-20 MINUTES

Hot soup is a very traditional and heart-warming food. One of the best things about it is that most of the myths are true. That chicken soup fed you by the loving, sympathetic spoonful when you were a sick child really did help make you well. Those cozy, old-time, cold-winter-night, hot-soup suppers were truly good for you.

Like hors d'oeuvres, soups are indispensable to the 40-minute 'Golden Door' plan for dining. Soup is especially indicated if you are having only a salad for luncheon. Hot or cold, soup can transform any ordinary mealtime into a 'Golden Door' luncheon or dinner.

If you have believed that making your own soup stock would be a time-consuming effort, think about it again. The initial work of preparing the stock takes time but can be done at your convenience. The later pay-off is quick,

quick meals. A frozen pint or quart of soup stock can be instantly transformed into a gourmet dish by the addition of almost any raw vegetable or combination thereof.

Here's a suggestion for almost-instantaneous creme soups: simply cook any vegetable until tender and reserve the broth. Puree the vegetable with its broth, add a touch of skim milk. Voila. Delicious Creme of Cauliflower, Creme of Celery, etc.

Because it stretches out the calories it contains, soup has always been every dieter's friend. Because it is inexpensive, soup is one of the deep pleasures shared, internationally, by the rich and the poor; cheap and filling, it can be augmented by any odds and ends — very attractive to thrifty housewives.

Vegetable Stock

1	whole celery or 1 small celery root
1	onion, peeled, studded with 4 cloves
2	leeks (white part only)
1	carrot
4	ripe tomatoes, quartered
1	turnip, small
1 teaspoon	dried whole thyme
2	bay leaves
10	peppercorns, crushed
12 cups	water
2 tablespoons	soy sauce (low sodium)
1 tablespoon	sea salt

Combine all ingredients in large stockpot. Slowly bring to boil. Simmer about 2 hours, reducing to about 10 cups. Strain liquid. Check seasoning.

Makes about 8 cups.

CALORIES PER CUP: 11

PREPARATION TIME: 2 HOURS 30 MINUTES

Vegetable Stock with Onions

6	onions, thinly sliced
1½ tablespoons	sesame-seed oil
2 teaspoons	dried whole thyme
2 teaspoons	vegetable seasoning
1 recipe	Vegetable Stock (at left) soy sauce (low sodium), to taste

Preheat oven to 325°.

In heavy skillet, heat oil and add onion slices. Sprinkle with thyme and vegetable seasoning, and stir with wooden spatula. Reduce fire. In about 10 minutes, when onions become translucent, remove from fire.

Place in baking dish. Bake about 25-30 minutes, till light golden brown. Transfer onions to stockpot. Add **Vegetable Stock**. Simmer 30 minutes, skimming off froth. Onions should be tender. Add soy sauce to taste.

Serve as soup, or strain to make onion-flavored vegetable stock.

Makes about 10 cups.

CALORIES PER CUP: 33

PREPARATION TIME: 1 HOUR 10 MINUTES

Chicken Broth

CHICKEN STOCK FOR

2 pounds	chicken backs and wings
3 quarts	water (12 cups)
1	onion, peeled, studded with 4 whole cloves
1	carrot
10	peppercorns, crushed
2 teaspoons	sea salt

BOUQUET GARNI, CONSISTING OF FOLLOWING
INGREDIENTS BOUND IN CHEESECLOTH

3	celery stalks
2	bay leaves
1 teaspoon	dried whole thyme (or 1 fresh sprig)
2-3	parsley sprigs

Combine all ingredients in stockpot. Simmer gently, uncovered, 2-3 hours. As it cooks, skim fat and froth. Reduce to 8-10 cups.

Ladle out chicken pieces and bouquet garni. Strain liquid. Skim fat. Refrigerate overnight, and skim fat again.

Makes approximately 8 cups.

CALORIES PER CUP: 30

PREPARATION TIME: 2½-3 HOURS

Golden Turkey Broth

2	turkey wings or backs (about 2¼ - 2½ pounds)
1	onion, peeled, studded with 4 cloves
3	celery stalks
1	carrot, medium size
1 teaspoon	dried whole thyme
2	bay leaves
10	peppercorns, crushed
1 teaspoon	sea salt
14 cups	water

Preheat oven to 350°.

Place turkey wings in shallow baking dish. Surround them with onion, celery, carrot, all sprinkled with thyme, bay leaves, and peppercorns. Bake about 1 hour and 15 minutes, till turkey and onions become golden brown.

Put all baked ingredients in large stockpot. Add water and sea salt. Simmer 3 hours, occasionally skimming fat and froth. Reduce to about 10 cups.

Ladle out turkey pieces with slotted spoon. Strain liquid. Skim remaining fat with kitchen paper towel (or refrigerate overnight and then skim fat).

Makes approximately 8 cups.

CALORIES PER CUP: 32

PREPARATION TIME: 4 HOURS 15 MINUTES

Fish Soup

1	onion, halved
2	celery stalks
3 quarts	Fish Bouillon (at right) or water
1 cup	broth, reserved
2	leeks (white parts only), julienne cut
2	carrots, medium, julienne cut
1	turnip, small, julienne cut
4 pieces	white sea bass, ling cod, or cabrilla (5 oz. each), cut in small pieces
12	raw shrimp, medium size, peeled, deveined
¼ cup	dry white wine
1 teaspoon	dried whole thyme
2	garlic cloves, minced
1	bay leaf
3 ounces	Neufchatel low-fat cream cheese
1 tablespoon	arrowroot
	cayenne pepper, to taste
	fresh lemon juice, to taste
garnish:	2 tablespoons fresh parsley or chives, chopped

Combine onion, celery, and **Fish Bouillon**. Simmer, uncovered, about 30 minutes, till tender. Drain, reserve broth, and set onion and celery aside.

In separate pan, simmer leeks, carrots, and turnips — barely covered in water — about 5 minutes, till cooked, but still crisp.

Preheat oven to 350°.

Place fish and shrimp pieces in shallow pan. Add wine, thyme, garlic, and bay leaf; cook over medium fire, covered, 2 minutes. Do not remove cover, and bake about 10 minutes.

Puree cooked celery and onion in blender with 1 cup of reserved broth. Add cream cheese and arrowroot. Blend till smooth. Pour mixture over fish and shrimp; bring to a simmer till sauce starts to thicken. Season with cayenne pepper and lemon juice.

Place mixture in hot serving dish. With slotted spoon, lift out leeks, carrots, and turnip. Place them on top of fish mixture. Garnish and serve.

SERVES 8 SMALL PORTIONS. CALORIES PER PORTION: 186

SERVES 4 LARGE PORTIONS. CALORIES PER PORTION: 372

PREPARATION TIME: 45 MINUTES

Fish Bouillon

2 pounds	fish heads, bones, and trimmings
3 quarts	water

BOUQUET GARNI, CONSISTING OF FOLLOWING INGREDIENTS BOUND IN CHEESECLOTH

3	celery stalks
1	bay leaf
1 teaspoon	dried whole thyme
2 or 3	parsley sprigs
10	peppercorns, crushed
2 teaspoons	sea salt
1	carrot

Combine all ingredients in stockpot. Simmer gently, uncovered, 2-3 hours. Be sure to skim foam. Reduce to 6-8 cups.

CALORIES PER CUP: 30

PREPARATION TIME: 2 HOURS

Chinese Vegetable Soup

4 cups	Vegetable Stock (page 47)
1½ cups	fresh vegetables: turnips, peeled, quartered, thinly sliced; cauliflower cut in 1″ flowerets; broccoli cut in 1″ flowerets; zucchini, halved lengthwise and thinly sliced lengthwise; bell pepper cut in 1″ strips; celery, cut in thirds, thinly sliced lengthwise
½ cup	Chinese pea pods, trimmed, halved lengthwise
½ cup	bean sprouts soy sauce (low sodium), to taste
garnish:	4 tablespoons carrots, grated, and 4 tablespoons scallions, chopped

Bring **Vegetable Stock** to boil. Add 1½ cups vegetables. Bring to boil again. Add pods and sprouts, and cook just a few seconds more. Add soy sauce. Vegetables should be crisp.

Garnish and serve immediately.

SERVES 4. CALORIES PER SERVING: 70
PREPARATION TIME: 25 MINUTES

Miso Soup

3½ cups	Vegetable Stock (page 47)
1½ tablespoons	miso paste
1 teaspoon	ginger, chopped
1 teaspoon	lemon zest, minced soy sauce (low-sodium), to taste
garnish:	4 teaspoons scallions, chopped

Place in blender **Vegetable Stock**, miso paste, ginger, lemon zest, and soy sauce; blend.

Heat to a simmer. Garnish and serve.

SERVES 4. CALORIES PER SERVING: 41
PREPARATION TIME: 15 MINUTES

Egg Soup

3 cups	Chicken Broth (page 48)
1	egg
1	egg white
2 tablespoons	Parmesan or Romano cheese, freshly grated
2 tablespoons	fresh parsley, chopped vegetable seasoning, to taste
garnish:	parsley sprigs

Bring **Chicken Broth** to a boil.

In blender, beat together egg, egg white, and cheese. Add parsley, and pulse in quickly.

When broth is boiling, gradually pour in egg mixture. Whisk vigorously with wire whisk till egg is cooked. Mixture will float to surface. Check the seasonings.

Garnish with parsley sprigs and serve.

SERVES 4. CALORIES PER SERVING: 68
PREPARATION TIME: 10 MINUTES

Minestrone Soup

2 teaspoons	olive oil
2 teaspoons	garlic, minced
1	onion, small, diced
1	bay leaf
1 teaspoon	dried whole thyme
	black pepper, freshly ground, to taste
4	tomatoes, large, peeled, seeded, and diced
1	leek, average size, trimmed, halved lengthwise, and sliced thin
1	carrot, peeled, thinly sliced
4	celery stalks, thinly sliced
1	turnip, quartered, thinly sliced
½ cup	tomato puree
5 cups	Vegetable Stock (page 47), heated
½ cup	green beans, sliced
⅓ cup	brown rice, cooked; or barley, cooked
1 cup	spinach, raw, coarsely chopped
	vegetable seasoning, to taste
	black pepper, freshly ground, to taste
¼ cup	fresh parsley, chopped
2 teaspoons	dried sweet basil
¼ cup	Parmesan or Romano cheese, freshly grated

In heavy saucepan, heat oil, add garlic and onion; gently saute till they begin to soften. Stirring with wooden spoon, add bay leaf, thyme, and dash of pepper. Add tomatoes, leek, carrot, celery, and turnip. Cover. Steam over low fire 8-10 minutes.

Add tomato puree and **Vegetable Stock**. Simmer gently, uncovered, 20 minutes.

Add green beans, rice, and spinach. Simmer 5 minutes. Check seasonings with vegetable seasoning and ground pepper, to taste.

Before serving, mix together parsley, basil, and cheese; stir into soup. Sprinkle with more cheese, if desired.

MAKES 8 SMALL PORTIONS. CALORIES PER PORTION: 107

MAKES 4 LARGE PORTIONS. CALORIES PER PORTION: 214

PREPARATION TIME: 1 HOUR

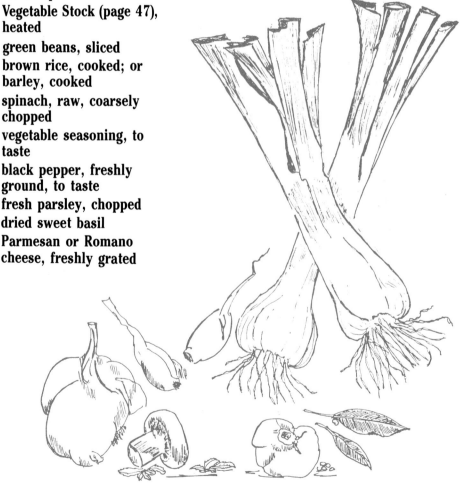

Hot and Sour Shrimp Soup

3 cups	Chicken Broth (page 48)
1 tablespoon	fresh lemon juice
½ cup	shrimp, raw, peeled, deveined, and chopped
1 cup	fresh mushrooms, thinly sliced
4 ounces	tofu (bean curd), drained, cut into ½″ discs
1 tablespoon	arrowroot, mixed with ¼ cup water
1½ tablespoons	white rice vinegar
1½ tablespoons	soy sauce (low sodium)
1½ tablespoons	Mirin (sweet Sake) Tabasco sauce, to taste
½ teaspoon	fresh ginger, minced
1 cup	celery, thinly sliced at angle
garnish:	3 tablespoons green onions, thinly sliced; 1 tablespoon lemon grass, thinly sliced (optional)

Bring **Chicken Broth** and lemon juice to boil. Stir in shrimp. Simmer. Add mushrooms and tofu; bring to boil. Stir in arrowroot mixed with water, and thicken lightly. Add vinegar, soy sauce, Mirin, Tabasco, and ginger. Simmer 5 minutes. Just before serving, add celery and cook a few minutes more. Celery should remain crisp.

Garnish and serve.

SERVES 4. CALORIES PER SERVING: 101

PREPARATION TIME: 15 MINUTES

Hot and Sour Chicken Soup

3 cups	Chicken Broth (page 48)
1 tablespoon	fresh lemon juice
2 ounces	chicken breasts, skinned, boned, chopped finely
1 cup	fresh mushrooms, thinly sliced
4 ounces	tofu (bean curd), drained, cut into ½″ discs
1 tablespoon	arrowroot, mixed with ¼ cup water
1½ tablespoons	white rice vinegar
1½ tablespoons	soy sauce (low-sodium)
1½ tablespoons	Mirin (sweet Sake)
few drops	Tabasco sauce
½ teaspoon	fresh ginger, minced
1 cup	Chinese pea pods, sliced lengthwise
garnish:	3 tablespoons green onions, thinly sliced

Bring **Chicken Broth** and lemon juice to boil. Stir in chicken. Simmer. Add mushrooms and tofu; bring to boil. Stir in arrowroot (mixed with water), and thicken lightly. Add vinegar, soy sauce, Mirin, Tabasco, and ginger. Simmer 5 minutes.

Just before serving, add pea pods and cook a few seconds more. Pods should remain crisp.

Garnish and serve.

SERVES 4. CALORIES PER SERVING: 99

PREPARATION TIME: 15 MINUTES

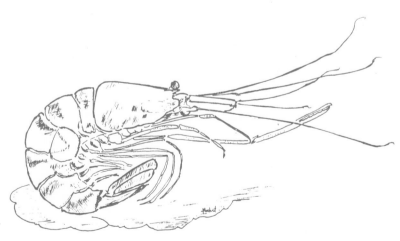

Fresh Chinese Pea Pod Soup

2 teaspoons	sesame-seed or safflower oil
2	onions, coarsely chopped
1 teaspoon	dried sweet basil
5 cups	Vegetable Stock (page 47), heated
3 ounces	Neufchatel low-fat cream cheese
¾ pound	fresh Chinese pea pods (snow peas), washed and trimmed
	vegetable seasoning, to taste
garnish:	parsley sprigs

In saucepan, heat oil and gently saute onion till glazed. Add basil and **Vegetable Stock.** Simmer very gently, uncovered, 30 minutes. Remove from fire. Cool 10 minutes.

In blender or food processor, puree broth with cream cheese and Chinese pea pods. Season with vegetable seasoning and bring to near boil. Garnish and serve immediately.

SERVES 4. CALORIES PER SERVING: 175

PREPARATION TIME: 45 MINUTES

Corn Chowder

¼ cup	onion, coarsely chopped
1 tablespoon	butter
2 teaspoons	whole-wheat flour
1 12-oz. can	creamed corn
4 cups	skim milk
1 teaspoon	Golden Door Herb Seasoning (page 5)
½ teaspoon	black pepper, freshly ground
1 tablespoon	fresh parsley, chopped fine
dash	paprika

Saute onion in butter till limp. Add flour, cook 1 minute, add remaining ingredients. Heat thoroughly but do not boil.

SERVES 6. CALORIES PER SERVING: 130

PREPARATION TIME: 20 MINUTES

Spinach-Pear Soup

2	leeks (white part only), cut in 1″ slices
1	onion, halved
3 cups	Vegetable Stock (page 47)
2 teaspoons	arrowroot, dissolved in 2 tablespoons water
1 cup	fresh spinach, chopped (or ½ cup frozen spinach, thawed and drained)
	white pepper, to taste
	vegetable seasoning, to taste
1 or 2 drops	Pernod liqueur
1	firm pear (not overly ripe) or apple, cored and thinly sliced

In **Vegetable Stock,** simmer leeks and onion 35 minutes, till tender. Remove from fire. Cool 10 minutes.

In food blender, puree leeks and onion with some of the broth till creamy and smooth. Add dissolved arrowroot. Return mixture to pot. Bring back to a boil. With wooden spatula, stir in spinach. Season with pepper and vegetable seasoning. Remove from fire, and add Pernod.

Place 2 or 3 slices of pear in each bowl, pour soup over, and serve immediately.

SERVES 4. CALORIES PER SERVING: 73

PREPARATION TIME: 1 HOUR

Broccoli Soup

WITH SESAME SEEDS

2 teaspoons	sesame-seed or safflower oil
1 teaspoon	garlic, minced
1	onion, diced
2 cups	broccoli stems and tops, cut in 1″ pieces
2 teaspoons	dried sweet basil
1 teaspoon	vegetable seasoning
4 cups	Vegetable Stock (page 47), heated
2 ounces	Neufchatel low-fat cream cheese
½ cup	broccoli flowerets
garnish:	2 tablespoons raw sesame seeds, freshly toasted

In heavy saucepan, heat oil. Gently saute garlic and onion till glazed. Add basil and broccoli stems and tops. Sprinkle with vegetable seasoning. Steam, covered, over medium-low heat 8-10 minutes. Add **Vegetable Stock**. Simmer gently, uncovered, 45 minutes, till vegetables are tender. Remove from fire.

In blender, combine soup mixture with cheese till smooth.

Reheat mixture to a boil. Quickly steam broccoli flowerets. They should still be crisp when added to soup.

Sprinkle sesame seeds over each bowl before serving.

SERVES 4. CALORIES PER SERVING: 144

PREPARATION TIME: 1 HOUR

Creme of Asparagus Soup

2 teaspoons	sesame-seed or safflower oil
1	onion, coarsely chopped
1 teaspoon	dried sweet basil
10 ounces	fresh asparagus, trimmed, peeled, cut in 1″ pieces
4 cups	Vegetable Stock (page 47), heated
2 ounces	Neufchatel low-fat cream cheese
	vegetable seasoning, to taste
garnish:	fresh parsley

Note: In trimming asparagus, do not use fibrous lower stems of spears, but reserve these for other uses, such as **Potassium Broth** (page 143).

In saucepan, heat oil. Gently saute onion till glazed. Add basil and asparagus. Steam gently, covered, 5-7 minutes. Add **Vegetable Stock**. Simmer, uncovered, 30 minutes. Remove from fire. Cool 10 minutes.

In blender, puree the mixture with cheese till smooth.

Reheat, season with vegetable seasoning. Garnish and serve.

SERVES 4. CALORIES PER SERVING: 108
PREPARATION TIME: 50 MINUTES

Fresh Watercress Soup

2 teaspoons	sesame-seed or safflower oil
1	onion, diced
1 teaspoon	garlic, minced
	dried whole thyme, to taste
4 cups	fresh watercress, with stems, coarsely chopped
3 cups	Vegetable Stock (page 47), heated
2 ounces	Neufchatel low-fat cream cheese
	vegetable seasoning, to taste
	cayenne pepper (optional), to taste
garnish:	watercress, chopped

In saucepan, heat oil. Gently saute onion and garlic till glazed. Add watercress and pinch of thyme. Steam, covered, over low fire, 3-4 minutes; stir occasionally.

Add **Vegetable Stock**. Simmer gently, uncovered, 20-25 minutes. Remove from fire. Cool 10 minutes.

In blender, combine soup mixture with cheese till creamy.

Reheat. Season with vegetable seasoning to taste, and cayenne pepper, if desired.

Garnish and serve.

SERVES 4. CALORIES PER SERVING: 96

PREPARATION TIME: 50 MINUTES

Curried Carrot Soup

2 teaspoons	sesame-seed or safflower oil
1	onion, coarsely chopped
1 teaspoon	dried whole thyme
1	bay leaf
4 or 5	carrots, average size, sliced
1 tablespoon	curry powder
5 cups	Vegetable Stock (page 47), heated
3 ounces	Neufchatel low-fat cream cheese
	vegetable seasoning, to taste
	cayenne pepper (optional), to taste
3 tablespoons	parsley, chopped
garnish:	parsley sprigs

In saucepan, over moderate fire, heat oil. Gently saute onions and stir with thyme and bay leaf till glazed. Add carrots. Stir in curry powder. Pour in **Vegetable Stock**. Simmer, uncovered, 40-50 minutes, till carrots are tender. Cool 10 minutes. Remove bay leaf.

In blender, blend soup mixture and cheese till smooth.

Return mixture to same saucepan. Reheat. Season with vegetable seasoning. Add chopped parsley and cayenne pepper (optional) to taste.

Garnish and serve.

SERVES 4. CALORIES PER SERVING: 151

PREPARATION TIME: 1 HOUR

Vichysoisse

2 teaspoons	sesame-seed or safflower oil
3	leeks (white part only), coarsely cut (about 1¼ cups)
1	onion, large, chopped fine
2	potatoes, peeled, diced, and rinsed
1	fresh thyme sprig (or ¼ teaspoon dried whole thyme)
1	bay leaf
3½ cups	Vegetable Stock (page 47)
3 ounces	Neufchatel low-fat cream cheese
	vegetable seasoning, to taste
garnish:	grated nutmeg, to taste, and ¼ cup chives or scallions, finely chopped

In heavy saucepan, heat oil and gently saute leeks and onions till slightly glazed. Add potatoes, thyme, and bay leaf. Steam, covered, over low fire 8-10 minutes. Add **Vegetable Stock**. Simmer 40 minutes till vegetables are tender.

Cool. Discard thyme (if fresh sprig was used) and bay leaf.

In blender, combine mixture with cheese and blend till smooth and creamy. Season with vegetable seasoning. Chill. Garnish and serve.

MAKES 8 SMALL PORTIONS. CALORIES PER PORTION: 73

MAKES 4 LARGE PORTIONS. CALORIES PER PORTION: 146

CAN BE PREPARED AHEAD

PREPARATION TIME: 1 HOUR

Clam Vichysoisse

	ingredients for Vichysoisse (at left), minus Vegetable Stock
3 cups	clam juice
1 cup	water
½ cup	clams (canned or steamed), chopped
	fresh lemon juice, to taste
garnish:	scallions, chopped

Prepare as for **Vichysoisse**, substituting clam juice and water for **Vegetable Stock**.

MAKES 8 SMALL PORTIONS. CALORIES PER PORTION: 85

MAKES 4 LARGE PORTIONS. CALORIES PER PORTION: 179

CAN BE PREPARED AHEAD

PREPARATION TIME: 1 HOUR

Grapefruit Gazpacho

2	tomatoes, medium size, peeled, seeded, and finely chopped
1 cup	cucumber, peeled and grated
½ cup	celery, finely chopped
½ cup	bell pepper, finely chopped
2 tablespoons	fresh parsley, chopped
1½ cups	fresh grapefruit juice
	fructose (optional), to taste
garnish:	parsley sprigs

Note: Grapefruit juice is sometimes slightly tart. Adjust taste with a little fructose.
Combine all ingredients by hand, or mix in blender on pulse cycle. Chill well (at least 2 hours).
Garnish and serve.

SERVES 4. CALORIES PER SERVING: 60

PREPARATION TIME: 20 MINUTES

Chilled Lemon Soup

4 cups	Chicken Broth (page 48)
¼ cup	white rice (long grain)
1 teaspoon	vegetable seasoning
2	eggs
¼ cup	fresh lemon juice
garnish:	mint sprigs and thin lemon slices

In 8-cup saucepan, bring **Chicken Broth** to boil. Add rice and vegetable seasoning. Reduce heat. Simmer, covered, 15-20 minutes, till rice is tender. Remove from fire.

In blender, beat eggs till light and fluffy; add lemon juice, and blend well. Add about 2 cups of hot soup mixture, blending constantly till smooth.

Return this mixture to remainder of soup, and beat with wire whisk to combine well and to thicken soup slightly. Cool; stir occasionally. Garnish and serve.

Note: This soup may also be served hot. Heat only to boil.

MAKES 8 SMALL PORTIONS. CALORIES PER PORTION: 59

MAKES 4 LARGE PORTIONS. CALORIES PER PORTION: 117

CAN BE PREPARED AHEAD

PREPARATION TIME: 45 MINUTES

Crab-and-Cucumber Bisque

1	European cucumber, peeled (1 cup sliced, 1 cup grated)
1 tablespoon	sesame-seed or safflower oil
2	onions, coarsely chopped
2	leeks, medium size (white part only), chopped
1	bay leaf
1	thyme sprig (or ½ teaspoon dried whole thyme)
6 cups	Vegetable Stock (page 47), heated
4 ounces	Neufchatel low-fat cream cheese
6 ounces	crab meat, cooked or canned; finely chopped
½ tablespoon	fresh lemon juice
	cayenne pepper, to taste
garnish:	2 tablespoons fresh parsley, finely chopped

In heavy saucepan, heat oil and gently saute onion, leeks, sliced cucumber, bay leaf, and thyme for 5 minutes; cover, steam over low heat 10 minutes.

Add **Vegetable Stock**. Bring to boil. Reduce fire; simmer gently, uncovered, 30 minutes. Remove from fire, and discard thyme sprig (if fresh thyme was used) and bay leaf. Cool 10 minutes.

In blender, combine broth mixture with cream cheese. Blend till smooth. Pour mixture in bowl. Add chopped crab meat, grated cucumber, lemon juice, and a dash of cayenne pepper. Mix well.

Refrigerate 2 hours.

Garnish and serve.

SERVES 8. CALORIES PER SERVING: 112

CAN BE PREPARED AHEAD

PREPARATION TIME: 1 HOUR

Basil Soup

5 cups	Vegetable Stock (page 47)
4	celery stalks, medium size, sliced
1	carrot, sliced
1	turnip, peeled, halved, sliced
2	leeks, average size, trimmed, sliced (or 2 onions)
1 cup	fresh green beans, French-cut
1	potato, medium size, diced small
2	tomatoes, medium size, peeled, seeded, and diced
3	garlic cloves, crushed in garlic press
1 tablespoon	olive oil
6	sprigs sweet basil (or ½ tablespoon dried sweet basil)
2 ounces	Jarlsberg or Gruyere cheese, freshly grated black pepper, freshly ground, to taste vegetable seasoning, to taste
garnish:	fresh parsley

In saucepan, bring **Vegetable Stock** to boil. Add celery, carrot, turnip, and leeks. Simmer gently 20 minutes.

Add beans, potato, and tomatoes. Simmer 10 minutes more.

In blender, puree garlic and olive oil with ⅓ cup hot soup broth, till really smooth. Add basil and puree briefly with garlic. Pour this mixture back into hot soup, and stir in cheese. Check the seasonings with pepper and vegetable seasoning.

Garnish, and serve piping hot.

MAKES 8 SMALL PORTIONS. CALORIES PER PORTION: 91

MAKES 4 LARGE PORTIONS. CALORIES PER PORTION: 182

PREPARATION TIME: 1 HOUR

Cold Cucumber Soup

1	cucumber, small, peeled, and grated (remove seeds only if they are very large)
1½ cups	plain, low-fat yogurt
1	garlic clove, small, crushed in garlic press
1 tablespoon	tarragon vinegar
½ teaspoon	lemon zest, grated
1 teaspoon	fresh dill, finely chopped (or ½ teaspoon dried dill weed, crushed) cayenne pepper, to taste
¼ cup	water
2 tablespoons	parsley, finely chopped

In blender, combine yogurt, garlic, vinegar, lemon zest, dill, and dash of cayenne pepper. Blend till garlic is pureed. Add water, and blend several seconds longer till soup is smooth.

Pour into bowl containing cucumber. Add chopped parsley, and stir.

Refrigerate 4 hours or more before serving.

SERVES 4. CALORIES PER SERVING: 75

CAN BE PREPARED AHEAD

PREPARATION TIME: 20 MINUTES

Court Bouillon

3	celery stalks
5	parsley sprigs (with roots, if possible)
1	lemon, cut in ½″ slices
2 teaspoons	sea salt
1 cup	white vinegar
1 cup	dry white wine (optional)
3 quarts	water

BOUQUET GARNI, CONSISTING OF FOLLOWING INGREDIENTS BOUND IN CHEESECLOTH

1	bay leaf
1	thyme sprig
10	peppercorns
1	clove

Combine all ingredients in stockpot. Simmer 30-40 minutes, reducing to 10 cups.

This broth is used to poach fish such as salmon, or seafood such as lobster or crayfish. The purpose of preparing court bouillon is to make a broth similar to sea water.

MAKES 10 CUPS. CALORIES PER CUP: 24

PREPARATION TIME: 40 MINUTES

Lima Bean Soup

1 cup	dried lima beans, soaked overnight in 4 cups water
1	celery stalk, chopped coarsely
2	onions, chopped coarsely
2 tablespoons	sesame-seed or safflower oil
1	bay leaf
1 teaspoon	celery seeds
¼ teaspoon	dried sweet basil
	fresh lemon juice, to taste

In large soup pot, saute onions and celery in oil till limp. Add beans and water in which they have soaked. Simmer 2½-3 hours, till beans are tender. Then puree in food processor or blender. Return to soup pot, add seasonings, and simmer 30 minutes more.

SERVES 4. CALORIES PER SERVING: 225

PREPARATION TIME: 15 MINUTES

COOKING TIME: 3-3½ HOURS

Peanut Butter Soup

1 tablespoon	corn-oil margarine
1	onion, medium size, diced
3	celery stalks, diced
3 ounces	pimiento, chopped
1 teaspoon	dried sweet basil
4 cups	Vegetable Stock (page 47), or water
4 tablespoons	crunchy peanut butter
¾ tablespoon	vegetable seasoning
1 tablespoon	cornstarch, diluted
1 cup	whole milk
	cayenne pepper, to taste

In margarine, saute onion, celery, and pimiento until softened. Add dried basil. Add **Vegetable Stock** and peanut butter. Simmer 15 minutes.

Add vegetable seasoning, thicken with cornstarch, and simmer 10 minutes more.

Before serving, add milk and dash of cayenne.

SERVES 4. CALORIES PER SERVING: 187

PREPARATION TIME: 40 MINUTES

Rancho La Puerta, the Golden Door's well-known predecessor and sister spa, for many years was totally vegetarian. (Now, fish is served there twice a week, but no other exceptions are made.) At its inception, in 1940, there were no handy volumes to explain how to guarantee complete proteins in a vegetarian menu. We had to work carefully and research widely to assemble balanced meals.

When vegetarianism became generally popular in the United States several decades ago, there was still no preeminent authority writing on the subject. As a result, much misunderstanding led to some badly deficient diets.

Then, in 1971, Frances Moore Lappe brought out Diet for a Small Planet. Still available in paperback from Ballentine Books, it remains the definitive volume on the tricky subject of combining incomplete proteins in order to make whole ones. I recommend it to you, along with the following vegetarian main dishes from the 'Golden Door.'

With the present problem of providing sufficient grain for cattle and crops for people, it behooves everyone to observe at least one vegetarian day now and then, preferably at least once a week. The lack of intelligently controlled acreage is more critical and worldwide than most people realize. Just now, Mexico, which has to import much of its beans, corn and other staple foods, is diverting its most valuable agricultural lands to cattle fodder, because of the country's demand for beef. And so it goes. Before it's all gone, vegetarianism—or, at least, controlled acreage—ultimately will have to solve the world food problem.

As you get into jogging and other exercise, inevitably you will choose occasional vegetarian meals and, ultimately, vegetarian days. It will all be part of your new BODY-PRIDE PACKAGE.

Broccoli/Broccoli

1	onion, large, halved and peeled
2 pounds	fresh broccoli
½ cup	reserved vegetable broth (optional)
4 ounces	Neufchatel low-fat cream cheese
½ teaspoon	vegetable seasoning
¼ teaspoon	grated nutmeg
1 teaspoon	arrowroot
¼ teaspoon	ground cardamom
	fresh lemon juice, to taste
	cayenne pepper, to taste
1	egg, hard-cooked, chopped
2 tablespoons	scallions, chopped
2 ounces	Monterey jack cheese, freshly grated

Place onion in saucepan and cover with water. Cook, covered, about 45 minutes, till onion is tender. Cool.

Trim stems from broccoli, leaving flowerets with 1½ " stems. Set flowerets aside. Peel stems, cut into 1" chunks, place in small saucepan, and cover with water. Cook, covered, about 25 minutes, till tender. Drain, reserving vegetable broth.

In blender or food-processor, puree onion, broccoli stems, and (if necessary) ½ cup reserved vegetable broth. Add Neufchatel cheese, vegetable seasoning, nutmeg, arrowroot, cardamom, squirt of lemon juice, and dash of cayenne pepper. Mix sauce well in blender till smooth and creamy. Place in saucepan, and warm over low fire. Check seasonings. Before serving sauce, add chopped egg and scallions.

Quarter broccoli flowerets, and steam about 7-10 minutes, till tender yet firm. Place in individual serving casseroles. Coat broccoli with sauce, sprinkle with grated jack cheese. Broil till cheese melts and browns slightly. Serve immediately.

Broccoli Filling for Crepes

Using same recipe, steam, drain, and chop broccoli flowerets. Make sauce as described above, combine with broccoli stems and reheat. Mixture will fill 8 **Whole-Wheat Crepes** (page 111).

SERVES 4. CALORIES PER SERVING: 213

PREPARATION TIME: 1 HOUR

Vegetable Pate

2	Whole-Wheat Crepes (page 111)
1½ cups	zucchini, grated
1 cup	spinach, cooked, drained, and chopped
1 teaspoon	dried sweet basil
½ teaspoon	vegetable seasoning
2½ cups	steamed and grated broccoli (approximately 2½ pounds)
1 cup	Brown Rice, cooked (page 114)
2 cups	carrots, grated
4 tablespoons	parsley, freshly chopped
1½ teaspoon	dried whole thyme
2	eggs
6	egg whites

Combine zucchini, spinach, basil, and vegetable seasoning; place in a strainer to drain.

Preheat oven to 350°.

Oil an 8½"x4½"x2½" loaf pan (preferably clay); place crepes on bottom.

Combine carrots with parsley and thyme.

Beat eggs and egg whites. Add ⅓ to zucchini mixture; ⅓ to broccoli; ⅓ to carrot mixture.

Press down broccoli mixture in loaf pan; add ½ **Brown Rice** as a layer, and smooth out; press down carrot mixture; add remainder of **Brown Rice**; as last layer, spread out zucchini mixture.

Cover with piece of oiled waxed paper; place in bain-marie (pan of water). Bake 1 hour and 20 minutes; uncover, and bake 15 minutes more. Set aside 10 minutes before slicing.

Serve hot with **Sauce Michel** (page 23); or cold with **Vincent Sauce** (page 20) or **Sauce Raifort** (page 19).

MAKES 8 SMALL PORTIONS. CALORIES PER PORTION: 96

MAKES 4 LARGE PORTIONS. CALORIES PER PORTION: 192

PREPARATION TIME: 15 MINUTES

BAKING TIME: 1 HOUR 35 MINUTES

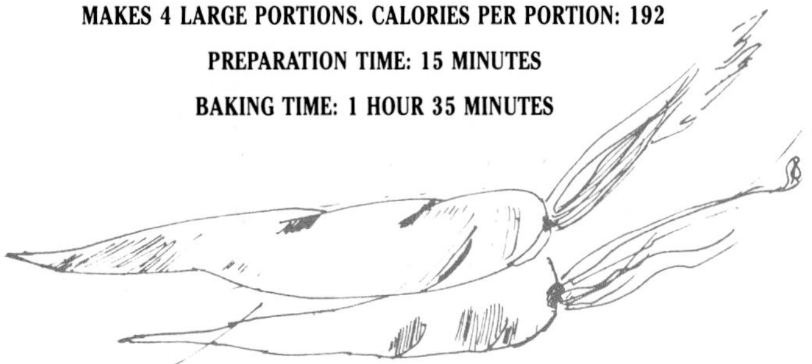

Carrot-Walnut Loaf

3 cups	carrots, grated
1 teaspoon	vegetable seasoning
1 teaspoon	dried whole thyme
2 teaspoons	olive oil
1 tablespoon	shallots, minced
1 teaspoon	garlic, minced
2 teaspoons	curry powder
3 tablespoons	fresh parsley, chopped
¼ cup	Danish blue cheese (for milder loaf, substitute another ¼ cup Neufchatel low-fat cream cheese)
¼ cup	Neufchatel low-fat cream cheese
½ cup	walnuts, freshly chopped
4	egg whites
1	egg sesame-seed or safflower oil
1 recipe	Sauce Michel (page 23)
garnish:	parsley sprigs

Preheat oven to 375°.

In large mixing bowl, combine grated carrots, vegetable seasoning, and thyme.

In small, heavy skillet, heat oil over low fire. Add shallots, garlic, and curry powder. With wooden spatula, mix to a paste, for about 4-5 minutes. Add to carrot mixture and stir. Add parsley, cheese, and walnuts. Mix well.

Lightly beat egg and egg whites till frothy. Fold into carrot mixture. Sprinkle 4-cup earthenware baking dish with a few drops of oil, spreading around bottom. Line bottom with waxed paper. Pour in carrot mixture. Pat down pate with your hand.

Cover pan loosely with grease-proof paper. Bake in bain-marie (pan of water) 1 hour and 10 minutes. Set aside 10 minutes.

Cut with knife around edges, and unmold. Top with **Sauce Michel.**

Garnish and serve.

SERVES 4. CALORIES PER SERVING: 141

PREPARATION TIME: 15 MINUTES

BAKING TIME: 1 HOUR 10 MINUTES

Parsnip Whip

2   parsnips, large (about 1¼ — 1½ pounds), peeled
⅓ cup   parsnip broth, reserved
2 ounces   Neufchatel low-fat cream cheese
     vegetable seasoning, to taste
garnish: parsley sprigs

Cut parsnips in 2″ chunks, cover with water, and simmer gently, covered, about 25 minutes, till tender.

With slotted spoon, remove parsnips. Puree in food processor with reserved broth, till smooth. Add cheese and vegetable seasoning, and process well. Heat mixture in double boiler, and serve, garnished.

MAKES 8 SMALL PORTIONS. CALORIES PER PORTION: 75

MAKES 4 LARGE PORTIONS. CALORIES PER PORTION: 150

PREPARATION TIME: 35 MINUTES

Braised Celery Hearts and Walnuts

2   celery hearts and stalks, 5″ long
½ cup   reserved celery broth
2 ounces   Neufchatel low-fat cream cheese
     grated nutmeg, to taste
     vegetable seasoning, to taste
     cayenne pepper, to taste
     fresh lemon juice, to taste
2 teaspoons   arrowroot
2 tablespoons   fresh parsley, chopped
garnish: 2 tablespoons walnuts

Cut each celery heart to about 5″ length, and remove 2 or 3 outer stalks. With potato peeler, peel outside stalks. Halve celery hearts lengthwise. Cover hearts and outside stalks with water. Simmer gently, about 15-20 minutes, till tender. Drain, reserving broth.

In blender, place ½ cup celery broth and 4 cooked outer stalks, and puree with cheese till smooth. Add nutmeg, vegetable seasoning, and cayenne pepper, to taste, with a squirt of lemon juice. Add arrowroot and parsley, and blend briefly.

Place celery in saucepan. Pour sauce over, and let bubble 2-3 minutes to thicken.

For best results, chop walnuts with knife, not food-processor.

Before serving, top with chopped walnuts.

SERVES 4. CALORIES PER SERVING: 85

PREPARATION TIME: 45 MINUTES

Yasai Itame

(STIR-FRIED ORIENTAL VEGETABLES AND TOFU)

1 tablespoon	sesame-seed or safflower oil
2 teaspoons	garlic, minced
1 teaspoon	ginger, minced
1 cup	mushrooms, sliced
½ cup	water chestnuts, sliced
½ cup	bell pepper, cut in 2" strips
½ cup	celery stalks, cut in 2" strips
½ cup	carrots, cut in 2" strips
3 tablespoons	soy sauce (low sodium)
½ cup	Vegetable Stock (page 47) or Chicken Broth (page 48), heated
½ cup	scallions, cut in 2" strips
1 cup	bean sprouts
1 cup	Chinese (Napa) cabbage, shredded
½ cup	Chinese pea pods
1½ cups	soybean sprouts
2 tablespoons	arrowroot, dissolved in ¼ cup water
1 cup	tofu, diced in ¼ cup Vegetable Stock or Chicken Broth
2 tablespoons	sesame seeds, freshly toasted

Separate hard vegetables (mushrooms, water chestnuts, bell pepper, celery, and carrots).

Soft vegetables are cooked later to ensure crispness — that is the secret of this dish. The whole process should take about 8-10 minutes. Use a wok or heavy skillet.

Heat oil and add, in rapid succession, garlic, ginger, mushrooms, water chestnuts, pepper, celery, and carrots. Stir well as vegetables cook. Sprinkle with soy sauce. Add **Vegetable Stock** or **Chicken Broth**; bring to a bubble. Add scallions, bean sprouts, cabbage, and Chinese pea pods. Thicken broth with arrowroot dissolved in water, and toss again.

Heat tofu in remaining **Vegetable Stock** or **Chicken Broth**; drain and add to vegetable mixture. Sprinkle more soy sauce. Add toasted sesame seeds, and serve immediately.

SERVES 4. CALORIES PER SERVING: 161
PREPARATION TIME: 25 MINUTES

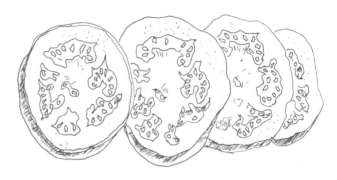

Eggplant Parmigiana

1	eggplant, small, sliced in 4 ¾" rounds (4 ounces, each); ends cut off
2 tablespoons	olive oil
2 cups	Tomato Sauce (page 24)
1 teaspoon	vegetable seasoning
½ teaspoon	dried whole oregano
1 cup	fresh mushrooms, sliced
½ cup	celery, diced
½ cup	bell pepper, diced
2 tablespoons	Parmesan or Romano cheese, freshly grated
2 tablespoons	fresh parsley, chopped
8 thin slices	mozzarella cheese (about 3 ounces)

Brush both sides of eggplant with oil. Broil on both sides till lightly browned but not cooked.

Place 1 cup **Tomato Sauce** in baking dish just large enough to hold eggplant slices; set slices on top of sauce. Sprinkle with vegetable seasoning and oregano.

Preheat oven to 350°.

Heat remainder of **Tomato Sauce** with mushrooms, celery, and pepper. Add grated cheese and parsley; cover eggplant with sauce. Cover each eggplant with 2 mozzarella slices; cover with lid or foil and bake 40 minutes, till done. Serve immediately.

SERVES 4. CALORIES PER SERVING: 263
PREPARATION TIME: 15 MINUTES
BAKING TIME: 40 MINUTES

Baked Potato Romanoff

4	baking potatoes
	sesame-seed or safflower oil
garnish:	4 tablespoons scallions, chopped; 1-ounce jar black caviar (lumpfish type)

MOCK SOUR CREAM:

½ cup	plain, low-fat yogurt
½ cup	low-fat cottage cheese
1 teaspoon	apple-cider vinegar
	cayenne pepper

Preheat oven to 325°.

Scrub potatoes and rub with a few drops of oil. Bake about 1 hour and 15 minutes, till done. Do NOT wrap in foil.

Prepare Mock Sour Cream: Combine yogurt, cottage cheese, cider vinegar, and a sprinkle of cayenne pepper in blender till smooth.

Slit each potato once lengthwise and twice crosswise. To open potatoes, press with your fingers, and spoon in Mock Sour Cream. Garnish and serve.

SERVES 4. CALORIES PER SERVING: 173

PREPARATION TIME: 5 MINUTES

BAKING TIME: 1 HOUR 15 MINUTES

Stuffed Eggplant

2	eggplants, small-to-average size
2 tablespoons	olive oil
1	onion, chopped
1 tablespoon	garlic, minced
1 tablespoon	whole dried oregano
½ teaspoon	ground cardamom
½ cup	red bell pepper (about 1 pepper), diced, or pimiento
1 cup	fresh mushrooms, sliced
1 tablespoon	vegetable seasoning
1 teaspoon	black pepper, freshly ground
½ teaspoon	fennel seeds
¾ cup	Brown Rice, cooked (page 114)
1 cup	tomatoes (about 2 tomatoes), peeled and diced
½ cup	walnuts, freshly chopped
⅓ cup	fresh parsley, chopped
garnish:	parsley sprigs or cilantro

Wash and trim top ends of eggplants. Halve lengthwise. Drop halves into boiling water. Simmer, covered, 10-15 minutes, till eggplants begin to soften. (Large eggplants may take longer.) Remove from water and cool.

In heavy skillet, heat oil and gently saute onion and garlic. Add oregano and cardamom. Stir with wooden spatula till onions are translucent. Add red pepper (or pimiento), mushrooms, vegetable seasoning, black pepper, and fennel. Cook about 5 minutes more. Remove from heat, and fold in **Brown Rice** and tomatoes.

Preheat oven to 350°.

With knife tip, gently carve out insides of cooked eggplants, leaving about ½″ of eggplant inside shells. Place shells on baking dish. Roughly chop scooped-out insides of eggplants, and add to stuffing mixture. Heat this mixture briefly. Add ¼ cup nuts and all the chopped parsley. Fill eggplant shells. Top with remaining nuts. Bake about 15-20 minutes, till piping hot.

Garnish and serve.

SERVES 4. CALORIES PER SERVING: 274

PREPARATION TIME: 50 MINUTES

Eggplant Florentine

1	eggplant, small, sliced in 4 ¾″ rounds (about 4 ounces, each); ends cut off
2 teaspoons	olive oil
	vegetable seasoning to taste
	dried whole oregano, to taste
1½ cups	fresh spinach, cooked, drained, and chopped
	vegetable seasoning, to taste
	grated nutmeg, to taste
¼ pound	fresh mushrooms
1	small onion
1	garlic clove, large
1 teaspoon	dried whole oregano
	vegetable seasoning, to taste
¼ teaspoon	black pepper, freshly ground
¼ teaspoon	dried whole oregano
¼ teaspoon	grated nutmeg
2 ounces	Monterey jack cheese, grated
2 tablespoons	chives, scallions, or fresh parsley, chopped
2 tablespoons	Parmesan or Romano cheese, freshly grated
1 cup	Tomato Concassee (page 24)
garnish:	watercress or parsley sprigs

Brush both sides of eggplant with oil. Broil on both sides till lightly browned but not cooked.

Place in non-aluminum baking dish just large enough to hold slices. Brush lightly with oil, and season with dash of vegetable seasoning and 1 teaspoon oregano. Set aside. Preheat oven to 350°.

Grate mushrooms, onion, and garlic in food processor, or by hand. Put into heavy skillet; add ¼ teaspoon oregano, vegetable seasoning, to taste, and black pepper. Cook, covered, over medium fire about 5 minutes, till all liquid has evaporated; stir occasionally.

Add nutmeg and jack cheese. Cook till cheese is melted and creamy. Sir in chives and spinach; blend in thoroughly. Spoon over eggplant slices; sprinkle with Parmesan cheese, and spoon **Tomato Concassee** around base of eggplant (not on top).

Bake about 30 minutes, till eggplant is tender.

Garnish and serve.

SERVES 4. CALORIES PER SERVING: 166
PREPARATION TIME: 20 MINUTES
BAKING TIME: 30 MINUTES

Carrot Loaf

1 tablespoon	sesame-seed or safflower oil
2	garlic cloves, minced
1	onion, diced finely
2 cups	carrots, thinly sliced
1½ cups	Vegetable Stock (page 47)
4	eggs
2 cups	fresh mushrooms, diced finely
1 cup	Swiss cheese, freshly grated
4 tablespoons	fresh parsley, chopped
½ teaspoon	turmeric
1 teaspoon	vegetable seasoning
⅛ teaspoon	white pepper

Heat oil, and saute garlic and onion to soften. Add carrots; saute a few minutes. Bring **Vegetable Stock** to boil, and add carrot mixture. Cover and simmer gently till vegetables are soft—around 20-30 minutes. Remove cover; stir occasionally. Boil till liquid evaporates.

Preheat oven to 350°.

Puree carrot mixture with eggs in blender, till smooth. Pour into bowl, and combine with mushrooms, cheese, parsley, turmeric, vegetable seasoning, and pepper.

Bake in oiled, 6-cup loaf pan set in bain-marie (pan of water), for 45 minutes to 1 hour, or till tester comes out dry and mixture is firm to touch.

MAKES 8 SMALL PORTIONS. CALORIES PER PORTION: 130
MAKES 4 LARGE PORTIONS. CALORIES PER PORTION: 259
PREPARATION TIME: 45 MINUTES
BAKING TIME: 45-60 MINUTES

Stuffed Zucchini Florentine

4	zucchini, medium size
	vegetable seasoning, to taste
	dried whole oregano, to taste
½ pound	fresh mushrooms
1	garlic clove
1	shallot, medium size
1 teaspoon	vegetable seasoning
½ teaspoon	dried whole oregano
¼ teaspoon	grated nutmeg
¼ teaspoon	black pepper, freshly ground
6 ounces	Monterey jack cheese, grated
2 cups	fresh spinach, cooked, well drained
½ cup	Brown Rice, cooked (page 114)
garnish:	red bell pepper strips (optional)

Preheat oven to 350°.

Wash zucchini well, and halve lengthwise. Cut crisscross pattern on inside of each zucchini half, allowing inside to cook faster without taking away outside firmness. Sprinkle with vegetable seasoning (to taste) and dash of oregano. Place in shallow baking pan. Add water to ½" depth, cover tightly, and bake 25-30 minutes, till tender. Remove from oven, uncover, and cool.

In food processor grate mushrooms, garlic, and shallot. Put into heavy skillet with 1 teaspoon vegetable seasoning, ½ teaspoon oregano, nutmeg, and black pepper. Cook over medium fire, stirring occasionally with wooden spoon till mushrooms are soft and moisture has evaporated. Add spinach and 4 ounces grated cheese; stir over fire till cheese is creamy. Remove from heat, add **Brown Rice**, and mix well.

Scoop out insides of zucchini halves, leaving about ¼" zucchini around edges, to hold shape. Drain scooped-out insides, and chop coarsely. Combine with mushroom mixture. Spoon filling into zucchini shells; return to baking pan to reheat. Top with remainder of cheese. Be sure some water remains in bottom of baking pan, to prevent sticking and burning. Heat about 10 minutes. Garnish, if desired, and serve.

SERVES 4. CALORIES PER SERVING: 218
PREPARATION TIME: 50 MINUTES

Lentil-Spinach Loaf

2 cups	lentils
2	bay leaves
1 cup	raw spinach, chopped coarsely
1	large onion, chopped coarsely
1	bell pepper, chopped coarsely
1	garlic clove, chopped
3	eggs, lightly beaten
1 tablespoon	soy sauce (low sodium)
½ cup	raw cashews, chopped
2 teaspoons	vegetable seasoning
⅛ teaspoon	black pepper, freshly ground

Soak lentils in water to cover, a few hours or overnight. Drain, place in cooking pot, and cover with a few inches of water; add bay leaves. Simmer, covered, till tender, about 1 hour. Drain.

Preheat oven to 325°.

Combine well lentils, spinach, onion, bell pepper, garlic, eggs, soy sauce, cashews, vegetable seasoning, and pepper.

Oil a loaf pan, and line bottom with waxed paper (oil paper as well). Pour mixture into pan, cover tightly with foil, and bake 45 minutes to 1 hour, or till firm. Remove from oven, and set aside at least 10 minutes before uncovering and unmolding.

Serve with **Tomato-Cilantro Sauce** (page 24).

SERVES 4. CALORIES PER SERVING: 194
PREPARATION TIME: 1 HOUR 10 MINUTES
(Not including soaking)
BAKING TIME: 45-60 MINUTES

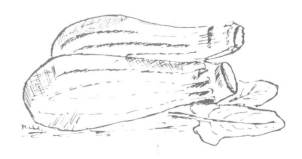

Irish Pie

3	potatoes, medium-size; peeled and cut in large chunks
2	leeks, large; trimmed and cut in large chunks
1	onion, peeled and cut in large chunks
2 teaspoons	dried whole thyme
½ teaspoon	sea salt
6 cups	water
2 tablespoons	corn-oil margarine
½ cup	fresh parsley, chopped
⅛ teaspoon	white pepper
½ cup	whole-wheat bread crumbs

Preheat oven to 350°.

Place potatoes, leeks, onion, thyme, and salt in heavy pan; add about 6 cups of water, or enough to nearly cover. Cook, covered, 30 minutes, or till vegetables are tender. Remove cover, and cook over high fire approximately 15 minutes, or till most of liquid has evaporated. (This mixture will thicken, and will require frequent stirring.) Remove from fire.

Add margarine, parsley, and pepper. Mash with a potato masher to combine.

Mixture need not be really smooth.

Grease with margarine a 7″x11″ baking pan. Pour potato mixture into pan, and sprinkle bread crumbs over top. Bake 15-20 minutes, or till bubbling hot.

MAKES 8 SMALL PORTIONS. CALORIES PER PORTION: 70

MAKES 4 LARGE PORTIONS. CALORIES PER PORTION: 140

PREPARATION TIME: 1 HOUR

Ratatouille

2 teaspoons	olive oil
2 teaspoons	garlic, chopped
1	onion, small, coarsely chopped
3	tomatoes, peeled and diced
1	bay leaf
2 teaspoons	dried whole oregano
½ teaspoon	black pepper, freshly ground
1	eggplant, pared and diced (about 1½ cups)
3	zucchinis, small, diced (1½ cups)
1	bell pepper, diced (1 cup)
½ pound	fresh mushrooms, diced vegetable seasoning
1 tablespoon	Parmesan or Romano cheese, freshly grated
3 tablespoons	chives, chopped
4 ounces	Monterey jack cheese, freshly grated
garnish:	alfalfa sprouts

In heavy saucepan, heat oil. Add garlic and onion; gently saute over moderate fire, and stir with wooden spatula till glazed.

Add tomatoes, bay leaf, oregano, and pepper. Simmer, covered, about 5 minutes.

Add eggplant, zucchini, bell pepper, and mushrooms; stir well. Simmer, covered, 5 minutes more. (Vegetables should still be crisp.) Yields 8 cups.

Season with vegetable seasoning to taste and add Parmesan cheese and chives.

Preheat oven to 375°.

Divide into 4 casserole dishes; spread 1 ounce jack cheese on each, and bake about 10 minutes.

Garnish, and serve piping hot.

MAKES 8 SMALL PORTIONS. CALORIES PER PORTION: 113

MAKES 4 LARGE PORTIONS. CALORIES PER PORTION: 226

PREPARATION TIME: 1 HOUR

Vegetables with Pasta

2 tablespoons	olive oil
3 teaspoons	garlic, minced
3	tomatoes, peeled and diced
2 tablespoons	fresh parsley, chopped
	black pepper, freshly ground, to taste
10	fresh mushrooms, sliced
3	zucchini, small, sliced and blanched
1 cup	broccoli, sliced and blanched
1½ cups	green beans, sliced
1 cup	Chinese pea pods, trimmed
6	fresh asparagus spears, peeled, sliced, and blanched
1 pound	spaghettini, cooked al dente
⅓ cup	butter, melted
⅓ cup	Parmesan or Romano cheese, freshly grated
1 cup	heavy cream, warm
2-3 tablespoons	fresh basil, chopped (or 1-2 tablespoons dried whole basil)
	vegetable seasoning
	black pepper, freshly ground to taste
garnish:	whole cherry tomatoes

In small pan, quickly saute garlic and tomatoes in 1 tablespoon oil. Sprinkle parsley, also black pepper, to taste.

In another pan, quickly saute mushrooms in 1 tablespoon oil. In rapid succession, add zucchini, broccoli, green beans, Chinese pea pods, and asparagus. Cook till vegetables are just heated; they should be crisp.

Cook spaghettini al dente, and drain.

With fork, mix spaghettini with melted butter, cheese, and cream. Add basil, dash of vegetable seasoning and ground pepper. Top with green vegetables and sauteed tomatoes. Garnish with cherry tomatoes, and serve with more cheese on side.

MAKES 8 SMALL PORTIONS. CALORIES PER PORTION: 439

MAKES 4 LARGE PORTIONS. CALORIES PER PORTION: 979

PREPARATION TIME: 35 MINUTES

Walnut-Stuffed Cabbage

1	Chinese (Napa) or Savoy cabbage head (about 1 pound)
½ pound	fresh spinach
1 teaspoon	garlic, minced
1	carrot, small, cut into 2″ julienne strips
1	celery stalk, small, cut into 2″ julienne strips
1	zucchini, small, cut into 2″ julienne strips
2	green onions, small, cut into 2″ julienne strips
¼ cup	walnuts, freshly chopped
⅛ teaspoon	Sansho pepper or freshly ground black pepper
3 tablespoons	soy sauce (low sodium)
½ cup	Chicken Broth, heated (page 48)
2 teaspoons	potato starch, dissolved in 4 tablespoons water
1 cup	bean sprouts

Remove 4 large outer leaves from cabbage and blanch in boiling water till barely wilted (about 4 minutes). Remove from water and cool. Shred about 2 cups of remaining cabbage; set aside.

Trim spinach, cutting only small root off base of each spinach bunch so stems will hold together. Place in skillet, add water to cover. Bring to boil to blanch briefly. Remove from heat, drain, and cool.

Heat oil in wok or heavy skillet. Saute garlic; add carrots, celery, zucchini, and green onions. Mix quickly. Add shredded cabbage; mix again. Stir in walnuts and pepper. Add drained spinach, soy sauce, and **Chicken Broth**. Bring to boil; add potato starch. Stir gently till mixture thickens. Add bean sprouts. Be sure vegetables remain crisp — do not overcook. Remove from heat to stuff cabbage leaves.

Preheat oven to 350°.

Divide vegetables among the 4 blanched cabbage leaves. Roll up leaves lengthwise to enclose vegetables. Place, folded-side down, in skillet; pour any remaining sauce over all. Reheat gently to serve.

SERVES 4. CALORIES PER SERVING: 137
PREPARATION TIME: 40 MINUTES

Tofu Cutlets with Oriental Vegetables

1-2 tablespoons	sesame oil
1 pound	firm tofu, cut in 8 equal slices
	dusting of whole-wheat flour
	sprinkle Sansho pepper (or vegetable seasoning)
1 teaspoon	garlic, minced
½ teaspoon	fresh ginger, minced
1	carrot, cut into thin strips
2	celery stalks, cut into thin strips
16	Chinese pea pods
¼ cup	scallions, chopped
1 tablespoon	soy sauce (low sodium)

In large skillet, heat oil. Pat tofu cutlets with paper towel, then dust each with flour and seasoning.

Saute cutlets on both sides till light golden brown. Place tofu on 4 warm plates and set aside.

In same skillet, in quick succession add garlic, ginger, carrot strips, celery, Chinese pea pods, and a few more drops of oil if necessary. Stir with wooden spatula till vegetables begin to cook.

Sprinkle with soy sauce and chopped scallions. Cover tofu cutlets with vegetable mixture and serve immediately.

SERVES 4. CALORIES PER SERVING: 111
PREPARATION TIME: 15 MINUTES

Artichokes Stuffed with Vegetables

4	artichokes, medium size
4	lemon slices, thick
1 cup	reserved artichoke broth
1 tablespoon	sesame-seed or safflower oil
1	onion, medium size, chopped
1 teaspoon	dried whole thyme
1 teaspoon	vegetable seasoning
¼ teaspoon	fennel seeds
¾ cup	fresh spinach (about 1 bunch), cooked, drained, and finely chopped
2 cups	broccoli flowerets, slightly steamed, coarsely chopped
4 ounces	Jarlsberg cheese, freshly grated
½ cup	Brown Rice, cooked (page 114)
½ teaspoon	black pepper, freshly ground
¼ teaspoon	grated nutmeg
garnish:	alfalfa sprouts and lemon wedges

Cut off stems flush with bottoms so artichokes stand upright. Cut down tops, leaving artichokes about 2½ - 3″ tall.

Set in saucepan (with a lemon slice tied beneath each artichoke) and cover with water; hold them down with a plate on top, and boil 25-30 minutes, till bottoms are tender when pierced with knife. Drain artichokes upside down, reserving 1 cup broth.

Heat oil in skillet, add onion, thyme, vegetable seasoning, and fennel seeds; gently saute till onion is translucent. Add spinach, broccoli, ½ the grated cheese, **Brown Rice**, pepper, and nutmeg. Stir and set aside.

Place artichokes in oven-proof pan. Scoop out middle leaves and chokes, being sure to leave hearts intact. Spoon in filling, pressing down into artichokes, and mound it on top. Sprinkle with remaining cheese. This step can be prepared in advance.

Preheat oven to 350°.

Add vegetable broth to artichoke pan, to about ½″ depth. Bake 15 minutes, till hot. Garnish and serve.

SERVES 4. CALORIES PER SERVING: 241

PREPARATION TIME: 50 MINUTES

Tecate Tostadas

4	corn tortillas
8 ounces	homemade refried beans
½ head	iceberg lettuce, shredded
1	tomato, medium size, chopped fine
4	radishes, sliced thin
4 ounces	Monterey jack cheese, grated
4	avocado slices

Preheat oven to 375°.

Heat tortillas 5-10 minutes, till crisp.

Spread each tortilla with beans; top with lettuce, tomato, radish slices, cheese, and an avocado slice.

Just before serving, warm in oven.

SERVES 4. CALORIES PER SERVING: 258

PREPARATION TIME: 30 MINUTES

SEAFOOD AND FISH

Most people who think they dislike seafood I'm sure had a poor introduction to it. They should erase that early memory and reintroduce themselves through recipes such as appear here — the 'Golden Door' specifies only the mildest and most agreeable of fish.

Once, we all had our origin in the sea. As various species evolved, birds and mammals developed the ability to store fat in true adipose tissue. This was a triumphant deviation which only recently has turned against us humans. Fat-free fish (only canned salmon contains any significant amount of fat) remains our dietary salvation, unless we become 100% vegetarian. If we don't make this adjustment before we're 80, we're in trouble.

Let's learn the bounty of the sea and the ways in which it pleases us best.

Consider color when you're buying shellfish and fish. Scallops, for instance, should not be greyish. Learn to tell the subtle difference in appearance between fresh and frozen fish. If you're fortunate enough to live where fresh fish are plentiful, never eat any other kind. And always buy it from a fish market.

Fresh or frozen, the fish should be looked right in the eye (eyes are to be clear). Again, note color — in this case, a good red in the gills.

Remember that truly fresh fish should neither smell nor taste fishy.

Greek Shrimp

2 teaspoons	olive oil
1 teaspoon	garlic, minced
16	large shrimp, raw; peeled and deveined
1 tablespoon	dried tarragon (or dried sweet basil)
¼ cup	dry white wine (such as Chablis or Chenin Blanc)
16	small black Greek olives
1 cup	fresh tomatoes, peeled, seeded, and diced
2 tablespoons	fresh lemon juice
3 tablespoons	feta cheese, freshly grated
¼ cup	scallions, chopped
⅛ teaspoon	black pepper, freshly ground

In heavy 8″ saucepan, quickly saute garlic in oil over medium fire. Add shrimp and tarragon; cook, covered, 4 or 5 minutes, tossing once. Add wine; cook, uncovered, a few seconds before adding olives, lemon juice, and tomatoes. Cook a few minutes more to soften tomatoes, and mix in cheese and pepper.

Spoon into 4 warmed ramekins. Sprinkle with scallions, and serve with **Brown Rice** (page 114), or sourdough bread.

SERVES 4. CALORIES PER SERVING: 212
PREPARATION TIME: 15 MINUTES

Yoshe Nabe*

1 tablespoon	sesame-seed or safflower oil
2	onions, sliced
1 pound	fresh (or precooked) lobster, cut into 1″ pieces
1 pound	sea bream, sea bass, cabrilla, or other white fish, cut into 1″ pieces
8	clams, medium size, scrubbed clean
6 cups	water or Fish Bouillon
1	carrot, diagonally sliced
4	spinach leaves with stems
1 1-pound head	Chinese (Napa) cabbage, quartered along core
½ cup	Sake
1 teaspoon	vegetable seasoning
1 tablespoon	soy sauce (low sodium)
4 ounces	tofu (soybean curd), diced, sprinkled with low-sodium soy sauce
garnish:	scallions, chopped

Heat oil in heavy skillet. Saute onions quickly till almost tender. Lower fire. Add lobster pieces, fish, and clams. Cover with about 6 cups water, and bring to boil. With spoon, skim off foam and fat.

Add vegetables. Season with Sake, vegetable seasoning, and soy sauce. Simmer 10 minutes. Make sure vegetables are not overcooked.

Add tofu. Sprinkle with scallions before serving piping hot.

MAKES 8 SMALL PORTIONS. CALORIES PER PORTION: 149

MAKES 4 LARGE PORTIONS. CALORIES PER PORTION: 297

PREPARATION TIME: 30 MINUTES

*For variation, you may use rice noodles, pieces of crab, large prawns, or even small pieces of chicken to enrich Yoshe Nabe, which means a gathering of seafood, shellfish, and vegetables in one pot.

San Francisco Cioppino

2 teaspoons	garlic, minced
1 tablespoon	olive oil
1 cup	Tomato Concassee (page 24)
1 teaspoon	dried whole oregano
½ cup	tomato puree (canned)
1 cup	leeks, julienne cut, 2″ long
6 cups	Fish Bouillon (page 49), heated saffron, to taste
8	clams, scrubbed clean
¾ pound	crab claws or crab pieces, cut in 1″ pieces
4 ounces	sea bass or other fish steak, cut in 1″ pieces
1 tablespoon	Pernod liqueur
2 tablespoons	fresh parsley, chopped

In 4-quart pot, gently saute garlic in olive oil. Add **Tomato Concassee**, oregano, tomato puree, and leeks. Simmer 5 minutes. Add **Fish Bouillon**, and simmer 10 minutes. Remove froth with spoon. Add saffron and clams. Simmer till clam shells open. Add crab and fish; simmer 5-7 minutes, till done.

Before serving, add Pernod and parsley.

Serve with breadsticks.

MAKES 8 SMALL PORTIONS. CALORIES PER PORTION: 138

MAKES 4 LARGE PORTIONS. CALORIES PER PORTION: 275

PREPARATION TIME: 30 MINUTES

Sea Bass Romaine

4	large outer leaves of romaine lettuce
1 tablespoon	sesame oil
4	sea-bass fillets (approx. 5 oz. each)
	dusting of unbleached white flour
4	fresh basil leaves, or 2 teaspoons dried whole basil
1 tablespoon	fresh lemon juice
1 cup	carrots and turnips, julienned and blanched
¼ cup	plain, low-fat yogurt
1 tablespoon	Dijon-type mustard
	cayenne pepper, to taste (optional)
garnish:	4 lemon wedges

Preheat oven to 350⁰.

Dip romaine leaves in boiling water; blanch 2 minutes. Drain vegetables in sieve, and refresh them under cold running water. Dry on paper towel. Heat oil in heavy skillet. Dust sea-bass fillets in flour. Quickly saute for 1 minute on each side.

Place each fillet on lettuce leaf. Set a basil leaf on each fillet; sprinkle with lemon juice and wrap fillet tightly.

Transfer fillets to lightly oiled baking dish just large enough to accommodate them. Cover. Bake 15-20 minutes, depending on thickness of fish. Meanwhile heat julienned carrots and turnips in a little vegetable broth. Mix yogurt and mustard with cayenne, if desired, to make Yogurt/Dijon Mustard Sauce. When fish is baked, place each fillet on a warm plate; cover with sauce and then with julienned vegetables. Garnish and serve.

SERVES 4. CALORIES PER SERVING: 165

PREPARATION TIME: 25 MINUTES

Hot Salmon Pate

1 pound	fresh salmon fillet, skinned, boned
6 ounces	bay shrimp, cooked
2 tablespoons	fresh lemon juice
¾ cup	Fish Bouillon (page 49), or Chicken Broth (page 48)
1 teaspoon	vegetable seasoning
	cayenne pepper, to taste
1	egg yolk
3	egg whites, slightly beaten
	sesame-seed or safflower oil
1 recipe	Sauce Michel (page 23)
1½ tablespoons	dried whole basil or tarragon
garnish:	2 tablespoons fresh parsley, chopped

Preheat oven to 375°.

In food processor, place all ingredients, except egg whites and oil and Sauce Michel with basil or tarragon. Puree with metal blade. Transfer to mixing bowl, and fold in egg whites with spatula.

Place mixture in 5-cup earthenware pate mold, slightly oiled. Cover tightly with foil. Set in hot bain-marie (pan of hot water). Bake 1 hour.

Remove from oven, and let settle 10 minutes. Remove foil. Top each serving slice with tarragon sauce (Sauce Michel with tarragon) or basil sauce (Sauce Michel with basil). Garnish and serve immediately.

MAKES 8 SMALL PORTIONS. CALORIES PER PORTION: 107

MAKES 4 LARGE PORTIONS. CALORIES PER PORTION: 214

PREPARATION TIME: 30 MINUTES

BAKING TIME: 1 HOUR

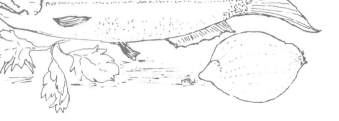

Fish with Vegetables (en Papillote)

4 pieces	aluminum foil, about 12" square
4	sea bass, rock cod, or cabrilla fillets, about 4-5 ounces each (thick and meaty)
4	tomato slices, thick
4	parsley sprigs
8	fresh mushrooms, sliced
4	fresh basil leaves (or 2 teaspoons dried whole basil)
4 teaspoons	fresh lemon juice
	black pepper, freshly ground

Preheat oven to 350°.

Place each fillet in a foil square. Atop each fillet put 1 tomato slice, 1 parsley sprig, 2 sliced mushrooms, 1 basil leaf, 1 teaspoon lemon juice, and ground pepper, to taste. Lift ends of foil and close tightly together to make a pouch.

Set foil-wrapped fillets on baking sheet. Bake 25-30 minutes. (Fish also may be barbecued over moderate fire.)

Serve fish in its pouch, steaming hot.

SERVES 4. CALORIES PER SERVING: 139

PREPARATION TIME: 30 MINUTES

Baked Dill Salmon

4 pieces	aluminum foil, about 12" square
1 pound	salmon fillets, cut into 4 portions
12	cucumber slices, ⅛" thick, peeled
4	lemon slices, peeled
1 teaspoon	dried dill
4	parsley sprigs
4	raw shrimp (optional), large, peeled, deveined

May be baked or barbecued. If baked, preheat oven to 375°.

Place salmon in foil squares. Spread 3 cucumber slices and 1 lemon slice on each fish portion. Sprinkle with dill; add 1 parsley sprig and, if desired, 1 shrimp. Lift ends of foil and close tightly together to make a pouch.

Put salmon about 3-4 inches above hot fire of barbecue grill, a little away from center of heat. Cook 15-20 minutes. Or put foil-wrapped salmon in baking dish and bake 20 minutes, till done.

Remove foil, and serve immediately with salads and **Crudites** (page 43).

SERVES 4. CALORIES PER SERVING: 156

PREPARATION TIME: 30 MINUTES

Fillet of Sole California Style

1 tablespoon	sesame-seed or safflower oil
1	egg, beaten
1 teaspoon	fresh parsley, chopped
1 teaspoon	dill weed
4	sole (or other fish) fillets, about 3½ ounces each
garnish:	lemon wedges and fresh parsley, chopped

Preheat oven to 375°.

In heavy skillet, heat oil. Beat egg, together with parsley and dill. Dip each fillet in the egg wash and place in heated skillet. Saute quickly on both sides.

Remove from skillet, and place in shallow baking dish. Bake 5-10 minutes (depending upon fillets' thickness). Garnish, and serve immediately.

SERVES 4. CALORIES PER SERVING: 154
PREPARATION TIME: 15 MINUTES

Fillet of Sole Florentine

4	sole (or other fish) fillets, about 3½ ounces each
4 tablespoons	dry white wine
4 teaspoons	fresh lemon juice
	dried whole oregano, to taste
8 drops	sesame-seed or safflower oil
2 cups	fresh spinach, cooked, but not overcooked, finely chopped
¼ teaspoon	grated nutmeg
4 tablespoons	Parmesan or Romano cheese, freshly grated
	paprika, to taste
garnish:	lemon wedges

Preheat oven to 350°.

In separate baking (gratine) dishes, place fillets. To each, add 1 tablespoon wine, 1 teaspoon lemon juice, sprinkle of oregano, and 2 drops of oil.

Bake, uncovered, 5-10 minutes (depending on fillets' thickness), till ¾ cooked. Remove from oven. Spread ½ cup spinach over each fillet to cover; sprinkle with a little nutmeg, and 1 tablespoon cheese. Top with paprika, to taste. Return to oven. Bake 8-10 minutes, till sides just begin to bubble.

Garnish and serve.

SERVES 4. CALORIES PER SERVING: 194
PREPARATION TIME: 20 MINUTES

Fillet of Sole with Dilled Cucumber Slices

4	fillets of sole (or other fish fillets), about 3½ ounces each
8 drops	sesame-seed or safflower oil
	white pepper, to taste
	dill weed
2	European cucumbers, peeled, thinly sliced
4 teaspoons	fresh lemon juice
	paprika
garnish:	parsley sprigs and lemon wedges

Preheat oven to 325°.

Place fillets in individual baking dishes. Put 2 drops of oil on each fillet. Add white pepper and dill weed. Cover fillets with cucumber slices, sprinkle more white pepper and dill weed on top. Cover baking dishes tightly. Bake 20-25 minutes, till done.

Remove fish from oven; uncover. Add 1 teaspoon lemon juice to each serving. Sprinkle with paprika, and garnish. Serve immediately.

SERVES 4. CALORIES PER TABLESPOON: 147
PREPARATION TIME: 30 MINUTES

Fillet of Sole California Style, with Grapes

1 recipe	Fillet of Sole California Style (page 76)
40	seedless grapes (not too sweet)
⅓ cup	Hungarian green wine (or other dry white wine)
garnish:	lemon wedges and parsley sprigs

In skillet, heat grapes with wine till grape skins begin to burst. Before serving and garnishing, arrange 10 grapes, with juice, around each fillet.

Garnish and serve.

SERVES 4. CALORIES PER SERVING: 192
PREPARATION TIME: 15 MINUTES

Baked Whole Fish Parmentiere

1	red snapper or rock cod, about 3-4 pounds
5	red potatoes, scrubbed, thinly sliced
1 tablespoon	olive oil
	sea salt, to taste
2	onions, thinly sliced
4	celery stalks
1	bay leaf
½ teaspoon	cracked black pepper
4	tomatoes, peeled and sliced
2 tablespoons	dried sweet basil
	black pepper, freshly ground, to taste
	vegetable seasoning, to taste

Under cold running water, wash and scale fish. With sharp knife, open belly; clean inside thoroughly (or have done by your fish merchant).

Preheat oven to 350°.

Spread potato slices to make 1 layer at bottom of deep baking dish adequate to hold whole fish. Sprinkle olive oil and sea salt over potatoes. Put sliced onions on top.

Stuff fish with celery, bay leaf, and cracked pepper. Place fish with belly spread open (do not lay fish on its side) in baking dish. Surround with tomato slices; sprinkle with basil, ground pepper, and vegetable seasoning. Also season fish.

Tightly cover baking dish with lid or foil (it should not touch fish). Bake about 1 hour and 20 minutes, allowing 30 minutes more for each additional pound.

Remove from oven, and let stand 10 minutes; uncover. With knife tip, carefully cut meat away from bones. Cover with its own juices. Serve with potato, onion, and tomato.

MAKES 8 SMALL PORTIONS. CALORIES PER PORTION: 203

MAKES 4 LARGE PORTIONS. CALORIES PER PORTION: 406

PREPARATION TIME: 10 MINUTES

BAKING TIME: 1 HOUR 20 MINUTES

Shrimp Sauce Kimini

1 recipe	Beans Niban Dashi (page 102)
16	raw shrimp, medium size, peeled, deveined, rinsed, and butterflied
1 tablespoon	sesame-seed or safflower oil
	Sansho or powdered ginger, to taste; or black pepper, freshly ground paprika, to taste
garnish:	lemon wedges and 2 teaspoons scallions, chopped

Spear 4 shrimp each on 4 bamboo skewers.

Heat a grill or cast-iron pan with oil.

Season shrimp with pepper (or ginger) and paprika. Quickly saute on both sides. Cook, covered, 5 minutes, till done.

Serve over **Beans Niban Dashi**, and spoon tofu sauce from beans over shrimp.

Garnish, and serve immediately.

SERVES 4. CALORIES PER SERVING: 174

PREPARATION TIME: 15 MINUTES

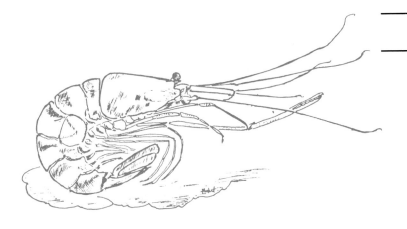

Shrimp Creole

1½ cups	Tomato Concassee (page 24)
½ cup	celery, sliced
½ cup	bell pepper, sliced
	black pepper, freshly ground, to taste
2 tablespoons	black olives, freshly chopped
½ cup	scallions (halve, if too thick), cut in 1″ pieces
2 teaspoons	garlic, minced
2 teaspoons	olive oil
20	raw shrimp, medium size, peeled, deveined, and butterflied
3 tablespoons	fresh parsley, chopped
garnish:	parsley sprigs and lemon wedges

Gently heat **Tomato Concassee**; stir in celery and bell pepper. Cook 8-10 minutes, till vegetables begin to soften. Season with pepper. Add olives and scallions. Set this Creole sauce aside.

In separate skillet, gently saute garlic in olive oil. Add shrimp, and cook on both sides till almost done. Pour Creole sauce over shrimp, and let bubble 5-7 minutes.

Before serving, sprinkle parsley over shrimp. Garnish.

Note: If you would prefer this recipe a little spicier, add 1 or 2 teaspoons dried hot chile flakes to the **Tomato Concassee**, with vegetables.

SERVES 4. CALORIES PER SERVING: 154
PREPARATION TIME: 20 MINUTES

Coquille Fruits de Mer

1	onion, halved
2 teaspoons	shallots (or white part of scallions), minced
1 teaspoon	sesame-seed or safflower oil
½ teaspoon	dried whole thyme
12 ounces	scallops, cut in small pieces
8 ounces	mushrooms, diced
4 ounces	raw shrimp, large (or small bay shrimp), diced
⅓ cup	dry white wine
¾ cup	juices from seafood, reserved
2 ounces	Neufchatel low-fat cream cheese
1½ tablespoons	arrowroot
2 teaspoons	fresh lemon juice
⅛ teaspoon	grated nutmeg
	cayenne pepper, to taste
3 ounces	crab meat, cooked or canned (optional)
garnish:	paprika and 2 tablespoons fresh parsley, chopped

In stainless-steel saucepan, cover onion with water. Simmer 30 minutes, till tender.

In heavy saucepan, gently saute shallots in oil over low heat. With wooden spatula, stir in thyme, scallops, mushrooms, shrimp, and wine. Cover; simmer slowly 5 minutes, till done. Stir to separate scallops, Strain juices from scallops and shrimp; reserve ¾ cup. (Add juice from boiled onion if necessary to make ¾ cup.) Set mixture aside, covered.

In blender, puree till very smooth onion, ¾ cup reserved juice from seafood, cheese, arrowroot, and lemon juice. Season with nutmeg and dash of cayenne pepper.

Pour this creamy sauce over scallops and shrimp; return to fire; simmer, and let bubble till slightly thick. Add crab meat, if desired.

Spoon into 4 scallop shells. Garnish and serve.

SERVES 4. CALORIES PER SERVING: 260
PREPARATION TIME: 45 MINUTES

Scallops in Leek Sauce

2	leeks, large (use white parts only), halved, and thinly sliced (2 cups)
1 pound	raw scallops, quartered
8	raw shrimp, medium size, peeled, deveined, cut in chunks
1 cup	dry white wine
1	bay leaf
¾ cup	seafood broth, reserved
3 ounces	Neufchatel low-fat cream cheese
1 tablespoon	fresh lemon juice
1 tablespoon	arrowroot
	grated nutmeg, to taste
	cayenne pepper, to taste
garnish:	2 tablespoons scallions, chopped

Cover leeks with water. Simmer, covered, 15 minutes, till tender.

Place scallops and shrimp in saucepan with wine and bay leaf. Slowly simmer, covered, over medium heat 5-10 minutes. Drain off ¾ cup broth; reserve. Set aside scallops and shrimp, covered.

With slotted spoon, remove ½ the leeks. In blender or food processor, puree them with seafood broth till very smooth. Add cheese, lemon juice, and arrowroot. Season with dash of nutmeg and dash of cayenne pepper.

Pour this blended sauce over scallops (making sure they have been drained of all liquid). Simmer a few minutes to thicken sauce. Pour into serving dish.

Heat remaining leeks, and drain well. Place them on top of seafood mixture. Serve in 4 scallop shells. Garnish.

SERVES 4. CALORIES PER SERVING: 266

PREPARATION TIME: 35 MINUTES

Seafood Curry

¾ cup	fresh pineapple, diced
½ cup	apple, peeled, diced
½	banana, sliced
2 tablespoons	curry powder
1¼ cups	bay shrimp (8 ounces), cooked
1¼ cups	crab meat (8 ounces), canned or cooked, with juice; cut in chunks
¾ cup	Sauce Michel (page 23)
	cayenne pepper, to taste
1 teaspoon	arrowroot (optional)
garnish:	4 lemon wedges; 2 tablespoons coconut, grated, freshly toasted; parsley sprigs

Heat pineapple, apple, banana, and curry powder in heavy skillet. Cook gently, and stir about 10 minutes, till moisture has evaporated from fruit, and banana has softened and thickened.

Add shrimp and crab; heat. Add **Sauce Michel** and blend well, heating till piping hot. Add dash of cayenne pepper.

Taste for seasoning. There should be a nice contrast between sweetness of fruit and sharpness of cayenne pepper.

If sauce is too thin, thicken with arrowroot.

Garnish and serve.

SERVES 4. CALORIES PER SERVING: 176

PREPARATION TIME: 20 MINUTES

Lobster Thermidor

1	onion, small
2	celery-heart stalks
2	lobsters, cooked (1¾ pounds each), halved
½ cup	vegetable broth, reserved
2 teaspoons	olive oil
1 tablespoon	shallots, minced
½ teaspoon	black pepper, freshly ground
3 ounces	Neufchatel low-fat cream cheese
1 teaspoon	arrowroot
1½ tablespoons	Dijon mustard
	cayenne pepper
1 teaspoon	fresh (or dried) tarragon, chopped
1 tablespoon	fresh parsley, chopped
garnish:	lobster roe (reserved); fresh parsley, chopped; lemon wedges; parsley sprigs

In just enough water to cover, gently simmer onion and celery, covered, about 45 minutes, till vegetables are tender. Drain, and reserve ½ cup of broth.

Remove meat from cooked lobster, saving shells. Trim out sinews and dark parts; save the roe. Slice meat in ¼″ slices.

Rinse shells in cold water and place on baking dish.

In saucepan, heat oil and gently saute shallots (seasoned with ground pepper). Add lobster meat, and heat over low fire.

In blender, puree vegetable broth, onion, and celery. Add cheese and arrowroot; blend well till very smooth. Pour over lobster meat, and heat till sauce thickens slightly. Add mustard, dash of cayenne pepper, tarragon, and 1 tablespoon chopped parsley. Stir well.

Heat lobster shells in oven about 10 minutes; fill them with lobster mixture.

Garnish with chopped roe mixed with chopped parsley — sprinkle on top of each shell; add parsley sprigs and lemon wedges. Serve.

SERVES 4. CALORIES PER SERVING: 194
PREPARATION TIME: 1 HOUR

Sashimi

¾ pound	bonito, tuna, or sea bass, boned and skinned; remove dark sinews
6	lettuce leaves
1 cup	lettuce, shredded
1 cup	daikon, grated
garnish:	red radishes, scallions, and lemon slices
2 teaspoons	Wasabi
4 teaspoons	water
1 teaspoon	soy sauce (low sodium)

Slice fish on a slant, cutting thin pieces about 1″ long. (Your fish merchant might do this for you, especially in Oriental markets.)

Spread lettuce leaves on elegant platter. Spread shredded lettuce in center, and place sashimi (slices of fish), like a fan, on top. Make little heaps of grated daikon. Add garnishes.

Separately, in small dish, mix Wasabi, water, and soy sauce to make a paste.

With chopsticks, dip each slice of sashimi into Wasabi sauce. Eat with grated daikon and garnishes.

SERVES 4. CALORIES PER SERVING: 93
PREPARATION TIME: 10 MINUTES

LET'S TALK ABOUT THESE RECIPES

FOIL BAKING: En papillote used to signify baking in an oiled paper bag but foil has made this technique obsolete.

Place food in center of squarish piece of foil, fold and crease, fold, crease and conclude with open ends which you fold over the bundle.

We are told that foods wrapped in heavy-duty aluminum foil may be placed directly on the oven rack, unless a recipe specifies differently. But you can always be sure all will go well if you place your foil-wrapped bundle on a cookie sheet.

Fish can be barbecued by use of triple thicknesses of foil.

Soaring sales figures show the American public's gratitude to the chicken, which lends itself to many enchanting recipes while keeping the daily calorie count within reason.

It is not necessary to make a pitch for chicken dinners. They're hard to dislike. But they taste even better if you buy poultry from a butcher or poultry shop. The extra expense is pretty well offset by the fact that these chickens will not shrink in the pan to the extent that supermarket fowl does. Moreover, since you eliminate the skin of the chicken in low-calorie recipes, the taste of the flesh becomes even more important. A chicken who has been kept awake all night with electric lights and never has been allowed to scratch on the ground simply won't do.

'Golden Door' chickens live happily just above the vegetable garden. At night they are fed grain but during the day they have as a treat vegetable scraps from the garden. (What is raked from the chicken yard goes into the compost heap for the garden — a perfect example of recycling.) They are not caged in chicken prisons where diseases are rampant, and hence they have no need for doses of penicillin.

Be very choosy about chicken. Never buy it cut up in plastic-wrapped packages. Insist that it be date-stamped. Smell it. Never store it uncooked in the refrigerator for more than two days (USDA advice).

Most of us are familiar with the story that fortified red wine historically was coupled with red meat because beef can develop some nasty bacteria. But how many are familiar with the fact that Consumer Reports testers recently found salmonella(e) in approximately 20% of chicken purchased on both the east and west coasts?

Cooking kills this bacteria. Be cautious in handling raw chicken. Clean the cutting board or any surface it touches, and thoroughly wash all plates and utensils with which it comes in contact.

Turkey is a splendid choice for your table, and provides a week of challenge as you think of ways to use the leftovers.

Of course, you never, never buy rolled, boneless preformed turkey (or r., b., p. anything).

Golden Door Breast of Chicken

---

2 ounces	Monterey jack cheese, cut into 4 pieces
4	chicken breast halves, skinned, trimmed of fat
2 tablespoons	unbleached flour
2	eggs, beaten
1 tablespoon	Parmesan or Romano cheese, freshly grated
1 tablespoon	chives, chopped
1 tablespoon	dried sweet basil, chopped
1 teaspoon	vegetable seasoning
2 teaspoons	sesame-seed or safflower oil
garnish:	4 parsley sprigs, 4 lemon wedges

Insert cheese into pouch of chicken breast (push finger along bone to make a pouch). Coat breast with flour, and dip into egg beaten with cheese, chives, sweet basil, and vegetable seasoning.

Preheat oven to 375°.

In heavy skillet, heat oil. Add chicken breasts, and brown on both sides. Remove from skillet; place in baking dish. Bake, uncovered, about 25-30 minutes, till chicken is tender.

Garnish and serve.

SERVES 4. CALORIES PER SERVING: 266
PREPARATION TIME: 40 MINUTES

Sesame Chicken Breast in Ginger

4	chicken breast halves, skinned, boned, and trimmed of fat
1 tablespoon	fresh ginger, minced
1 tablespoon	soy sauce (low sodium)
2 tablespoons	sesame-seed or safflower oil
4 teaspoons	garlic, minced
1 cup	fresh asparagus, trimmed, cut into pieces 2″ long
1 cup	zucchini, cut into pieces 2″ long
1 cup	scallions (green part), cut into pieces 2″ long
½ cup	Chicken Broth (page 48), heated
3 cups	bean sprouts
	soy sauce (low sodium)
	vegetable seasoning
1 tablespoon	arrowroot (dissolved in 2 tablespoons water)
1 teaspoon	lemon zest, grated
3 tablespoons	sesame seeds, freshly toasted

Marinate chicken breasts in ginger and mild soy sauce for 1 hour. Cut chicken breasts into thin strips 2″ long.

In heavy skillet, quickly heat 1 tablespoon oil and 2 teaspoons garlic. Stir in chicken strips until lightly sauteed.

Cover, set aside.

Use a wok to stir-fry vegetables: Heat remainder of oil and garlic, and in quick succession add asparagus, zucchini, peppers. Stir-fry till vegetables begin to cook. Add chicken strips and scallions; mix again. Add **Chicken Broth** and bean sprouts; sprinkle with soy sauce and vegetable seasoning. When broth comes to a boil, thicken with dissolved arrowroot.

Whole process should take about 10 minutes.

Before serving, sprinkle with lemon zest and sesame seeds.

SERVES 4. CALORIES PER SERVING: 274

CAN BE PREPARED 1 HOUR AHEAD

COOKING TIME: 15 MINUTES

Broiled Cornish Game Hen Golden Door

2	Cornish game hens (1 pound, 5 ounces each), halved
2 tablespoons	soy sauce (low sodium)
1 teaspoon	ginger, minced
⅓ cup	pineapple juice
8	thin orange slices
2 teaspoons	coconut, grated and freshly toasted
garnish:	parsley sprigs

For 2 hours, refrigerate game hens in marinade of soy sauce, ginger, and pineapple juice, covered.

Preheat broiler. Preheat oven to 350°.

Remove hens from marinade. Put marinade aside.

Place hens in skillet; broil 5 minutes on each side. (If barbecuing, brown them on both sides, and follow remainder of recipe.)

Bake hens, uncovered, 30 minutes, till done.

In same skillet, pour marinade over hens and mix with pan juices. Simmer 2-3 minutes, to reduce juice.

Serve hens in their juice. Top with orange slices and coconut sprinkle. Garnish and serve.

SERVES 4. CALORIES PER SERVING: 285

PREPARATION TIME: 45 MINUTES

Chicken Paprika

2 teaspoons	sesame-seed or safflower oil
1	onion, small, chopped
1	bell pepper (optional), small, diced fine
½ teaspoon	dried whole marjoram
1½ tablespoons	paprika, Hungarian-style
4	chicken breast halves, skinned, trimmed of fat
¾ cup	Chicken Broth (page 48), heated
3 ounces	Neufchatel low-fat cream cheese
1 teaspoon	arrowroot
	vegetable seasoning, to taste
garnish:	2 tablespoons fresh parsley or scallions, chopped

Preheat oven to 350°.

In heavy skillet, heat oil and gently saute onion and bell pepper till glazed. Sprinkle with marjoram and 1 tablespoon paprika. Stir with wooden spatula over low heat (onion and bell pepper must not stick to pan). Sprinkle remaining paprika over chicken breasts, and place them over onions. Cover; bake 35-40 minutes, till done.

Remove from oven. Add **Chicken Broth**, and simmer 2-3 minutes. Remove chicken breasts onto a plate. Blend broth, cooked onions, cheese, and arrowroot in blender till smooth.

Replace chicken breasts in skillet, pour sauce over chicken, and cook about 5 minutes to reduce.

Season with vegetable seasoning. Garnish and serve.

SERVES 4. CALORIES PER SERVING: 219

PREPARATION TIME: 10 MINUTES

BAKING TIME: 35-40 MINUTES

Curried Chicken Breast

2 teaspoons	sesame-seed or safflower oil
1 teaspoon	fresh ginger, minced
1 tablespoon	scallion or shallot, chopped
4	chicken breast halves, skinned and trimmed of fat
	vegetable seasoning
¾ cup	pineapple, diced
1 tablespoon	curry powder
1	banana, small, sliced
3 tablespoons	tomato puree
½ cup	Chicken Broth (page 48), heated
2 ounces	Neufchatel low-fat cream cheese
1 teaspoon	arrowroot
	cayenne pepper, to taste
	saffron (optional)
garnish:	2 teaspoons coconut, grated and freshly toasted

Preheat oven to 350°.

In heavy skillet, heat oil and gently saute ginger with scallion or shallot. Place chicken meat-side down; saute quickly. Turn over, bone-side down, sprinkle with vegetable seasoning, cover tightly, and bake 30-35 minutes.

In stainless-steel pan, heat pineapple 5 minutes or till it starts to release juice. Add curry powder, mixing well. Stir in banana and tomato puree. Add **Chicken Broth.** Simmer gently, uncovered, 15 minutes. Let cool.

In blender, puree fruit mixture with cream cheese and arrowroot. Add cayenne pepper, if desired. Pour mixture over cooked chicken. Simmer gently 5 minutes. Add dash of saffron, and check seasonings. Garnish and serve.

Serve with a vegetable such as broccoli or carrots.

SERVES 4. CALORIES PER SERVING: 248

PREPARATION TIME: 45 MINUTES

Breast of Chicken Florentine-Parmesan

4	chicken breast halves, boned, skinned, and trimmed of fat
1	egg, beaten
1 teaspoon	dried sweet basil
2 tablespoons	Parmesan or Romano cheese, freshly grated
1 tablespoon	sesame-seed or safflower oil
1 cup	spinach, cooked and well drained
1 ounce	Monterey jack cheese, freshly grated
	grated nutmeg
4	mozzarella slices (about 2 ounces)
1½ cups	Tomato Concassee (page 24)
garnish:	2 tablespoons fresh parsley, chopped

Preheat oven to 350°.

Beat egg with basil and Parmesan cheese. Dip chicken breasts into egg wash. Heat heavy skillet with oil; saute chicken on both sides till golden brown. Place skillet in oven. Bake 20-25 minutes till chicken is moist and almost done.

Chop spinach coarsely. Heat with jack cheese and pinch of nutmeg till cheese is creamy. Spread this mixture in 4 separate baking dishes.

Place each chicken breast on top of spinach mixture. Cover with mozzarella slices, and return to oven for 15 minutes.

Heat **Tomato Concassee**. Remove chicken from oven, and pour tomato sauce around the individual servings.

Garnish, and serve immediately.

SERVES 4. CALORIES PER SERVING: 312

PREPARATION TIME: 1 HOUR

Chicken Yakitori

4	chicken breast halves, skinned, boned, and trimmed of fat
3 tablespoons	Sake
1 tablespoon	soy sauce (low sodium)
1 teaspoon	fresh ginger, minced
½	eggplant, cut into ¾″ squares (16 cubes)
garnish:	2 tablespoons sesame seeds, freshly toasted; 2 tablespoons scallions, chopped

Cut trimmed chicken breasts into ¾″ squares. Marinate in Sake, soy sauce, and ginger. To moisten well, turn pieces in marinade. Cover with plastic wrap; refrigerate overnight.

Spear chicken pieces on 8 6″-long bamboo skewers; place eggplant cube on each end.

Reserve marinade.

Preheat hibachi or charcoal grill (or heat 1 teaspoon sesame oil in cast-iron pan). Broil skewers about 3″ from heat for 4-5 minutes, turning once. Dip skewers in reserved marinade, and broil additional 4-5 minutes.

Garnish. Serve 2 skewers per person, steaming hot, on same platter with **Yasai Itame** (page 64), and lightly coat skewers with **Ponzu Dip** (page 22).

SERVES 4. CALORIES PER SERVING: 197

PREPARATION TIME: 25 MINUTES

Chicken Ratatouille

1 teaspoon	olive oil
1	onion, thinly sliced
1 teaspoon	garlic, minced
2 teaspoons	dried sweet basil
4	chicken breast halves, skinned, trimmed of fat
	vegetable seasoning
4 cups	Ratatouille (page 68)
2-3 ounces	Jarlsberg (or thinly sliced mozzarella) cheese, freshly grated
2 tablespoons	fresh parsley, chopped

Preheat oven to 375°.

In heavy cast-iron skillet, heat oil. Add onion and garlic. Gently saute a few minutes till onion softens. Sprinkle basil over mixture, and place chicken breasts over onion and garlic. Sprinkle lightly with vegetable seasoning. Cover tightly, and cook 3-4 minutes.

Bake 20-25 minutes. Remove from oven. Chicken breasts should be very nice and juicy.

Remove rib bones from breasts. Line 4 baking dishes (or 1 large one) with onion mixture and juices. Place chicken breasts on top of onion. Cover each chicken breast with 1 cup **Ratatouille**. Sprinkle cheese over each breast and return to oven to bake 15 minutes, or till top of each breast is light brown. Sprinkle with parsley, and serve.

SERVES 4. CALORIES PER SERVING: 333

PREPARATION TIME: 50 MINUTES

Almond Chicken

4	chicken breast halves, trimmed of fat
	sea salt, to taste
	black pepper, freshly ground
	dried whole marjoram
1 teaspoon	olive oil
1 tablespoon	shallots, chopped
1	garlic clove, small, minced
2 tablespoons	almonds, freshly sliced (about 1 ounce)
¼ cup	dry white wine or Vermouth
2 teaspoons	fresh lemon juice
1 teaspoon	butter
1 teaspoon	fresh parsley, chopped
garnish:	¼ avocado (optional), sliced; 4 small bunches seedless grapes; 4 parsley sprigs; 4 lemon wedges

Preheat oven to 350°.

Season chicken with salt, pepper, and marjoram. In skillet just large enough to hold chicken breasts, heat oil and saute both sides of chicken about 5 minutes, till lightly browned. Remove from pan.

To same pan, add shallots and garlic; gently saute till they soften. Arrange chicken breasts on top of shallots and garlic in skillet, so that they are touching. Sprinkle sliced almonds over top. Bake, uncovered, about 20-25 minutes, till chicken is done.

Remove chicken from skillet and keep warm on hot platter. Add wine and lemon juice to same skillet. Cook over medium heat and stir to reduce sauce, about 3-5 minutes. Add butter and parsley. Blend well.

Spoon sauce onto serving plates, then place chicken on top (this keeps almonds crisp). Garnish with fruit, and serve.

SERVES 4. CALORIES PER SERVING: 196 WITH AVOCADO: 220

PREPARATION TIME: 45 MINUTES

Foil-Wrapped Baked Chicken

4 pieces	aluminum foil, about 12″ square
4	chicken breast halves, skinned and trimmed of fat
1 teaspoon	vegetable seasoning
4 tablespoons	celery, minced
4 tablespoons	onion, minced
4 tablespoons	fresh parsley, chopped
4	fresh thyme sprigs, small (or ¾ teaspoon dried whole thyme)
4 tablespoons	fresh lemon juice
4 tablespoons	dry white wine
garnish:	1 tablespoon fresh parsley, chopped

Preheat oven to 375°.

Place chicken breasts on foil squares. Season with vegetable seasoning. Sprinkle celery, onion, and parsley over chicken; add thyme, lemon juice, and wine. Bring ends of foil together over chicken and bend ends upward (to prevent juice from running out). Seal ends and top by folding foil over into tight roll. Bake on baking tray, 30-35 minutes.

Before serving, open foil packets and place chicken on heated serving plate. Discard thyme sprigs, pour juices over chicken. Garnish and serve.

SERVES 4. CALORIES PER SERVING: 145

PREPARATION TIME: 40 MINUTES

Turkey Breast Minceur

1	turkey breast, whole or split (4½ to 6 pounds)
1 tablespoon	vegetable seasoning
½ teaspoon	dried whole thyme
½ teaspoon	dried whole oregano
1	onion, whole, stuck with 6 cloves
1	celery heart, small
1	turnip, peeled
1	bay leaf
1 teaspoon	black pepper, freshly ground

BASIC SAUCE MICHEL:

1½ cups	Chicken Broth (page 48), approximately — added to reserved turkey broth to make 1¾ cups
3 ounces	Neufchatel low-fat cream cheese
1 tablespoon	arrowroot
2 teaspoons	fresh lemon juice cayenne pepper
¼ teaspoon	grated nutmeg
garnish:	2 tablespoons fresh parsley, chopped

Preheat oven to 350°.

Place turkey breast-side down in roasting pan just large enough to hold it plus the vegetables. Sprinkle with vegetable seasoning, thyme, and oregano. Add onion (stuck with cloves), celery heart, turnip, bay leaf, and pepper. Bake, tightly covered, 1 hour at 350°. Reduce heat to 325°; bake 4½-pound breast another hour, add 20 minutes for larger breast. Do not remove cover till turkey is done.

Remove turkey from roasting pan. Pour pan juices into measuring cup. Carefully spoon out excess fat, and blot fat with paper towels. To pan juices, add enough **Chicken Broth** to make 1¾ cups. Remove cloves from onion. In blender or food processor, puree onion, celery, broth, cream cheese, arrowroot, lemon juice, nutmeg, and dash of cayenne pepper. (This is **Sauce Michel** (page 23).)

Pour **Sauce Michel** into pan, heat, and let bubble a few minutes. Remove skin from turkey breast. Slice breast into 3½-4-ounce portions. Coat each serving with about 3 tablespoons of sauce.

Garnish and serve.

SERVES 4. CALORIES PER SERVING 292

PREPARATION TIME: 15 MINUTES

BAKING TIME: 2 HOURS

Variations of Turkey Breast Minceur

Spinach Sauce

See page 23.

CALORIES PER TABLESPOON: 8
PREPARATION TIME: 10 MINUTES

Mushroom Sauce

2 cups	fresh mushrooms, sliced
1 tablespoon	fresh lemon juice
¼ cup	water
1 teaspoon	vegetable seasoning
½ teaspoon	black pepper, freshly ground
¼ cup	scallions, chopped

Steam mushrooms in saucepan, covered, with lemon juice, water, vegetable seasoning, and pepper, 5 minutes. Add mushroom mixture to **Sauce Michel** (page 23). Heat to a simmer. Add scallions.

CALORIES PER TABLESPOON: 6
PREPARATION TIME: 10 MINUTES

Sauce Aurore

Cook turkey breast along with:

2	carrots, medium size
1	onion
1	celery stalk, small

Save these vegetables, and add to following ingredients:

2 cups	broth from turkey bones; if necessary, add Chicken Broth (page 48)
3 ounces	Neufchatel low-fat cream cheese
	cayenne pepper
	grated nutmeg
2 teaspoons	fresh lemon juice
2 teaspoons	sesame-seed or safflower oil
1 tablespoon	curry powder
	vegetable seasoning, to taste
garnish:	fresh parsley

Puree carrots, onion, celery, broth, cream cheese, dash of cayenne pepper, dash of nutmeg, and lemon juice in blender or food processor (as in **Sauce Michel**, page 23).

Heat oil and curry powder in small skillet; cook a few minutes. Add sauce. Taste for seasonings, add vegetable seasoning, and heat to a simmer.

Garnish and serve.

CALORIES PER TABLESPOON: 7
PREPARATION TIME: 15 MINUTES

Culturally, Americans have been conditioned to think meat is desirable and beefsteak is king.

We recoil from the Oriental custom of eating grasshoppers. But grasshoppers and cattle forage in the same fields. Basically, they are all second-hand foods. That is to say, the animal kingdom consumes cereal and grains in order to produce nutrients which we humans could process for ourselves by eating good basic foods.

At the 'Golden Door' we serve veal or lamb once or twice a week. Beef never. I look forward to the time when all our guests will consent to its complete elimination in their at-home menus.

If you must eat meat, satisfy your desire with the best lean grade, perfectly prepared—and eat it less frequently. Reduce your cholesterol and do great things for the world food supply.

Buy only from an old-fashioned butcher. Avoid meat that has been sprayed with preservative and red dye. In other words, avoid all prepackaged meat.

Veal Roulade

4 thin slices	veal scallopini (about 3 ounces, each)
2 teaspoons	dried sweet basil
	black pepper, freshly ground, to taste
	vegetable seasoning, to taste
1 cup	fresh spinach, cooked, drained, and chopped
2 ounces	Monterey jack or Jarlsberg cheese, freshly grated
	grated nutmeg, to taste
8	pine nuts (optional)
2 teaspoons	sesame-seed or safflower oil
¼ cup	dry Vermouth
1 tablespoon	fresh lemon juice
2-3 tablespoons	corn-oil margarine
1 tablespoon	Parmesan or Romano cheese, freshly grated
	paprika, to taste
	fresh parsley, chopped, to taste
2 cups	pasta, freshly cooked

Pound veal with cleaver (or ask butcher to prepare for you). Season each slice with basil, and with black pepper to taste, and dash of vegetable seasoning.

Preheat oven to 350°.

Heat spinach with jack cheese and nutmeg; stir with wooden spatula till cheese is melted. Remove from fire. Spread each scallopini with spinach mixture. Place 2 pine nuts in center of each, if desired, and roll up, securing with toothpick.

Heat oil in heavy skillet. Gently brown scallopinis on both sides. Cover skillet, and bake about 10 minutes.

Remove veal from pan, also removing toothpicks. To same pan add Vermouth and lemon juice. Reduce for 2-3 minutes. Add margarine; stir till melted. Return veal to pan, and roll it in juices.

Sprinkle with Parmesan cheese, paprika to taste, and chopped parsley. Serve immediately, with pasta.

SERVES 4. CALORIES PER SERVING: 250
PREPARATION TIME: 20 MINUTES

Veal Scallopini

4	veal scallopini (white veal), 2½-3 ounces each unbleached white flour, to dust
1	egg, beaten
2 teaspoons	dried whole oregano
2 tablespoons	Parmesan cheese, freshly grated
1 tablespoon	olive oil
2 tablespoons	butter or corn-oil margarine
1 tablespoon	chives or scallions, minced
1 cup	cooked artichoke hearts (fresh or canned), diced
2 cups	fresh mushrooms, sliced
½ teaspoon	black pepper, freshly ground
½ cup	dry white wine
½ cup	Chicken Broth (page 48), heated
¼ cup	fresh lemon juice
4 tablespoons	parsley, freshly chopped

Preheat oven to 350°.

To beaten egg, add 1 teaspoon oregano and 1 tablespoon cheese. Quickly dust scallopini in flour and dip in egg wash.

In large heavy skillet over low fire, heat olive oil and quickly saute scallopini 2 minutes on each side, till golden brown. Place in baking dish, cover loosely with foil, and set in oven for no more than 10 minutes while preparing sauce:

In skillet heat butter and saute 1 tablespoon shallots. Add 1 teaspoon oregano, and cook briefly. Add artichokes and mushrooms, and stir with wooden spatula till mushrooms begin to cook. Sprinkle with pepper. Pour over wine, **Chicken Broth**, and lemon juice. Reduce for 3-4 minutes, and add 1 tablespoon butter.

Remove scallopini from oven; again place in skillet, to soak up sauce. Sprinkle with 1 tablespoon cheese and with parsley. Serve immediately.

Accompany this dish with Jerusalem artichokes and spaghetti.

SERVES 4. CALORIES PER SERVING: 240

PREPARATION TIME: 1 HOUR

Fricassee of Veal

1 pound	white stewing veal, cubed
2 cups	water
¼ teaspoon	dried whole thyme
1	bay leaf, small
2 teaspoons	vegetable seasoning
2	leeks (white part), diced in large pieces (if leeks aren't available, substitute 1 onion, diced, plus 2 celery stalks cut in ½″ pieces)
1 cup	fresh white mushrooms, thickly sliced
¾ cup	veal broth, reserved
4 ounces	Neufchatel low-fat cream cheese
1½ teaspoons	arrowroot
1½ teaspoons	fresh lemon juice grated nutmeg, to taste
garnish:	parsley sprigs

Place veal cubes in 2-quart pan with water; add thyme, bay leaf, vegetable seasoning, and leeks. Simmer gently, covered, 1 hour, till veal is tender. Add mushrooms, and simmer 5 minutes more.

Drain broth, reserving ¾ cup (save remainder for other purposes). In blender combine reserved broth with cream cheese and arrowroot, till smooth. Pour this mixture over veal; add lemon juice. Heat veal with sauce to thicken slightly. Sprinkle dash of nutmeg, and mix.

Garnish and serve.

SERVES 4. CALORIES PER SERVING: 336

PREPARATION TIME: 1 HOUR 15 MINUTES

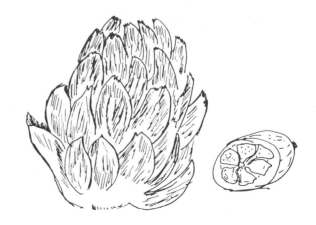

Veal Roast

2 pounds	veal roast (top or bottom round), lean
1	onion, small; halved and stuck with 6 cloves
1	fresh thyme sprig (or 1 teaspoon dried whole thyme)
1	bay leaf
	black pepper, freshly ground, to taste
¾ pound	fresh mushrooms, diced
¾ cup	water
1 tablespoon	fresh lemon juice
1 tablespoon	arrowroot, dissolved in 2 tablespoons water
	vegetable seasoning, to taste
	cayenne pepper, to taste
2 tablespoons	pimientos (if fresh, blanch them first), diced
3-4 tablespoons	scallions, chopped

Preheat oven to 350°.

Place roast in pan; surround with onion, thyme, and bay leaf. Add ground pepper. Cover tightly and bake 1 hour and 20 minutes.

Cook mushrooms 5 minutes in water and lemon juice.

When roast is done, drain juice into mushrooms. Reduce to ½ by boiling uncovered. When sauce is reduced, skim off any fat with spoon. Meanwhile, keep roast covered and warm.

Add dissolved arrowroot, plus vegetable seasoning and cayenne pepper, to taste. Simmer to thicken.

Add pimientos and ½ the scallions.

Slice roast, coat with sauce; garnish with remainder of scallions, and serve.

MAKES 8 SMALL PORTIONS. CALORIES PER PORTION: 260

MAKES 4 LARGE PORTIONS. CALORIES PER PORTION: 520

PREPARATION TIME: 10 MINUTES

BAKING TIME: 1 HOUR 20 MINUTES

Pot au Feu

1½ pounds	lean shortribs
10-12 cups	water (approximately), to cover
1 teaspoon	sea salt
1½ cups	vegetable medley (onion, turnip, parsnip, leek, carrot), thickly sliced
2	potatoes, peeled and diced
garnish:	scallions, chopped; Dijon mustard; cornichons

BOUQUET GARNI, CONSISTING OF FOLLOWING INGREDIENTS BOUND IN CHEESECLOTH:

¼ teaspoon	dried whole thyme
½ teaspoon	peppercorns
1	garlic clove
3	cloves
4	parsley sprigs
1	bay leaf
2	celery stalks

Place meat in heavy soup kettle. Cover with water. Add salt and bouquet garni. Bring to a boil; skim off fat and foam as they rise. Simmer gently 3 hours, till meat is tender. Discard bouquet garni. Cool. Refrigerate overnight.

Next day, remove fat. Bring to boil again. Add vegetable medley. Simmer 30 minutes, till vegetables are tender.

In separate pot, blanch sliced potatoes in water for 5 minutes. Drain and add to pot. Check seasoning.

First, serve broth and vegetables, topped with scallions. Meat is served separately, with Dijon mustard and cornichons.

SERVES 4. CALORIES PER SERVING: 289

PREPARE DAY AHEAD

COOKING TIME: 3 HOURS

FINAL PREPARATION TIME: 40 MINUTES

Spinach-Meat Loaf

1 pound	veal, lean, ground
1	onion, small, minced
2 teaspoons	garlic, minced
½ teaspoon	dried whole thyme
1	egg
2	egg whites
½ teaspoon	black pepper, freshly ground
2 teaspoons	soy sauce (low sodium)
1 slice	Tecate Bread (page 109), grated, or whole-wheat bread, dried and crumbled
	sesame-seed or safflower oil
½ cup	fresh spinach, cooked, drained, and coarsely chopped
1-2 ounces	Monterey jack cheese, cut in thin strips
1	bay leaf
1 recipe	Tomato Concassee (page 24)
garnish:	parsley sprigs

Mix veal, onion, garlic, thyme, egg, egg whites, pepper, soy sauce, and bread till well combined. Use a 8½″x4½″x2½″ baking dish; oil the bottom.

Preheat oven to 350°.

Place about ½ of mixture in baking dish. Pat down with hand to fill corners. Make indentation in middle of meat; put spinach there. Spread cheese on top of spinach. Add remaining mixture; pat down again. To shape loaf, moisten your hand with water. Make a crisscross design with knife. Top with bay leaf. Place in bain–marie (pan of water), and bake 1 hour to 1 hour and 15 minutes. Cool 5-10 minutes before serving (it will be easier to slice).

Serve with **Tomato Concassee**, and garnish.

MAKES 8 SMALL PORTIONS. CALORIES PER PORTION: 163

MAKES 4 LARGE PORTIONS. CALORIES PER PORTION: 327

PREPARATION TIME: 15 MINUTES

BAKING TIME: 1 HOUR 15 MINUTES

Mexican Meatballs

1 pound	veal, lean, ground
1	egg
1	egg white
¼ cup	Tecate Bread (page 109) or whole-wheat bread, dried and crumbled
½ teaspoon	chili powder
1	onion, small, grated
1	bell pepper, small, chopped fine
½ teaspoon	vegetable seasoning
3 cups	Chicken Broth (page 48)
1	bay leaf
2 tablespoons	dry Sherry wine
2 tablespoons	scallions, chopped

Mix veal, egg, egg white, bread crumbs, chili powder, onion, pepper, and vegetable seasoning till well combined. Shape into 1″ or smaller meatballs.

In skillet, heat **Chicken Broth** with bay leaf 10 minutes. Add meatballs one at a time. Simmer 30 minutes.

Before serving, add Sherry and scallions. Serve with **Ignacio's Salsa** (page 23).

SERVES 4. CALORIES PER SERVING: 338

PREPARATION TIME: 45 MINUTES

Greek Meatballs

2 tablespoons	bran flakes
3 tablespoons	Tecate Bread (page 109) or whole-wheat bread, dried and crumbled
1 tablespoon	whole-wheat flour
½ cup	plain, low-fat yogurt
¾ pound	lamb, ground
2 tablespoons	fresh mint, chopped
1	tomato, large; peeled, seeded, and chopped
1 tablespoon	Parmesan or Romano cheese, freshly grated
4 tablespoons	scallions, chopped
1½ cups	fresh spinach, cooked, drained, and chopped
1 teaspoon	garlic, minced
garnish:	1 large tomato, diced; fresh parsley, chopped

Mix bran, bread crumbs, flour, and yogurt. Let stand 5 minutes.

Add lamb, mint, tomato, cheese, and scallions. Combine well. Form 1″ meatballs, and place in heavy skillet.

Broil meatballs (several inches from broiler) 10-15 minutes, till brown; or bake 15 minutes in center of preheated 375° oven.

In separate skillet, heat spinach with garlic. Transfer to platter. Serve meatballs on top of spinach; pour over excess juice from meat. Garnish and serve.

MAKES 8 SMALL PORTIONS. CALORIES PER PORTION: 135

MAKES 4 LARGE PORTIONS. CALORIES PER PORTION: 270

PREPARATION TIME: 30 MINUTES

Curried Leg of Lamb

1	onion, medium, diced
1 tablespoon	garlic, minced
1 pound	lamb, lean, diced into ¾″ cubes
1½ - 2 tablespoons	curry powder
1	tomato, large; peeled and diced (or 4 canned tomatoes)
1	rosemary sprig
2 cups	eggplant, diced into ½″ cubes
2 teaspoons	vegetable seasoning
1 cup	fresh applesauce
1	banana, small
3 ounces	Neufchatel low-fat cream cheese
½ cup	Vegetable Stock (page 47), or Chicken Broth (page 48)
½ cup	fresh orange juice cayenne pepper, to taste
garnish:	2 tablespoons coconut, freshly grated and toasted

Preheat oven to 350°.

In heavy covered saucepan, steam onion, garlic, and lamb over medium fire 5-10 minutes, till meat begins to cook. Sprinkle curry powder; stir with wooden spatula to coat meat. Add tomato and rosemary. Bake, tightly covered, about 40 minutes.

Add eggplant and vegetable seasoning. Stir together well. Cover again, and cook 15 minutes more.

In food processor, puree together applesauce, banana, cheese, and **Vegetable Stock** till smooth. Pour over curried lamb. Add orange juice; let bubble 5 minutes. Sprinkle dash of cayenne pepper, and season to taste. Sprinkle with coconut.

MAKES 8 SMALL PORTIONS. CALORIES PER PORTION: 210

MAKES 4 LARGE PORTIONS. CALORIES PER PORTION: 420

PREPARATION TIME: 30 MINUTES

BAKING TIME: 40 MINUTES

Broiled Lamb Chops

4 loin lamb chops (5-6 ounces with fat and bone; or 4½ - 5 ounces, trimmed)
rosemary, to taste
black pepper, freshly ground, to taste

Trim excess fat from chops.

Place on broiler pan and sprinkle with rosemary and pepper. Broil 10-12 minutes on each side, till done.

SERVES 4. CALORIES PER SERVING: 230
PREPARATION TIME: 15-20 MINUTES

Ground Lean Lamb

1 pound lean lamb, ground
2 teaspoons garlic, minced
1 tablespoon dried whole oregano
1 eggplant, average size, pared and diced
2 teaspoons vegetable seasoning
1 teaspoon ground cardamom
2 teaspoons curry powder (mild)
1 bell pepper, diced
3 tomatoes, peeled, seeded, and diced
1 tablespoon fresh lemon juice
4 tablespoons fresh parsley, chopped
2 tablespoons walnuts, freshly chopped (optional)

In heavy skillet, brown lamb about 10 minutes; stir with wire whisk. Add garlic, oregano, and eggplant; stir with wooden spatula. Season with vegetable seasoning, cardamom, and curry powder. Simmer, covered, over low fire 8-10 minutes, till eggplant is soft. Add bell pepper and tomatoes; stir with spatula, and simmer 2-3 minutes more. Sprinkle with lemon juice and 2 tablespoons chopped parsley.

Serve over **Brown Rice** (page 114)—about ¼ cup per serving. Sprinkle with remaining parsley and, if desired, walnuts.

MAKES 8 SMALL PORTIONS. CALORIES PER PORTION: 158
MAKES 4 LARGE PORTIONS. CALORIES PER PORTION: 316
PREPARATION TIME: 30 MINUTES

Niku Dango Meat Roll

2	Chinese (Napa) cabbage leaves, large, or 4 Whole Wheat Crepes (page 111)
¾ pound	veal, lean, ground
3	raw shrimp, large; peeled, deveined, and chopped
1	egg
5	almonds, freshly chopped
1 teaspoon	garlic, minced
2 tablespoons	chives or scallions, chopped
2 tablespoons	soy sauce (low sodium)
1 teaspoon	vegetable seasoning
½ teaspoon	Sansho pepper or black pepper, freshly ground
½ teaspoon	fresh ginger, minced Japanese pickled ginger (optional)
garnish:	parsley sprigs

Blanch cabbage leaves in boiling water 2-3 minutes. Drain and cool. (Or prepare crepes.)

Combine veal, shrimp, egg, almonds, garlic, chives, soy sauce, vegetable seasoning, Sansho pepper, and fresh ginger. Mix well, and split into 2 equal portions. (If using crepes, divide into 4 portions.) Place inside cabbage leaves (or crepes) to form a log shape. Make a groove in center of meat, and fill with Japanese pickled ginger, if desired, pressing meat around ginger to seal. Roll cabbage leaves (or crepes) around meat filling. Place rolls in large skillet, adding water to ½″ depth. Steam gently, covered, about 30-35 minutes (better in a steamer or on a rack).

Remove from skillet, and slice each roll into 6 equal portions (3 equal portions, if making crepes). Serve 3 slices of meat roll over **Yasai Itame (Oriental Stir-Fried Vegetables)** (page 64). Spoon **Ponzu Dip** (page 22) over meat roll.

SERVES 4. CALORIES PER SERVING (WITH CABBAGE LEAVES): 231

CALORIES PER SERVING (WITH CREPES): 280

PREPARATION TIME: 55 MINUTES

VEGETABLES

The crisper, the fresher, the prettier, the better. Those are the requirements for the vegetables you buy. Best of all, try to grow a vegetable garden of your own, however small. There's no substitute for homegrown and fresh picked.

There was an old folk belief that people should eat three times as many vegetables as fruits. Today we recognize that as a fairly good ratio, but it was established long before anyone knew the nutritive properties of various foods. The old reasoning was that vegetables were more important because they were closer to the rich earth.

This European feeling for the soil and its products probably accounted for the enthusiastic acceptance of the Schreibergarten. It was introduced during World War I in Austria, where Dr. Schreiber advocated that vacant city land become communal gardens for apartment dwellers.

Today, this idea is being revived, right here in the United States.

If you have or know of unused land, investigate to see how it can be planted to vegetables.

That America leads the world in food production is no very great surprise. We began as a nation of farmers. This feeling for the good soil is latent in us all. Plant a kitchen garden, and you will find that not only your table and your nutrition will benefit. You too will feel more fulfilled.

Dilled Cucumber

1	European cucumber
2 tablespoons	dill weed
2 teaspoons	sesame-seed or safflower oil
½ cup	water
2 teaspoons	butter
2 tablespoons	fresh parsley, chopped vegetable seasoning, to taste (optional)

Peel cucumber; trim ends. Halve lengthwise, and cut into 2"-long chunks. Roll chunks in dill weed, to coat.

Sprinkle oil into heavy skillet, add cucumbers and water. Cook, tightly covered, 5-7 minutes, over low fire. Turn cucumber chunks over. Cover again, and cook 5-7 minutes more, till tender.

Add butter, parsley, and vegetable seasoning. Serve immediately.

SERVES 4. CALORIES PER SERVING: 49

PREPARATION TIME: 15 MINUTES

Carrots Vichy

½	white onion, small, chopped fine
1 pound	baby carrots, cleaned, peeled, sliced at an angle
½	bay leaf
	pure bottled spring water, to cover carrots
garnish:	2 tablespoons scallions or chives, chopped fine

Place onion, carrots, bay leaf, and water in saucepan. Gently cook, covered, till tender but firm, about 8-10 minutes. Drain, garnish, and serve.

SERVES 4. CALORIES PER SERVING: 42

PREPARATION TIME: 15 MINUTES

Steamed Onions and Spinach

4	onions, peeled, trimmed, halved horizontally
2 tablespoons	Neufchatel low-fat cream cheese
¾ cup	fresh spinach, cooked, drained well (or ½ spinach, ½ fresh sorrel) grated nutmeg, to taste
2 tablespoons	Parmesan or Romano cheese, freshly grated vegetable seasoning, to taste
garnish:	pine nuts

Preheat oven to 350°.

Place onion halves in heavy skillet. Add water, about ¼″ deep; cover tightly. Bring onions to boil, then place in oven for about 45 minutes. Remove, uncover, and cool a few minutes.

With slotted spoon, remove onions. Place in shallow baking dish. Lift out the insides, leaving about 3 or 4 outer rings.

Put insides of onion into food processor, and puree. Add cream cheese and spinach, and process, leaving mixture chunky. Season with dash of nutmeg and vegetable seasoning. Fill onion halves with mixture. Top with 3-4 pine nuts, grated. Return to oven, uncovered, and reheat 10 minutes, till hot.

SERVES 4. CALORIES PER SERVING: 108

PREPARATION TIME: 15 MINUTES

BAKING TIME: 45 MINUTES

Golden Potato Skins

4	baking potatoes, large
1 tablespoon	sesame-seed or safflower oil
1 teaspoon	vegetable seasoning

Preheat oven to 375°.

Wash and scrub potatoes. Rub with a little oil. Bake about 1 hour and 15 minutes, till done. Remove from oven, place a damp towel over potatoes (prevents skins from drying out), and cool. This step can be prepared several hours in advance.

Again preheat oven to 375°.

Halve cooled potatoes lengthwise. Scoop out insides, and put aside. (Leave about ½″ of potato next to skin.) Season skins with vegetable seasoning and brush lightly with oil. Bake 30 minutes more, till crisp and lightly browned. Serve immediately.

SERVES 4. CALORIES PER SERVING: 40

PREPARATION TIME: 15 MINUTES

BAKING TIME: 1 HOUR 45 MINUTES

Tomato Parmesan

4	tomatoes, halved
4	bread sticks
½ teaspoon	garlic, minced
½ teaspoon	dried whole oregano
2 tablespoons	fresh parsley, chopped
2 tablespoons	Parmesan or Romano cheese, freshly grated
½ teaspoon	black pepper, freshly ground

Place tomatoes in baking dish.

In food processor, place balance of ingredients (except oil). Process to a fine-crumb mixture, and sprinkle over each tomato.

Preheat oven to 325°.

Sprinkle each tomato with few drops of oil. Bake 20-25 minutes, till tomatoes are tender. Serve immediately.

SERVES 4. CALORIES PER SERVING: 117
PREPARATION TIME: 30 MINUTES

Brussels Sprouts with Sesame Seeds

1 pound	Brussels sprouts
2 tablespoons	sesame seeds, freshly toasted
1 tablespoon	corn-oil margarine vegetable seasoning, to taste

Trim and clean sprouts. With small knife, slit bottoms, to make an "X." Place in water ¾" deep, in shallow pan. Steam gently, tightly covered, about 15 minutes, till tender.

When sprouts are cooked, drain, add margarine, sprinkle with vegetable seasoning. Roll sprouts in sesame seeds, to coat. Serve at once.

SERVES 4. CALORIES PER SERVING: 98
PREPARATION TIME: 25 MINUTES

Green Beans Summer Savory

¾ – 1 pound	fresh green beans, sliced
1 teaspoon	olive oil
½	onion, chopped fine
1	garlic clove, small, minced
1 teaspoon	summer savory
2	tomatoes, large, peeled, seeded, diced
	vegetable seasoning, to taste
garnish:	2 tablespoons fresh parsley, chopped

Steam beans 5-10 minutes; keep green and crispy.

In skillet, heat oil. Gently saute onions and garlic till they soften. Add summer savory and tomatoes, and toss with drained, steamed beans.

Season lightly. Garnish, and serve immediately.

SERVES 4. CALORIES PER SERVING: 68
PREPARATION TIME: 15 MINUTES

Beans Japanese Style
Niban Dashi

¾ pound	Japanese beans or green beans, cut lengthwise
2 cups	water
4 ounces	tofu
2 tablespoons	Mirin (sweet Sake)
2 tablespoons	soy sauce (low sodium)
1 teaspoon	ginger, coarsely chopped
1 teaspoon	garlic, coarsely chopped
1	lemon zest, ½" wide, 2½" long
2 teaspoons	miso paste
¾ cup	vegetable broth reserved from beans, or Vegetable Stock (page 47), heated
2 teaspoons	arrowroot
garnish:	½ cup scallions, chopped; 2 tablespoons sesame seeds, freshly toasted

In 2 cups water, steam beans in covered pan 5-7 minutes, till done but still crisp. Drain, reserving ¾ cup broth.

In blender, puree till smooth the tofu, Mirin, soy sauce, ginger, garlic, lemon zest, and miso paste, together with vegetable broth. Add arrowroot, and blend again. Pour over beans, and bring to simmer to thicken sauce.

Garnish beans and serve.

SERVES 4. CALORIES PER SERVING: 103

PREPARATION TIME: 15 MINUTES

Curried Carrots

2 teaspoons	sesame-seed or safflower oil
4 tablespoons	onion, chopped
4-6	carrots, medium size, sliced (2½ cups)
½ cup	water
½ teaspoon	curry powder
1 teaspoon	unbleached white flour
⅓ cup	low-fat milk, plus 2 tablespoons carrot broth, reserved
¼ teaspoon	vegetable seasoning
garnish:	2 tablespoons fresh parsley, chopped

In heavy saucepan, heat oil and saute onions over low fire.

In separate saucepan, covered, cook carrots in water about 5 minutes, till done but still firm. Drain, reserving broth.

Add carrots to onions. Stir with wooden spatula. Sprinkle curry powder, and toss to coat carrots. Sprinkle flour, and stir again with spatula. Add milk and broth, stirring till sauce is smooth and thick. (Add more carrot broth, if necessary.)

Season, garnish, and serve.

SERVES 4. CALORIES PER SERVING: 62

PREPARATION TIME: 15 MINUTES

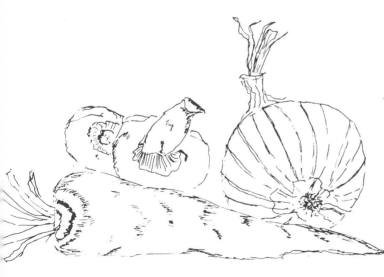

Artichokes with Puree of Leeks

3	artichokes, average size
3	lemon slices
2 teaspoons	fresh lemon juice
1	leek (white part only), large, washed, halved lengthwise
2	cups water
¼ cup	leek broth, reserved
1 ounce	Neufchatel low-fat cream cheese
	vegetable seasoning, to taste
	white pepper, to taste
garnish:	parsley sprigs

Trim artichokes. With a lemon slice tied beneath each artichoke, cook, covered, in boiling water to cover, with lemon juice for 35-40 minutes, till tender. Drain and cool. Remove all leaves and the chokes. This step may be prepared in advanced.

In separate saucepan, place leek in 2 cups water. Cook gently, covered, 30 minutes, till tender.

In food processor, puree cooked leek, ¼ cup reserved leek broth, and cream cheese till smooth. Season with vegetable seasoning and white pepper, to taste. Spoon into artichoke bottoms.

Garnish and serve.

Note: This puree can become a low-cal **Creme of Artichoke Soup**. To 1 **Artichokes with Puree of Leeks** recipe, add 2 cups **Chicken Broth** (page 48). Cut artichoke bottoms in pieces, puree, and add to mixture. Reheat, et voila!

SERVES 4. CALORIES PER SERVING: 61

PREPARATION TIME: 50 MINUTES

Zucchini Fans

1 tablespoon	olive oil
1	onion, medium size, halved and sliced
1	garlic clove, minced
1 teaspoon	dried whole thyme
1	bay leaf
4	zucchini, medium size
2	tomatoes, medium size
½ teaspoon	vegetable seasoning
garnish:	lemon wedges and parsley sprigs

In heavy skillet, heat oil. Add onion, garlic, thyme, and bay leaf. Cook till glazed.

Preheat oven to 350°.

Cut off zucchini ends. At one end of each zucchini, make 2½″ lengthwise slices ¼″ deep, creating a circular fan shape. Place a tomato slice between each cut of zucchini. Place over onions in skillet—alternate direction of each fanned-out zucchini. Season, and cover tightly. Bake 30 minutes, till zucchini is tender.

Serve immediately, topping each zucchini with onions and garnish.

SERVES 4. CALORIES PER SERVING: 49

PREPARATION TIME: 40 MINUTES

Stuffed Potato

4	baking potatoes, large
1 tablespoon	sesame-seed or safflower oil
1 cup	broccoli flowerets
1 cup	celery, diced
1 teaspoon	dried whole thyme vegetable seasoning, to taste
2 tablespoons	Parmesan cheese, freshly grated
8	thin mozzarella slices (about 3 ounces) paprika

Preheat oven to 375°.

Wash and scrub potatoes. Rub with a little oil. Bake 1 hour and 15 minutes, till done. Do NOT wrap in foil.

Meanwhile steam broccoli flowerets, covered, in smallest possible amount of water for 3-4 minutes. (Flowerets should be very green.) Drain broccoli. Steam celery with thyme for 3-4 minutes. Drain celery. Halve potatoes lengthwise, and scoop out insides, leaving about ½″ of potato next to skin. Season potato skin lightly and set aside.

While insides of potato are still steaming, chop with knife. Put into mixing bowl; mix in celery and broccoli flowerets. Season lightly with vegetable seasoning. Add Parmesan. Fill potato halves. Top with mozzarella slice and sprinkle with paprika. Return to oven and bake at 325° 15-20 minutes, till potato centers are heated.

Serve immediately.

SERVES 4. CALORIES PER SERVING: 186

PREPARATION TIME: 15 MINUTES

BAKING TIME: 1 HOUR 35 MINUTES

Cauliflower Whip

1	cauliflower head, pared and trimmed
3-4 tablespoons	cauliflower broth, reserved
1 tablespoon	Neufchatel low-fat cream cheese
1 teaspoon	corn-oil margarine grated nutmeg, to taste vegetable seasoning, to taste
garnish:	2 tablespoons Parmesan or Romano cheese, freshly grated; fresh parsley, chopped

Place cauliflower in saucepan. Cover with water, and simmer gently, covered, 20-25 minutes, till tender.

With slotted spoon, remove cauliflower from water and place in food processor with reserved cauliflower broth. Puree till smooth. Add cheese, margarine, nutmeg, and vegetable seasoning; puree again. Keep warm in double boiler.

Garnish and serve.

SERVES 4. CALORIES PER SERVING: 64

PREPARATION TIME: 30 MINUTES

Broccoli Spears

1 pound	fresh broccoli spears
¼ cup	fresh lemon juice
4 teaspoons	unsalted butter

Steam broccoli spears till tender. Do not overcook.

Warm lemon juice, melt butter, and pour both over spears. Serve immediately.

SERVES 4. CALORIES PER SERVING: 116

PREPARATION TIME: 15 MINUTES

Corn with Mint

4 ears	fresh, tender corn
2 quarts	water
handful	fresh mint leaves
4 teaspoons	butter

Bring water to rolling boil. Drop in corn and mint; boil gently 6-10 minutes, till corn is tender.

Drain. Melt 1 teaspoon butter over each ear of corn.

SERVES 4. CALORIES PER SERVING: 132

PREPARATION TIME: 15 MINUTES

Cauliflower Flowerets

1 head	cauliflower, broken into flowerets
2	eggs, hard-cooked
1 small bunch	fresh parsley, chopped fine
1 cup	whole-wheat bread crumbs, crushed fine
¼ cup	melted butter

Steam cauliflower till tender. Meanwhile, press eggs through sieve; mix parsley with bread crumbs. Add melted butter to these ingredients, and pour over steamed cauliflower. Serve at once.

SERVES 4. CALORIES PER SERVING: 120

PREPARATION TIME: 15 MINUTES

Vegetable Melange

1 cup	fresh broccoli flowerets
1 cup	fresh cauliflower flowerets
1 cup	fresh carrots, sliced coarsely
1 tablespoon	butter
2	breadsticks, crushed fine
1	garlic clove, crushed paprika, to taste

Steam vegetables separately, till each is tender. Meanwhile, melt butter in small pan; add crushed breadsticks, garlic, and paprika.

Mix together steamed vegetables, top with bread crumbs, and serve.

SERVES 4. CALORIES PER SERVING: 65

PREPARATION TIME: 15 MINUTES

Acorn Squash

2	acorn squash, medium size
1 tablespoon	butter, melted
2 teaspoons	brown sugar
1 teaspoon	ground cinnamon
¼ teaspoon	grated nutmeg
dash	allspice

Preheat oven to 350°.

Cut squash in two, scooping out seeds.

In separate dish, combine melted butter, sugar, and spices. Divide mixture equally into center of each squash half. Place halves in baking dish filled with water to depth of 2″. Cover with foil and bake 45-60 minutes, till tender.

SERVES 4. CALORIES PER SERVING: 135

PREPARATION TIME: 10 MINUTES

BAKING TIME: 45-60 MINUTES

Creamed Spinach

2 pounds	fresh spinach (or 10½ ounces frozen spinach, thawed)
	vegetable seasoning, to taste
⅛ teaspoon	grated nutmeg
1½ ounces	Monterey jack cheese, freshly grated

Wash and trim spinach. Put in saucepan with ½″ water. Weight down spinach with plate. Cook till just wilted. Drain well. Chop spinach coarsely, and season with nutmeg and vegetable seasoning. Place in saucepan; add cheese and heat, stirring with wooden spoon till cheese has melted.

Note: Frozen spinach (1 package equals 1 cup) has already been blanched; therefore, there's no need to cook it. Simply thaw, drain, chop, and heat. Then proceed to add seasonings and heat spinach with cheese.

SERVES 4. CALORIES PER SERVING: 81

PREPARATION TIME: 10 MINUTES

Puree St. Germain

¼ cup	Vegetable Stock (page 47)
2 teaspoons	butter
1 10-ounce package	frozen petit peas, thawed
2	fresh basil leaves (or ¼ teaspoon dried sweet basil)
	vegetable seasoning (optional)
garnish:	pimientos, or thin radish slices

Heat butter with **Vegetable Stock** till butter melts. Add thawed, drained peas. Simmer, covered, 3-4 minutes, till peas are just heated. Be sure they do not discolor or become mushy.

In food processor, puree cooked peas with basil. Add touch of vegetable seasoning if desired.

Garnish, and serve.

Note: This puree is outstanding for filling small, hollowed tomatoes, tiny cucumber boats, or artichoke bottoms.

SERVES 4. CALORIES PER SERVING: 72

PREPARATION TIME: 10 MINUTES

Zucchini Saute

4	zucchini, medium size, sliced in rounds
1 teaspoon	sesame-seed or safflower oil
1 teaspoon	butter
1 teaspoon	dried sweet basil
1 teaspoon	dried whole oregano
½ teaspoon	vegetable seasoning
¼ teaspoon	black pepper, freshly ground

In pan, melt butter with oil till butter foams. Add zucchini slices and seasonings. Cook till tender, and serve immediately.

SERVES 4. CALORIES PER SERVING: 105

PREPARATION TIME: 15 MINUTES

LET'S TALK ABOUT THESE RECIPES

BLANCHED SPINACH: Ideally, fresh spinach should be used in all recipes. But if you must resort to the frozen kind, ignore the recipe's direction to blanch the spinach (meaning, bring it to a boil and then immediately pour off the water), since frozen spinach is already cooked.

CHINESE (NAPA) CABBAGE: This odorless cabbage resembles romaine lettuce. Avoid very large or very firm heads, for they may be bitter.

PARSNIPS: If you have an unpleasant childhood memory of the parsnip, that's because it was cooked in its skin and hence made bitter. Don't reject parsnips till you have tried the Golden Door's Parsnip Whip.

SAVOY CABBAGE: A red variety of Chinese (Napa) Cabbage, it too is best selected in the medium-size head.

BREADS, CRUSTS AND GRAINS

On any diet, carbohydrates are essential to life. A piece of bread can be an important addition to a meal (particularly if the whole wheat in the bread combines advantageously with some other protein you are eating). Even lowest-calorie dieters need a piece of real bread daily because it contains crucial B vitamins. Buy your flours where you buy your whole grains and seeds — from a health-food store. And buy only the small quantity you need.

Your pleasure in eating a 'Golden Door' pastry can be doubled by knowledge that it contains a healthful whole grain. And that grains are called Nutrient Dense because of the amount of their good nutrients in proportion to calories contained. The findings of the Senate Select Committee on Diet and Nutrition revealed that Americans should be eating twice as many healthful, fibre-rich carbohydrates as are now being consumed. The 'Golden Door' and Rancho La Puerta diets have always relied on whole grains and other nourishing carbohydrates.

Included in the following recipes is a mainstay of Rancho La Puerta so enjoyed by guests there that it was demanded by 'Golden Door' guests, too. Called Tecate Bread, this recipe is a simplification of the Rancho bread which originally was made with sourdough.

If you don't wish to bake, examine the freezer section of your health-food store. Or, even better, ask around and find young people who specialize in turning out especially good whole-grain loaves from home ovens. A real plus is home-made bread baked with sprouted grains (a practice we began at La Puerta in the early 1940's).

Tecate Bread

(WHOLE-WHEAT BREAD)

½ ounce	dry active yeast (2 packets)
4 cups	water, lukewarm
¼ cup	corn oil
¼ cup	honey
10-10½ cups	whole-wheat flour
1 heaping cup	miller's bran, unprocessed
1 teaspoon	sea salt

Place yeast in large bowl. To dissolve, gradually add lukewarm water. Stir in oil and honey. Add flour, bran, and salt. Blend together with your hands. Knead till dough no longer is sticky or adhering to your hands. It should feel tough and elastic. (Add more flour if necessary.)

Lightly coat dough with oil, top and bottom. Place in bowl, and cover with towel not touching dough. Let rise in warm, draft-free area till doubled in size (about 1-2 hours).

Punch dough down. Placing on lightly greased board, knead about 1 minute. Divide into 3 equal parts, and throw dough against board 3 times. Generously oil 3 8½" x4¼"x2½" loaf pans (preferably clay); line bottoms with wax or parchment paper. With a little oil on your hands, shape dough into loaf shapes; place into pans, pressing gently. Run knife tip down center of each loaf. Cover again with towel, and let sit 30 minutes.

Preheat oven to 350°.

Bake 1 hour and 15 minutes, till well browned. Remove from oven, unmold by running knife around edges. Wrap in towels and plastic bags till cool. Rewrap in plastic, and refrigerate or freeze.

This bread is most enjoyable when toasted before serving.

CALORIES PER LOAF: 1,657

CALORIES PER SLICE (16 slices per loaf): 104

PREPARATION TIME: 2 HOURS

BAKING TIME: 1 HOUR 15 MINUTES

Pear-and-Zucchini Whole-Wheat Bread

1	pear, ripe; cored, quartered, and thinly sliced
	zucchini, grated (enough to make 2 cups when combined with pear)
¾ cup	walnuts, freshly chopped
1½ cups	sesame-seed or safflower oil
1¼ cups	honey
1 teaspoon	baking powder
¾ teaspoon	baking soda
1 teaspoon	sea salt
1 teaspoon	ground cloves
2	eggs
3 cups	whole-wheat pastry flour
1 tablespoon	grated lemon peel

Preheat oven to 325°.

Combine pear and zucchini with walnuts; set this bowl aside.

In food processor, mix oil and honey; add baking powder, baking soda, sea salt, and cloves. Combine. Add ½ the flour, and process well. Add eggs, and whirl in lemon peel and balance of flour. Pour mixture into zucchini-pear bowl, and mix well with spatula.

Oil 2 8½″x4½″x2½″ loaf pans; line the bottoms with waxed paper. Divide mixture into 2 baking dishes. Bake 1 hour and 20 minutes, or till tester comes out dry and middle of cake bounces back to touch.

Freezes well.

MAKES 32 SLICES. CALORIES PER SLICE: 195

PREPARATION TIME: 10 MINUTES

BAKING TIME: 1 HOUR 15 MINUTES

Persimmon-Walnut Whole-Wheat Bread

1½ cups	safflower oil
¾ cup	honey
1	persimmon, soft; peeled to make 1 cup (or 1 cup ripe apricots)
1 teaspoon	baking soda
¾ teaspoon	baking powder
1 teaspoon	sea salt
1 tablespoon	grated lemon peel
3 cups	whole-wheat pastry flour
2	eggs
½ cup	fresh orange juice
¾ cup	walnuts, freshly and coarsely chopped

Preheat oven to 325°.

Preferably using a food processor's metal blade, combine oil and honey. Add persimmon, baking soda, baking powder, salt, and lemon peel. Whirl briefly. Add ½ the flour, plus eggs. Whirl again, till smooth. Add remaining flour, plus orange juice. Whirl. Add walnuts, and whirl briefly. (Do not chop walnuts into extremely small pieces.)

Oil 2 8½″x4½″x2½″ loaf pans; line the bottoms with waxed paper. Divide mixture into 2 baking dishes. Bake 1 hour and 15 minutes, or till tester comes out dry and middle of cake bounces back to touch.

Freezes well.

Note: Some food processors do not have a sufficiently powerful motor. In this case it will slow down, and the mixture will not combine well.

MAKES 32 SLICES. CALORIES PER SLICE: 202

PREPARATION TIME: 10 MINUTES

BAKING TIME: 1 HOUR 15 MINUTES

Whole-Wheat Crepes

1 cup	whole-wheat pastry flour
3	eggs
2 teaspoons	soy sauce (low sodium)
2 teaspoons	Mirin (sweet Sake)
1½ cups	low-fat milk
¼ cup	water
	sesame-seed or safflower oil

Place flour in mixing bowl, and make a well in center. Add eggs, soy sauce, and Mirin. With wire whisk, begin to break up eggs, gradually stirring in about 2-3 tablespoons flour. Pour in milk gradually, and whisk till well blended. Add water and mix again. Let batter stand at least 1 hour (or overnight, if refrigerated and then brought back to room temperature) before making crepes.

Heat 8″ crepe pan or iron skillet with a little oil. When hot, drain off excess oil. Pour into skillet about ¼ of batter, and quickly tilt pan to coat evenly. Cook over medium fire about 30 seconds, till crepes are lightly browned. Turn over and cook briefly on reverse side. Turn out onto plate. Repeat cooking process with remaining batter, oiling lightly when necessary.

Makes about 10-12 crepes.

CALORIES PER CREPE: 52 (if you make 12)

CAN BE PREPARED AHEAD

PREPARATION TIME: 15 MINUTES

Whole-Wheat Pastry for Quiches

2 cups	whole-wheat pastry flour
3 ounces	corn-oil margarine, cut in small pieces
½ teaspoon	baking powder
½ teaspoon	sea salt
1	egg, beaten with ⅓ cup cold water

Preheat oven to 350°.

Knead together flour, margarine, baking powder, and salt till mixture is grainy but not too fine. Add egg-and-water mixture. Knead till dough is elastic and bounces back when pressed lightly.

Lightly grease with margarine 2 9″ pie plates. Split dough into 2 equal portions; roll out each portion on board. Place dough in plates, and pierce with fork. Bake 15 minutes before adding any filling.

Makes 2 bottom crusts.

Instead of 2 cups of whole-wheat pastry flour, you may use 1 cup, plus 1 cup of unbleached white flour.

CALORIES PER CRUST: 739

PREPARATION TIME: 30 MINUTES

Banana-Nut Whole-Wheat Bread

1½ cups	safflower oil
1¼ cups	honey
1 teaspoon	sea salt
1 teaspoon	baking powder
¾ teaspoon	baking soda
1 teaspoon	ground cloves
1 tablespoon	grated lemon peel
2	medium-sized bananas, sliced
3 cups	whole-wheat pastry flour
2	eggs
¾ cup	walnuts, freshly and coarsely chopped

Preheat oven to 325°

Preferably using a food processor's metal blade, combine oil and honey. Add salt, baking powder, baking soda, cloves, lemon peel, and bananas. Whirl well. Add ½ the flour, plus eggs. Whirl again till smooth. Add remaining flour, and whirl. Add walnuts, and whirl briefly (do not chop walnuts into extremely small pieces).

Oil 2 8½″ x 4½″ x 2½″ baking dishes; line bottoms with waxed paper. Divide mixture into 2 baking dishes. Bake 1 hour and 15 minutes — then test with sharp knife, which should come out dry.

Note: Some food processors do not have a sufficiently powerful motor. In this case, it will slow down, and the mixture will not combine well.

CALORIES PER LOAF: 3,229

CALORIES PER SLICE (16 slices per loaf): 202

PREPARATION TIME: 10 MINUTES

BAKING TIME: 1 HOUR 15 MINUTES

Corn Bread Chile Verde

1 recipe	Corn Bread (page 113)
1 7-ounce can	whole jalapeno chiles; spread open and drained

Follow recipe for **Corn Bread**. Place ½ batter in baking dish; spread chiles over batter. Top with remainder of batter and bake as directed.

NOTE: IF YOU PREFER VERY BLAND CHILES, CAREFULLY REMOVE ALL SEEDS.

MAKES 8 SMALL PORTIONS. CALORIES PER PORTION: 200

MAKES 4 LARGE PORTIONS. CALORIES PER PORTION: 400

PREPARATION TIME: 10 MINUTES

BAKING TIME: 35-40 MINUTES

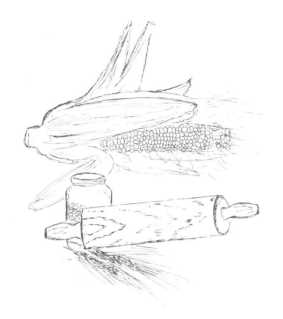

Sprouted Wheat Bread

1 cup	red cereal wheat
1 quart	water
3 tablespoons	black raisins (plumped in fresh lemon juice, grated lemon rind, and vanilla extract to cover) or white raisins
2 tablespoons	caraway seeds (pre-soaked)

Soak wheat for 3 days, drain and change water every 24 hours.

If plumped raisins are desired, soak 4 hours or overnight.

Grind wheat in meat grinder or food processor (gluten causes wheat to be very sticky).

Preheat oven to 275°.

Fold in other ingredients.

On lightly floured board, roll out wheat into 1½″ balls.

Bake on oiled cookie sheet 45 minutes (or place in sun 4-5 hours).

Turn out onto waxed paper; leave out 24 hours before storing. Keep in covered jar no more than 3 days.

MAKES 24 BALLS. CALORIES PER BALL: 18

PREPARATION TIME: 20 MINUTES

BAKING TIME: 45 MINUTES

Corn Bread

1 cup	creamed corn
¾ cup	yellow corn meal
1 teaspoon	baking soda
1 teaspoon	baking powder
3	eggs, beaten
¾ cup	low-fat yogurt
1 tablespoon	sesame-seed oil
½ cup	whole-wheat pastry flour
1 tablespoon	honey
½ tablespoon	butter
½ tablespoon	corn oil
2 tablespoons	Parmesan cheese

Preheat oven to 350°.

Mix corn, corn meal, baking soda, baking powder, eggs, yogurt, oil, flour, and honey with a whisk or in a mixer till well combined. In 10″ x 8″ baking dish, place butter and corn oil. Heat in oven till sizzling. Pour in batter, sprinkle with cheese. Bake 35-40 minutes, till dry and loaf when tested in center springs back to touch.

MAKES 8 SMALL PORTIONS. CALORIES PER PORTION: 190

MAKES 4 LARGE PORTIONS. CALORIES PER PORTION: 380

PREPARATION TIME: 10 MINUTES

BAKING TIME: 35-40 MINUTES

Brown Rice

¾ cup	short-grain brown rice, rinsed
1½ cups	water
⅛ teaspoon	fennel seeds (optional); or ¼ teaspoon dried whole marjoram; or ¼ teaspoon dried whole thyme; or 1-2 bay leaves and/or 1 garlic clove, large, crushed in press
¼ cup	green onions, sliced soy sauce (low sodium), optional

Place rice, water, and any of the optional seasonings into a small pot. Cover tightly, and bring to boil. Lower to simmer, and cook 25 minutes. Turn off fire but do not remove pot or lid; let sit on burner 15 minutes. Serve immediately.

SERVES 4. CALORIES PER SERVING: 143

PREPARATION TIME: 40 MINUTES

Wild Rice and Mushrooms

¾ cup	wild rice, rinsed
1½ cups	Vegetable Stock (page 47) or water
1 tablespoon	sesame-seed oil
1	garlic clove, minced
1½ cups	fresh mushrooms, sliced
¼ cup	low-fat yogurt
½ cup	scallions, chopped soy sauce, low sodium (optional)

Boil **Vegetable Stock** or water and pour over rice in cooking dish. Stir, cover, and let stand 4 hours or overnight.

Preheat oven to 350°.

Simmer rice, covered, 15-20 minutes more, till water evaporates. Set aside, covered, 10 more minutes.

Heat oil in skillet. Stir-fry garlic and mushrooms.

With fork, fold mushroom mixture into rice. Add yogurt and scallions. Heat in oven 10-15 minutes, covered.

Season with soy sauce to taste (if desired). Serve at once.

SERVES 4. CALORIES PER SERVING: 160

PREPARATION TIME: 45 MINUTES

Herbed Vegetable Rice

1 cup	short-grain brown rice, rinsed
2 cups	water
½ teaspoon	anise seeds
2 teaspoons	olive oil
2 teaspoons	garlic, minced
½ cup	celery, diced
½ cup	red or green bell pepper, diced
½ cup	fresh mushrooms, sliced
2 teaspoons	curry powder
2 tablespoons	soy sauce (low sodium)
1 teaspoon	lemon zest, grated dash of vegetable seasoning
garnish:	½ cup scallions, diced

For 30 minutes, gently boil rice and anise seeds, covered. Set aside, still covered, for 15 minutes to let rice swell.

While rice cooks, prepare remaining ingredients: In skillet, heat oil and gently saute garlic. Add celery, peppers, mushrooms. Sprinkle curry, and cook briefly.

Add vegetables to cooked rice, and fluff mixture together. Season with soy sauce, lemon zest, and vegetable seasoning. Garnish and serve.

Serve as a vegetarian main course, or as a side dish with chicken, fish, or veal. Other vegetables — such as zucchini, kohlrabi, cauliflower, broccoli, etc. — can be added.

MAKES 8 SMALL PORTIONS. CALORIES PER PORTION: 111

MAKES 4 LARGE PORTIONS. CALORIES PER PORTION: 222

PREPARATION TIME: 1 HOUR

Brown Rice, Chinese Stir-Fried

½ cup	Brown Rice (page 114)
1	onion, diced
2	garlic cloves, minced
1 cup	fresh mushrooms, sliced
½ cup	water chestnuts, sliced
½ cup	celery, diced
4	eggs, beaten
1 tablespoon	soy sauce (low-sodium)
½ cup	scallions, chopped

Heat oil and saute onion till it starts to soften. Add celery, mushrooms, and water chestnuts till they begin to soften. Add beaten eggs. Mix for a few seconds with wooden fork. While mixture is still loose, add **Brown Rice** and soy sauce; cook till they start to dry.

Remove from fire, add scallions, and serve.

SERVES 4. CALORIES PER SERVING: 189

PREPARATION TIME: 20 MINUTES

Austrian-Style Polenta with Yogurt-Paprika

8	Polenta pieces (at right)
1	onion, thinly sliced
1 tablespoon	safflower or sesame-seed oil
1 teaspoon	dried whole thyme
2 teaspoons	paprika
¾ cup	bell pepper, finely chopped
1½ cups	low-fat yogurt
2 tablespoons	feta cheese, grated

Preheat oven to 375°.

Saute onion in oil; add thyme, paprika, and bell pepper. Cook till mixture starts to soften.

In lightly oiled 8″ x 8″ baking dish, place 4 **Polenta** pieces. Over them, divide ½ the onion mixture, then ½ the yogurt and ½ the cheese. Position remainder of **Polenta** pieces on top of stacks, and repeat layering process.

Bake 25-30 minutes.

SERVES 4. CALORIES PER SERVING: 278

PREPARATION TIME: 45 MINUTES

Polenta

2½ cups	water
1 teaspoon	vegetable seasoning
¾ cup	yellow or white corn meal
1 teaspoon	summer savory
1 tablespoon	sesame-seed oil
2 tablespoons	Parmesan cheese cayenne pepper

Bring water to boil. Add vegetable seasoning. With wire whisk vigorously whisk in corn meal. Add summer savory. Let bubble 2-3 minutes, then transfer mixture to double boiler. Cover, and cook 25-30 minutes, till mixture becomes thick and firm. With wooden spatula, mix in oil, cheese, and cayenne pepper to taste.

Pour into lightly oiled 9″ x 5″ pan and use rubber spatula to spread mixture evenly. Cover with waxed paper. Set aside to cool 4 hours or overnight.

Cut into 8 even rectangular pieces, and use as basis for **Austrian-Style Polenta with Yogurt-Paprika** (at left), **Polenta Parmesan** (page 116), and **Polenta Chile Verde** (page 116).

MAKES 8 PIECES. CALORIES PER PIECE: 130

PREPARATION TIME: 40 MINUTES

Polenta Chile Verde

8	Polenta pieces (page 115)
1	onion, thinly sliced
1 tablespoon	safflower or sesame-seed oil
½ teaspoon	chile flakes (optional)
2 teaspoons	dried whole oregano
1 7-ounce can	whole jalapeno chiles; spread open and drained
8 thin slices	tomato
2 tablespoons	sharp cheddar cheese, freshly grated
	dried whole oregano

Preheat oven to 375°.

Saute onion in oil with chile flakes (optional) and 2 teaspoons oregano.

In lightly oiled 8″ x 8″ baking dish, place 4 **Polenta** pieces. Over them, divide ½ onion mixture, then ½ the chiles, ½ the tomato slices, and top with ½ the cheese.

Position remainder of **Polenta** pieces on top of stacks, then add remaining onion, tomato slices, chile, a sprinkle of oregano, and ½ the cheese.

Bake 25-30 minutes.

NOTE: IF YOU PREFER VERY BLAND CHILES, CAREFULLY REMOVE ALL SEEDS.

SERVES 4. CALORIES PER SERVING: 220

PREPARATION TIME: 45 MINUTES

Polenta Parmesan

8	Polenta pieces (page 115)
1½ cups	Tomato Concassee (page 24)
1 tablespoon	dried whole oregano
½ cup	celery, diced
½ cup	fresh mushrooms, sliced black pepper, freshly ground
2 tablespoons	Parmesan cheese
4 thin slices	mozzarella cheese (about 1½-2 oz.) paprika

Preheat oven to 350°.

In lightly oiled 8″ x 8″ baking dish, place 4 **Polenta** pieces. Cover with about ¾ cup **Tomato Concassee**. Atop pieces, sprinkle ½ tablespoon oregano, then all the celery and mushrooms. Add pepper to taste, and sprinkle with Parmesan.

Position remainder of **Polenta** pieces on top of stacks, and spread with remainder of **Tomato Concassee**. Sprinkle with remaining oregano; cover with mozzarella slices. Sprinkle with paprika.

Bake 20-25 minutes, or until topping starts to bubble.

SERVES 4. CALORIES PER SERVING: 25

PREPARATION TIME: 45 MINUTES

Indian Chappatis

¾ cup   whole-wheat flour
1¼ cup   white corn flour
1 cup   cold water
         pinch of sea salt
         dab of butter

Combine ingredients, then set aside for 15 minutes.

Heavily sprinkle table with whole-wheat flour. Roll ingredients into 4 balls, then roll out 4 8″ rounds.

In heated cast-iron skillet or on hot plate or barbecue, cook chappatis 3-4 minutes, till it starts to puff and brown. With spatula, flip onto other side and cook another 3-4 minutes or till puffed and turning brown. Brush with butter.

Serve with **Ignacio's Salsa** (page 23).

SERVES 4. CALORIES PER SERVING: 222

PREPARATION TIME: 25 MINUTES

Barley Pilaf

1   onion, large, chopped fine
½ pound   fresh mushrooms, coarsely chopped
¼ cup   unsalted butter
1 cup   pearl barley
2 cups   Chicken Broth (page 48)

Preheat oven to 350°.

Saute onion and mushrooms in butter till tender. Add barley, and brown lightly. Pour into buttered casserole dish. Pour 1 cup **Chicken Broth** over barley mixture. Bake, covered, 25 minutes. Uncover, add 1 cup **Chicken Broth**, and bake till liquid is absorbed and barley done — about 25 minutes.

SERVES 4. CALORIES PER SERVING: 120

PREPARATION TIME: 10 MINUTES

BAKING TIME: 50 MINUTES

Barley and Walnut Casserole

2 cups   barley, cooked (¾ cup barley cooked in 2 cups water)
2 tablespoons   sesame-seed oil
1   large onion, minced
1 teaspoon   dried rosemary
         black pepper, freshly ground
½ cup   walnuts, freshly chopped
1¼ cup   low-fat yogurt
1 cup   fresh carrots, finely grated

Prepare uncooked barley by rinsing and covering with water. Cover, bring to boil, then lower fire and simmer 45 minutes. Turn off fire; let covered barley pan remain on burner 15 minutes. Drain.

Preheat oven to 350°.

Heat oil and saute onion with rosemary and pepper to taste. Add cooked barley, walnuts, and yogurt. Bake 10-15 minutes.

Top with grated carrots and serve.

SERVES 4. CALORIES PER SERVING: 361

PREPARATION TIME: 1 HOUR 25 MINUTES

Couscous

1 cup	couscous
1 cup	boiling water
1 tablespoon	olive oil or butter (optional)
1 tablespoon	olive oil
1	onion, diced
1¼ teaspoon	ground cloves
¼ teaspoon	ground cinnamon
¼ teaspoon	ground cardamom
1 cup	carrots, diced
1 cup	parsnips, peeled and diced
1 cup	zucchini, diced
2 tablespoons	raisins (plumped in water; or in fresh lemon juice, grated lemon rind, and vanilla extract, to cover)
½ cup	fresh parsley, chopped
½ cup	almonds, freshly sliced and toasted

Pour boiling water over couscous; add 1 tablespoon olive oil or butter (if desired) and stir with fork to prevent lumps. Let stand 15 minutes. Drain in fine strainer. Position strainer over boiling water (don't let couscous touch water) and steam 5 minutes. Makes 2 cups.

In skillet heat 1 tablespoon oil and saute onion with cloves, cinnamon, and cardamom till onion starts to soften. Add carrots, parsnips, and zucchini; saute gently till vegetables begin to soften but are still crisp. Mix in cooked couscous, raisins, parsley and almonds. Serve at once.

SERVES 4. CALORIES PER SERVING: 349

PREPARATION TIME: 50 MINUTES

Rice and Lentil Pilaf

1 cup	lentils, cooked (½ cup lentils in 1¼ cup water)
1	onion, minced
1 teaspoon	dried whole thyme
2 teaspoons	curry powder
1 tablespoon	olive oil
1 cup	fresh mushrooms, sliced
1 cup	celery, diced
1 cup	Brown Rice (page 114)
3 tablespoons	pine nuts, freshly toasted
½ cup	fresh parsley, chopped
¼ cup	Parmesan cheese (optional)

Prepare uncooked lentils by rinsing and covering with water. Cover and simmer gently ½ hour. Drain.

Preheat oven to 350°.

Heat oil and saute onion, thyme, and curry. Add mushrooms and celery; saute till they start to soften.

With a fork carefully fold into vegetable mixture the **Brown Rice**, lentils, and pine nuts, alternately. Put into baking dish. Heat in oven 10 minutes.

Fold in parsley and cheese (if desired), and serve.

SERVES 4. CALORIES PER SERVING: 318

PREPARATION TIME: 50 MINUTES

Steamed Millet and Herbs

¾ cup	millet
2 cups	water
½ teaspoon	dried whole thyme
½ cup	fresh parsley, chopped
1 teaspooon	grated lemon peel (optional)

In heavy saucepan, combine millet, water, and thyme. Simmer, covered, 20 minutes. Turn off fire but leave covered 10-15 minutes. With fork, fluff in parsley (and lemon peel, if desired). Serve.

Note: For an even more interesting dish, you may add ½ cup of finely diced celery, pimiento, carrots, or any vegetable of your choice.

SERVES 4. CALORIES PER SERVING: 142

PREPARATION TIME: 45 MINUTES

Millet Pimiento Souffle

1½ cups	Steamed Millet and Herbs (at left)
1 cup	low-fat milk
2 teaspoons	dill weed
3 ounces	Monterey jack cheese, freshly grated
½ teaspoon	grated nutmeg
¼ cup	pimientos, chopped
3	egg yolks
6	egg whites, room temperature
	cream of tartar

Preheat oven to 350°.

Oil 1 1½-quart souffle mold. Cook **Steamed Millet and Herbs** in sauce pan with milk and dill approximately 5 minutes, with constant gentle stirring till thick. Mix in cheese, nutmeg, and pimientos. Remove from fire.

Add egg yolks to millet mixture by gradually blending small amounts of hot mixture into yolks, and then combining all.

Beat egg whites with pinch of cream of tartar till stiff. Gently fold into millet mixture.

Pour into souffle dish. Bake 35-40 minutes.

SERVES 4. CALORIES PER SERVING: 330

PREPARATION TIME: 20 MINUTES

BAKING TIME: 35-40 MINUTES

DESSERTS

'Golden Door' guests are allowed one dessert a day, at the evening meal. But if you are accustomed to a luncheon dessert, continue to eat it. A good diet plan cannot be based upon deprivation. Preferably, make that second dessert a simple one. After all, it's just a taste of sweet that you crave.

Here are useful suggestions for occasions when you want a simple dessert or haven't time to follow a recipe:

An apple half, sliced or wedged, plus 1-10 raisins.

A small orange, cut in thin slices, topped with a teaspoon of toasted coconut, garnished with fresh mint.

A bowl of 6-8 strawberries.

A cantaloupe wedge, garnished.

A chilled grapefruit half, garnished with strawberries. Grapes and cheese.

A few drops of Kirsch on a thin pineapple slice.

A few drops of Amaretto on melon balls, strawberries, or pineapple.

Any berry (strawberries, blueberries, raspberries) becomes an instant dessert sauce when pureed. Use over mousses, frozen yogurt, or whole fruit.

Slice the top off an orange; hollow out. Fill with frozen yogurt and top with a few whole raspberries.

Freeze seedless grapes. Combine one bunch of purple and one bunch of white frozen grapes.

Puree any sweet fruit (peaches, pineapples, papayas), add crushed ice. Freeze 1-2 hours for a light, cool frappe, perfect for ending any meal.

Steam a whole peach, pear, or apple. Serve with a pureed berry sauce.

Arrange pineapple, orange, and kiwi slices in a tall dessert glass. Serve a small ginger snap on the side.

Drizzle one-half jigger of Grand Marnier liqueur over one-half cup mandarin-orange slices. Place each serving next to a tiny dish containing a tablespoon of powdered sugar. Dip soaked orange slices into sugar.

In a small parfait glass, layer plain frozen yogurt and Creme de Menthe liqueur, alternating several times. Freeze till serving time.

Always eat dessert with a demitasse spoon or a demitasse fork, prolonging the pleasure.

Desserts serve a useful function, for they stretch a meal, they relax, and they reward.

Fresh Fruit Macedoine

4 cups	seasonal fruit, cut up*
1 cup	fresh orange juice
½ teaspoon	almond extract
garnish:	4 tablespoons almonds, toasted and sliced; fresh mint

Combine ingredients, and mix well. Cover and refrigerate. Garnish and serve.

MAKES 8 SMALL PORTIONS. CALORIES PER PORTION: 94

MAKES 4 LARGE PORTIONS. CALORIES PER PORTION: 189

PREPARATION TIME: 10 MINUTES

*Use any combination of fruits in season, such as apples, pears, grapes, melons, pineapple, strawberries, bananas, oranges, etc.

Strawberries and Raspberries

1 recipe	Strawberry Strawberries (page 126), without Grand Marnier
1 cup	raspberries (fresh or slightly sweetened frozen berries)
1 tablespoon	Framboise Liqueur (in place of Grand Marnier)

Follow instructions for **Strawberry Strawberries** recipe, deleting Grand Marnier; add raspberries and Framboise. Chill and serve as directed.

SERVES 8. CALORIES PER SERVING: 74

PREPARATION TIME: 10 MINUTES

Hot Spiced Apple in Papaya Sauce

1 tablespoon	sun-dried raisins, soaked in 1 tablespoon Sherry wine, plus 1 tablespoon water
4	apples, small, crisp; cored and cut into 10-12 wedges with skin
¾ cup	apple juice (unfiltered)
1 tablespoon	fresh lemon juice
⅛ teaspoon	ground cloves
1	papaya, halved and seeded (or 1 mango, peeled and cut away from pit)
garnish:	kiwi slices

Soak raisins several hours or overnight in Sherry and water.

In stainless-steel pan, covered, cook for 10 minutes raisins (with Sherry and water), apple wedges, apple juice, lemon juice, and cloves. (Apples should still be crisp.)

Scoop out papaya pulp. Put in blender with part of cooked-apple juice. Blend to smooth puree. Pour over hot apples, away from fire. Fold in mixture. (Papaya thickens apple juice into light-custard consistency.)

Garnish and serve immediately.

Note: Very good as dessert, or with **Broiled Cornish Game Hen Golden Door** (page 84), or with roast duckling.

SERVES 4. CALORIES PER SERVING: 134

PREPARATION TIME: 20 MINUTES

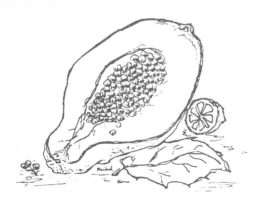

Pears in Burgundy Wine and Cassis

2 tablespoons	sun-dried currants
2 tablespoons	Creme de Cassis liqueur
2 tablespoons	Burgundy wine
¾ cup	Burgundy wine
½ cup	water
1 tablespoon	fresh lemon juice
1 tablespoon	honey
2	cloves
2	pears, large, ripe; halved lengthwise and cored
garnish:	mint sprigs and lemon slices

Soak currants in Cassis liqueur and 2 tablespoons Burgundy.

Bring to boil ¾ cup Burgundy, water, lemon juice, honey, and cloves. Simmer 5 minutes. Drop in pear halves and gently poach, uncovered, 10 minutes, till tender but still a little firm. With slotted spoon, remove pears. Reduce liquid by ⅓. Remove from heat; add currants.

Cool liquid and pour over pears.

Chill. Garnish and serve.

This recipe can be prepared a day in advance.

SERVES 4. CALORIES PER SERVING: 163

PREPARATION TIME: 20 MINUTES

Baked Apples

4	apples (golden delicious or pippin)
	ground cinnamon, to taste
¼ cup	apple juice (unfiltered)
½ cup	fresh papaya or mango pulp, or sun-dried raisins
1 teaspoon	candied ginger, minced
garnish:	mint sprigs

Preheat oven to 325° if using glass baking dish; 350°, if tin.

Standing apples up, cut horizontally. Core, and place in baking dish. Sprinkle with cinnamon. Add apple juice and cover tightly. Bake about 45 minutes, till tender. Cool.

Pour juice from baking dish into blender. Add papaya or mango pulp or raisins; puree till smooth. Add minced ginger, and quickly pulse into puree.

Coat each apple half with sauce, and garnish.

This is very pleasant with **Broiled Cornish Game Hen Golden Door** (page 84).

If the seasonal fruit is unavailable, place 5 or 6 sun-dried raisins in center of each cored apple before baking.

MAKES 8 SMALL PORTIONS. CALORIES PER PORTION: 45

MAKES 4 LARGE PORTIONS. CALORIES PER PORTION: 91

PREPARATION TIME: 10 MINUTES

BAKING TIME: 45 MINUTES

Hot Bananas and Blueberries

4	bananas, ripe
⅓ cup	apple juice (unfiltered)
½ cup	blueberries (or 2 teaspoons candied ginger)
1 tablespoon	Cointreau or Grand Marnier orange liqueur
garnish:	mint sprigs, strawberries, or kiwi slices

Place bananas in skillet with apple juice. Simmer gently, covered, 4-5 minutes, till bananas start to soften. Turn bananas over. Cook, uncovered, 3-4 minutes more, to reduce liquid to ½. Add berries or ginger.

Remove from heat. Add liqueur. Shake to roll bananas in liquid.

Serve immediately with juice, garnished.

MAKES 8 SMALL PORTIONS. CALORIES PER PORTION: 60

MAKES 4 LARGE PORTIONS. CALORIES PER PORTION: 121

PREPARATION TIME: 10 MINUTES

Mango-Lime Paradise

2 cups	mango pulp (from ripe, sweet mango)
1 tablespoon	fresh lime or lemon juice
½ cup	fresh orange juice
1 tablespoon	honey (omit if mango is very sweet)
garnish:	kiwi slices; raspberry or small strawberry for decoration

In food processor, puree mango pulp, lime juice, orange juice, and honey till smooth. Pour into 4 individual dessert cups. Garnish.

Heavenly when served cool!

CALORIES PER SERVING: 94

PREPARATION TIME: 10 MINUTES

Mango Creme

1	mango, ripe (about 1 pound); peeled and seeded
1 tablespoon	fresh lime or lemon juice
garnish:	kiwi slices, berries, or mint sprigs

Puree ingredients in food processor till very smooth. Garnish and serve.

For variety, this may be combined ½ and ½ with other fruit such as ripe fresh peaches, strawberries, or ripe apricots.

SERVES 4. CALORIES PER SERVING: 24

PREPARATION TIME: 10 MINUTES

Apricot Creme

8 ounces	ricotta cheese
1 16-ounce can	sugar-free apricots (1 cup)*
2 tablespoons	juice from apricots
3½ tablespoons	honey
1 tablespoon	fresh lemon juice
1 tablespoon	Grand Marnier orange liqueur (optional)
garnish:	kiwi or other fresh-fruit slices

Combine all ingredients in food processor; blend till very smooth, about 3-4 minutes.

Pour into separate dessert dishes. Chill.

Garnish and serve.

MAKES 8 SMALL PORTIONS. CALORIES PER PORTION: 101

MAKES 4 LARGE PORTIONS. CALORIES PER PORTION: 202

PREPARATION TIME: 5 MINUTES

*When fresh, juicy, ripe apricots are in season, they make an even more delicious cream. Use less honey, if desired.

Kiwi on Snow

4 ounces	Neufchatel low-fat cream cheese
4 ounces	ricotta cheese
2 tablespoons	honey
¼ cup	low-fat milk
1 tablespoon	Grand Marnier orange liqueur
1 tablespoon	fresh lemon juice
1 tablespoon	lemon zest, grated
1 tablespoon	coconut, freshly shredded and lightly toasted
garnish:	2 kiwi fruits, peeled and sliced; 4 raspberries or small strawberries

In food processor, blend cream cheese, ricotta, honey, and milk. Add liqueur, lemon juice, and lemon zest. Blend again briefly.

Pour this creme into 4 shallow dessert dishes. Sprinkle coconut in center, and arrange fruit garnish for color. Serve immediately.

MAKES 8 SMALL PORTIONS. CALORIES PER PORTION: 61

MAKES 4 LARGE PORTIONS. CALORIES PER PORTION: 122

PREPARATION TIME: 10 MINUTES

Carob Creme

¼ cup	low-fat milk
1 tablespoon	carob powder
1 teaspoon	instant decaffeinated coffee
1 pound	ricotta cheese
2½ tablespoons	honey
1 tablespoon	Amaretto liqueur
garnish:	almonds, freshly sliced and toasted; carob powder or instant-coffee granules

In double boiler, heat milk, carob powder, and coffee; stir frequently, till carob and coffee dissolve.

In food processor, puree cheese, honey, and liqueur. While machine is running, pour in milk mixture. Combine till very smooth. Cool.

Serve in individual dessert cups. With a sieve, sprinkle with coffee or carob powder. Garnish with almond slices, and serve.

MAKES 8 SMALL PORTIONS. CALORIES PER PORTION: 145

MAKES 4 LARGE PORTIONS. CALORIES PER PORTION: 290

PREPARATION TIME: 10 MINUTES

Apricot-Cheese Mold

¾ cup	apricots (around 4 or 5), pitted
¼ cup	fresh orange juice, or apricot nectar
1 teaspoon	honey
12 ounces	Neufchatel low-fat cream cheese
¾ cup	low-fat milk
4 tablespoons	honey
3-4 tablespoons	fresh lemon juice
2	eggs, room temperature
3	egg whites, room temperature
	grated lemon zest, from 1 lemon
garnish:	kiwi slices, strawberries, or raspberries

In covered saucepan, gently cook apricots, orange juice, and honey 10-15 minutes, till tender. Cool.

Preheat oven to 350°.

In food processor, puree cheese, milk, honey, and lemon juice till smooth.

In mixing bowl, beat eggs and whites with wire whisk till well combined and frothy. Add to cheese mixture in food processor. Blend well. Remove to a bowl.

With slotted spoon, remove apricots; puree in food processor. Add this to cheese mixture, whisking in well with the lemon zest.

Oil 8″ spring-form pan; line bottom with wax paper. Pour in mixture. Place pan in bain-marie (pan of water). Bake 1 hour. Be careful water does not evaporate completely.

Cool, then refrigerate. Unmold before serving, and garnish.

SERVES 8. CALORIES PER SERVING: 207

PREPARATION TIME: 20 MINUTES

BAKING TIME: 1 HOUR

Lemon Mousse

1 envelope	unflavored gelatin (1 tablespoon), dissolved in ¼ cup warm water
1	mango, medium size, ripe (¾ cup when pureed)
1 cup	fresh orange juice
2 teaspoons	honey
2 tablespoons	Grand Marnier or Cointreau orange liqueur
2 envelopes	unflavored gelatin (2 tablespoons), dissolved in ½ cup warm water
1 pound	ricotta cheese
5 tablespoons	honey
8 tablespoons	fresh lemon juice
1 tablespoon	Cointreau orange liqueur
1 tablespoon	lemon zest, grated
4	egg whites, room temperature
¼ teaspoon	cream of tartar
	sea salt, to taste
1 teaspoon	fructose
garnish:	mint leaves, berries, or kiwi slices

For topping, prepare 6-cup mold by oiling lightly. Puree mango in food processor till smooth. Add orange juice, 2 teaspoons honey, and 2 tablespoons liqueur; process. Add 1 envelope dissolved gelatin, and process again. Pour mixture into mold. Set in freezer till jelled, being careful not to freeze. (Or refrigerate overnight to jell.)

For mousse, puree in food processor ricotta cheese, 5 tablespoons honey, lemon juice, 1 tablespoon liqueur, and lemon zest till very smooth. Add 2 envelopes dissolved gelatin. Process again. Pour into bowl. Refrigerate till mixture thickens slightly.

Beat egg whites with cream of tartar, sea salt, and fructose till stiff and smooth. Gently fold whites into mousse mixture, ½ at a time, till well combined. Pour over jelled mango topping. Refrigerate at least 4 hours, or overnight.

Unmold before serving, and garnish.

MAKES 8 SMALL PORTIONS. CALORIES PER PORTION: 105

MAKES 4 LARGE PORTIONS. CALORIES PER PORTION: 209

PREPARE 4 HOURS AHEAD

PREPARATION TIME: 45 MINUTES

Strawberry Strawberries

3 cups	strawberries, sliced
½ cup	fresh orange juice
1 tablespoon	Grand Marnier orange liqueur
1 cup	mango pulp (or canned sugar-free apricots)
1 tablespoon	honey (optional)
garnish:	1 kiwi, sliced

In mixing bowl, combine strawberries, orange juice, and Grand Marnier. Cover and refrigerate 1 hour.

In food processor or blender, puree until smooth mango pulp and honey with part of juice from strawberries. Add 1 cup strawberry mixture, and combine briefly. (Strawberries should be a little chunky.) Add to sliced strawberries; gently mix with spatula.

Serve chilled, garnished; or serve as sauce.

SERVES 8. CALORIES PER SERVING: 66

PREPARATION TIME: 15 MINUTES

Apple Mousse

3	apples, golden delicious (about ¾ pound); peeled, cored, and sliced
⅓ cup	water
	fresh lemon juice, to taste
1 envelope	unflavored gelatin (1 tablespoon), dissolved in 3-4 tablespoons hot cooking liquid from apples
1 tablespoon	fructose
1 tablespoon	lemon zest, grated
¼ cup	water
1 tablespoon	Cointreau or Grand Marnier orange liqueur
2 teaspoons	candied ginger, chopped
2	egg whites, room temperature
	sea salt
garnish:	kiwi slices, berries, or mint leaves

In covered stainless-steel pan, gently cook apples with ⅓ cup water and few drops of lemon juice 10-15 minutes, till tender. Remove from heat. Cool 10 minutes.

In food processor, puree apples with their remaining liquid till smooth. Add fructose and dissolved gelatin; process till well combined. Pour into mixing bowl.

In ¼ cup water, blanch lemon zest; strain. Add liqueur. Fold into apple mixture. Place in freezer to cool completely. Stir occasionally, making sure it does not jell.

Beat egg whites with a pinch of sea salt till whites are stiff but still smooth. Gently fold apple mixture into whites, a little at a time, till smooth.

Pour into 4 1-cup dessert dishes or single 1¾-cup dessert dish. Refrigerate at least 1 hour, or overnight.

Garnish and serve.

MAKES 8 SMALL PORTIONS. CALORIES PER PORTION: 51

MAKES 4 LARGE PORTIONS. CALORIES PER PORTION: 102

PREPARE 1 HOUR AHEAD

PREPARATION TIME: 30 MINUTES

Mocha Mousse

6 tablespoons	ice water
½ cup	nonfat dry-milk powder
6 tablespoons	brewed coffee, chilled
4 teaspoons	sugar
½ teaspoon	vanilla extract
¼ teaspoon	almond extract

Pour ice water into bowl of electric mixer. Turn on mixer and gradually add nonfat dry milk till mixture resembles soft whipped cream. Continue to mix as you dribble in chilled coffee and add sugar and flavorings. Spoon into 4 dessert glasses. Chill no longer than 1½ hours.

SERVES 4. CALORIES PER SERVING: 115

PREPARATION TIME: 15 MINUTES

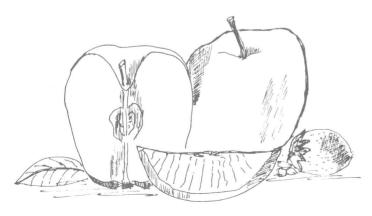

Apricot Mousse

1 pound	apricots, ripe, pitted
⅓ cup	water
1 envelope	unflavored gelatin (1 tablespoon), dissolved in 3-4 tablespoons hot cooking liquid from apricots
2 tablespoons	fructose
1 tablespoon	lemon zest, grated
¼ cup	water
1 tablespoon	Cointreau or Grand Marnier orange liqueur
2	egg whites, room temperature
	sea salt
garnish:	kiwi slices, berries, or mint leaves

In covered stainless-steel pan, gently cook apricots with ⅓ cup water 8-10 minutes, till tender. Remove from heat. Cool 10 minutes.

In food processor, puree apricots with their remaining liquid till smooth. Add fructose and dissolved gelatin; process till well combined. Pour into mixing bowl.

In ¼ cup water, blanch lemon zest; strain. Add liqueur. Fold into apricot mixture. Place in freezer to cool completely. Stir occasionally, making sure it does not jell.

Beat egg whites with a pinch of sea salt till whites are stiff but still smooth. Gently fold apricot mixture into whites, a little at a time, till smooth.

Pour into 4 1-cup dessert dishes or single 1¾-cup dessert dish. Refrigerate at least 1 hour, or overnight.

Garnish and serve.

MAKES 8 SMALL PORTIONS. CALORIES PER PORTION: 48

MAKES 4 LARGE PORTIONS. CALORIES PER PORTION: 97

PREPARE 1 HOUR AHEAD

PREPARATION TIME: 30 MINUTES

Carob Mousse

1 recipe	Carob Creme (page 125)
1 envelope	unflavored gelatin (1 tablespoon), dissolved in ¼ cup warm water
3	egg whites, room temperature
	sea salt to taste
¼ teaspoon	cream of tartar
2 teaspoons	fructose
	sesame-seed or safflower oil

While food processor is running with preceding **Carob Creme** recipe, add gelatin dissolved in water. Combine well. Remove to large bowl and refrigerate.

Lightly oil 4-cup souffle dish. For souffle effect, extend height of dish by applying 2″ collar of foil (oil lightly, and attach with tape).

Beat egg whites with dash of sea salt, cream of tartar, and fructose till whites are smooth but stiff. Gently fold whites into mixture, ½ at a time. Pour into mold. Refrigerate 3-4 hours or overnight.

Remove collar, garnish, and serve.

MAKES 8 SMALL PORTIONS. CALORIES PER PORTION: 79

MAKES 4 LARGE PORTIONS. CALORIES PER PORTION: 158

PREPARE 4 HOURS AHEAD

PREPARATION TIME: 20 MINUTES

Pumpkin Custard

1 ¼ cups	pumpkin pulp (fresh or canned)
¼ teaspoon	ground cloves
¼ teaspoon	ground cinnamon
3 tablespoons	honey
1 ½ cups	low fat milk
2	eggs, room temperature
2	egg whites, room temperature
garnish:	mint leaves or berries

Preheat oven to 350°.

In food processor, process pumpkin, cloves, cinnamon, and honey till smooth.

Scald milk. In bowl, beat eggs and egg whites till well combined and frothy. Slowly add milk to egg mixture, whisking well. Add egg mixture to pumpkin mixture in processor; combine well.

Pour into 4 ¾- to 1-cup dishes, or 1 large dish. Bake in bain-marie (pan of water) about 1 hour, till tester comes out clean.

Remove from oven. Place custard on rack. Put plastic wrap or wax paper over top to keep custard moist while cooling.

Garnish. May be served warm, room temperature, or cold.

MAKES 8 SMALL PORTIONS. CALORIES PER PORTION: 75

MAKES 4 LARGE PORTIONS. CALORIES PER PORTION: 151

PREPARATION TIME: 10 MINUTES

BAKING TIME: 1 HOUR

Frozen Pumpkin Dessert

1 cup	pumpkin pulp (fresh or canned)
1 cup	plain low-fat yogurt
¼ cup	fresh orange juice
¼ teaspoon	ground cinnamon
¼ teaspoon	ground cloves
2 tablespoons	honey
garnish:	mint leaves or cranberries

In food processor, blend all ingredients till smooth. Pour into 4 chilled dessert dishes. Freeze about 4 hours, maximum. Dessert mixture should be smooth, and not solid ice.

Garnish and serve.

SERVES 4. CALORIES PER SERVING: 103

PREPARE 4 HOURS AHEAD

PREPARATION TIME: 10 MINUTES

Vanilla Custard

2 cups	skim milk
2	egg yolks
¼ cup	sugar
1 teaspoon	vanilla extract
1	egg white, room temperature

In small pan combine milk, yolks, and sugar. Cook over low fire, stirring occasionally with wooden spoon till mixture thickens. Cool, and add vanilla. Beat egg white. Fold into mixture, and pour into 5 custard cups.

Refrigerate till serving time.

SERVES 5. CALORIES PER SERVING: 108

PREPARATION TIME: 25 MINUTES

Chocolate Souffle

2 ounces	semi-sweet chocolate
½ cup	low-fat milk
	sesame-seed or safflower oil
1½ pounds	ricotta cheese
1 envelope	gelatin (1 tablespoon), dissolved in ¼ cup warm water
½ cup	fructose or 5 tablespoons honey
1 tablespoon	instant decaffeinated coffee
2 tablespoons	Amaretto liqueur
6	egg whites (room temperature)
½ teaspoon	cream of tartar
	sea salt
garnish:	chocolate powder or granules of decaffeinated coffee

In double boiler, dissolve chocolate in milk.

Lightly oil 5-6-cup souffle dish. For souffle effect, extend height of dish by applying 2½ " collar of foil (oil lightly, and attach with tape).

In food processor, puree ricotta till very smooth. Add dissolved gelatin (stir to dissolve — gelatin should be smooth, not grainy) to ricotta, and blend well.

Stir melted chocolate and milk. Add fructose or honey and instant coffee; stir to dissolve. Strain this into ricotta mixture. Puree together till smooth. Add liqueur and blend well. Pour this mixture into bowl and refrigerate. Cool completely.

In bowl, beat egg whites with cream of tartar and pinch of sea salt till stiff but still smooth. With rubber spatula, quickly fold in a quarter of egg whites, and then gently fold in remainder to just combine mixture — do not over-mix. Pour into souffle dish. Refrigerate at least 3-4 hours, or overnight.

Remove collar; garnish, and serve.

SERVES 8. CALORIES PER SERVING: 252

PREPARE 3-4 HOURS AHEAD

PREPARATION TIME: 40 MINUTES

Mango Creme with Ricotta

1	mango, ripe; peeled and seeded
8 ounces	ricotta cheese
1-2 tablespoons	honey (depending upon sweetness of mango)
1 tablespoon	fresh lime juice
1 tablespoon	Grand Marnier orange liqueur (optional)
garnish:	kiwi slices, berries, mint sprigs, or other fresh fruit

Combine all ingredients in food processor till well blended and smooth. Pour into individual dessert dishes. Chill. Garnish and serve.

MAKES 8 SMALL PORTIONS. CALORIES PER PORTION: 84

MAKES 4 LARGE PORTIONS. CALORIES PER PORTION: 168

PREPARATION TIME: 10 MINUTES

Melon Balls Amaretto

½	cantaloupe, medium size
½	honeydew, medium size
½	crenshaw or casaba melon, medium size
4 ounces	Amaretto liqueur

Cut and seed melons. Using melon scooper, form melon balls. Put an assortment of melon balls into 4 dessert glasses. Top each with 1 ounce Amaretto.

SERVES 4. CALORIES PER SERVING: 127

PREPARATION TIME: 20 MINUTES

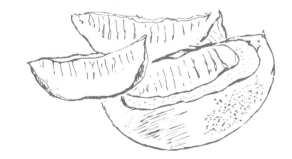

Cantaloupe Sherbet

1	cantaloupe (about 1¾ pound)
1 cup	fresh orange juice
2 tablespoons	honey
2	ice cubes
garnish:	fresh fruit

Halve cantaloupe; scoop out seeds and discard them. Scoop out cantaloupe pulp (not green part). This should amount to about 3 cups.

In blender, puree cantaloupe, orange juice, honey, and ice cubes till smooth.

Pour into mixing bowl. Freeze 3-4 hours; occasionally stir with wire whisk.

This sherbet does not store in freezer more than 12 hours! It will become solid ice.

Serve, garnished, in 4 dessert dishes.

DIRECTIONS FOR ICE-CREAM MACHINE:

If you have a sorbetiere (ice-cream machine), blend cantaloupe, orange juice, and honey in blender till smooth. Put into sorbetiere; pack ice around, and top with rock salt. Let machine rotate about 1 hour to 1 hour and 15 minutes; occasionally, add more ice and rock salt.

Note: For cantaloupe, you may substitute peaches, apricots, or berries. When using berries, reduce orange juice to ½ cup; if desired, add 1 extra tablespoon honey.

SERVES 4. CALORIES PER SERVING (CANTALOUPE OR BERRIES): 96

CALORIES PER SERVING (PEACHES): 133

CALORIES PER SERVING (APRICOTS): 162

PREPARE 4 HOURS AHEAD

PREPARATION TIME: 10 MINUTES

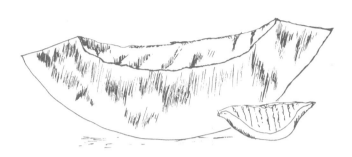

Chilled Melon Soup

3 cups	pulp from ripe cantaloupe or honeydew
1 teaspoon	fructose (or more, to taste)
1 teaspoon	grated lemon rind
½ cup	fresh orange juice
2 tablespoons	fresh lime juice
½ cup	whipping cream
garnish:	mint leaves or berries

Puree till smooth melon pulp, fructose, lemon rind, orange juice, and lime juice. Refrigerate till mixture is ice cold.

This step can be prepared several hours ahead.

Before serving, whip cream to soft peaks. Fold melon mixture into cream. Garnish and serve.

Delightfully refreshing on a hot summer day.

SERVES 4. CALORIES PER SERVING: 167

PREPARATION TIME: 20 MINUTES

Apricot Souffle

12-14 ounces	apricots, fresh, ripe; pitted
1½ tablespoons	honey
¼ cup	apricot nectar or (unfiltered) apple juice
2 tablespoons	fructose
1	egg yolk
1 tablespoon	Triple Sec or Grand Marnier orange liqueur
3	egg whites, room temperature
	sea salt, to taste
¼ teaspoon	cream of tartar

In covered stainless-steel pan, gently simmer apricots, honey, and juice about 5-10 minutes, till apricots are tender. Remove from fire. Cool about 10 minutes.

With slotted spoon, lift apricots out of their liquid; discard liquid. Puree apricots in food processor till smooth. Taste. With 1 - 1½ tablespoons fructose, adjust sweetness of puree, which depends upon ripeness of fruit.

Pour mixture into mixing bowl, and whisk in egg yolk and liqueur. Cool completely. This step can be prepared in advance.

Preheat oven to 350°.

In bowl, beat egg whites, dash of sea salt, ½ tablespoon fructose, and cream of tartar till stiff and smooth. Gently and quickly, fold ½ the mixture into puree, then the remainder.

Pour into 4 1¼-cup souffle dishes. Fill almost to top, piling higher in center.

Place on sheet tray; bake 25 minutes. Serve immediately.

Note: In season, fresh peaches may be substituted for apricots.

SERVES 4. CALORIES PER SERVING: 123

PREPARE AHEAD

PREPARATION TIME: 40 MINUTES

Peppermint-and-Rose-hip Sherbet

4	peppermint tea bags
4	rose-hip tea bags
4 cups	boiling water
1 10¾-ounce can	dietetic peaches (1 cup)
2 tablespoons	crystalized ginger, minced
3 tablespoons	fructose

Steep tea bags in boiling water for 30 minutes.

Cool completely.

Combine all ingredients in a blender, and blend till smooth. Pour into ice-cream machine, and whirl into a smooth sherbet. Serve the same day.

If you do not have an ice-cream machine, pour mixture into bowl and place in freezer 4-6 hours; stir occasionally with a wire whisk till icy.

MAKES 8 SMALL PORTIONS. CALORIES PER PORTION: 28

MAKES 4 LARGE PORTIONS. CALORIES PER PORTION: 56

PREPARATION TIME: 45 MINUTES

Mango Frozen Yogurt

1 cup	plain low-fat yogurt
1 cup	mango pulp (approximately 1 large, ripe mango)
½ cup	fresh orange juice
1 tablespoon	fresh lime juice
2-3 tablespoons	honey
garnish:	kiwi slices, blueberries, or other fresh fruit

Puree all ingredients in blender till very smooth. Pour into 4 8-ounce glasses. Chill in freezer, allowing maximum of 2 hours to set. If more time is needed, refrigerate. Dessert should not crystalize.

Garnish and serve.

Note: This frozen yogurt can be made with a variety of fresh ripe fruit, such as peaches, cantaloupe, honeydew, or pears; also with berries, such as strawberries or raspberries, with 1 extra tablespoon honey, if desired. Berries should not be pureed too fine, for their seeds become tart if pulverized.

SERVES 4. CALORIES PER SERVING: 120

PREPARATION TIME: 10 MINUTES

FREEZING TIME: 1 HOUR

Banana Ice Cream

4	bananas, small and ripe
	fresh lemon juice
1 teaspoon	vanilla extract
½ cup	low-fat milk
garnish:	strawberries, kiwi slices, or other fresh fruit

Peel bananas, cut out tips and brown spots, remove strings. Squeeze lemon juice over bananas. Wrap in plastic bag and freeze till solid.

Chill 4 champagne glasses or bowls.

Near serving time, cut bananas into small pieces. Blend in food processor with vanilla extract and milk till very smooth. If mixture becomes too thick, add more milk.

Pour into 4 chilled glasses or bowls. Return to freezer for not longer than 2 hours.

Garnish and serve.

Note: 12 large strawberries may be added, to give this ice-cream dessert a pink color.

SERVES 4. CALORIES PER SERVING: 95

PREPARE 4 HOURS AHEAD

PREPARATION TIME: 10 MINUTES

Strawberry Ice

6 cups	whole fresh strawberries
3 cups	crushed ice

In blender, puree 2 cups strawberries to 1 cup ice; repeat till all are pureed.

Spoon into 4 dishes; freeze 2-4 hours.

SERVES 4. CALORIES PER SERVING: 90

PREPARATION TIME: 15 MINUTES

Peach with Mango Sauce

2 cups	fresh peaches, sliced in small wedges
1 cup	Mango Lime Paradise (page 123), cooled
1 tablespoon	Grand Marnier orange-flavored liqueur
garnish:	fresh mint leaves

Mix all ingredients with spatula. Pour into 4 chilled wine glasses. Garnish and serve.

Note: Ripe, juicy apricots or nectarines may be substituted for peaches.

SERVES 4. CALORIES PER SERVING: 91

PREPARATION TIME: 15 MINUTES

Pear Souffle

3	pears (about 2 cups), ripe, peeled, cored, and sliced
½ tablespoon	honey
	ground cloves
1 teaspoon	fresh lemon juice
¼ cup	pear or (unfiltered) apple juice
1	egg yolk
1 teaspoon	Pernod liqueur
3	egg whites, room temperature
	sea salt
¼ teaspoon	cream of tartar
½ tablespoon	fructose

In covered stainless-steel pan, gently simmer pears, honey, dash of cloves, lemon juice, and pear juice about 15 minutes, till pears are tender. Remove from fire. Cool about 10 minutes.

With slotted spoon, lift pears out of their liquid; discard liquid. Puree pears in food processor till smooth. Pour into mixing bowl. Cool. Whisk in egg yolk and liqueur. Cool completely. This step can be prepared in advance.

Preheat oven to 350°.

In bowl, beat egg whites, pinch of sea salt, tartar, and fructose till stiff and smooth. Gently and quickly, fold ½ the mixture into puree, then the remainder.

Pour into 4 1¼-cup souffle dishes. Fill almost to top, piling higher in center.

Place on sheet tray; bake 25 minutes. Serve immediately.

SERVES 4. CALORIES PER SERVING: 131

PREPARATION TIME: 30 MINUTES

BAKING TIME: 25 MINUTES

Pear Flan

2	pears, ripe; peeled, cored, and diced
4 teaspoons	sun-dried raisins
¼ teaspoon	ground cloves
½ cup	pear or unfiltered apple juice
2 teaspoons	fresh lemon juice
	Pernod liqueur or sweet Sherry wine, to taste
2	eggs, room temperature
2	egg whites, room temperature
1 teaspoon	vanilla extract
1 cup	low-fat milk
1 tablespoon	honey
	ground nutmeg, to taste

Preheat oven to 350°.

For about 10 minutes, gently cook, covered, the pears, raisins, cloves, lemon juice, and pear juice.

Divide cooked pears and their juice into 4 1¼-cup baking dishes. Put dash of Pernod or Sherry in each cup.

In bowl, beat eggs and egg whites with vanilla extract. Scald milk with honey. Beat hot milk into egg mixture. Strain this mixture, and pour over pears.

Sprinkle pears with dash of nutmeg, and bake in bain-marie (pan of water) about 45 minutes to 1 hour, till done.

Immediately remove cups from water. Place on rack, and put wax paper or plastic wrap over tops to keep flan moist while cooling. When flan is at room temperature, refrigerate.

May be served warm, room temperature, or cold.

SERVES 4. CALORIES PER SERVING: 186

PREPARATION TIME: 15 MINUTES

BAKING TIME: 45 MINUTES

Tofu Cheesecake

4 ounces	whole-wheat honey-graham crackers
2 tablespoons	corn-oil margarine
1¼ cups	pineapple juice
1½-2 tablespoons	agar-agar
1 pound	tofu
5½ tablespoons	honey
6 tablespoons	fresh lemon juice
1 tablespoon	lemon peel, grated
1 teaspoon	candied ginger, minced

Preheat oven to 350⁰.

Finely crumble graham crackers with margarine, in food processor. Lightly grease 9″ pie plate with margarine, and evenly spread crumbs on it by hand. Press another 9″ pie plate into crumbs till surface is smooth.

Bake 10 minutes. Cool.

Heat pineapple juice to near-boil, add agar-agar, and whisk well. Simmer 5 minutes to dissolve agar-agar. Cool 5 minutes.

In blender, combine tofu, honey, lemon juice, lemon peel, candied ginger, and pineapple juice; blend up to 1 minute, till smooth and creamy.

Gently pour mixture into baked crust. Refrigerate 3-4 hours.

Garnish and serve.

SERVES 8. CALORIES PER SERVING: 190
PREPARATION TIME: 40 MINUTES

Glazed Pineapple

3 cups	fresh pineapple, cubed
2 tablespoons	brown sugar
3 tablespoons	dark rum

In medium-sized bowl, mix pineapple and brown sugar. Leave at room temperature 30 minutes. Then mix thoroughly with rum and spoon into 4 dessert glasses. Refrigerate till serving time.

SERVES 4. CALORIES PER SERVING: 100
PREPARATION TIME: 10 MINUTES

Cold Lemon Souffle

½ pint	whipping cream (1 cup)
3	egg yolks
1 cup	fresh lemon juice
¼ cup	honey
⅓ cup	fructose
3 envelopes	unflavored gelatin, dissolved in ⅔ cup hot water
1 tablespoon	lemon peel, grated
1 tablespoon	Grand Marnier liqueur
4	egg whites, room temperature
¼ teaspoon	cream of tartar
⅛ teaspoon	iodized sea salt
garnish:	lemon peel or other fresh fruit

Lightly oil 5-6 cup souffle dish. Make 2½″ collar with foil and oil lightly. Secure collar to dish with tape.

Whip cream to soft peaks and refrigerate.

In double boiler over fire, beat with wire whisk till thick and frothy the egg yolks, lemon juice, honey, and ½ fructose. Do not bring mixture to boil, or eggs will scramble.

Remove from fire and gradually whisk in dissolved gelatin and grated lemon peel. Place mixture over ice and beat till it cools and starts to thicken, about 5 to 10 minutes. As mixture begins to jell, whisk to keep smooth. Add Grand Marnier.

Beat egg whites with cream of tartar, salt, and remainder of fructose till they form soft peaks. With rubber spatula, gently fold whites and whipped cream into mixture.

Pour into prepared souffle dish and refrigerate 2-3 hours. Carefully remove collar and garnish. Serve at once.

SERVES 8. CALORIES PER SERVING: 212
PREPARATION TIME: 1 HOUR 15 MINUTES

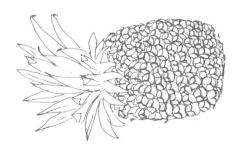

BEVERAGES

There is something so very gracious about a refreshing beverage served in a chilled crystal glass.

A refreshment break gives you a chance to pause, change your breathing pattern, savor a pleasurable moment, and give your blood sugar a boost. Such breaks are part of the 'Golden Door's daily schedule.

Nature lets us experience thirst so that we will be motivated to maintain the body's water balance. She does not favor our having a cola balance. Your body is 70% water, and you owe it a supply of pure water as well as pure air and food.

Unfortunately, the prevalence of bottled soft drinks (why "soft?" with all their chemicals and sugar, they can't feel soft to an empty stomach) has perverted the custom of the refreshment break. All such drinks contain an appalling total of calories; their so-called low-calorie spinoffs harbor even more hidden salt than is found in the non-diet variety.

Hidden salt has become the new buzz-word phrase. Good! Be aware of it, particularly when shopping for soda water for some of the following recipes.

Spiced-Apple-and-Camomile Tea

2 cups	camomile tea (double strength), cooled
	honey to taste, or 1 teaspoon fructose
⅛ teaspoon	ground cinnamon
⅛ teaspoon	ground ginger
⅛ teaspoon	ground cloves
1 to 1½ cups	apple juice (unfiltered)
garnish:	thin apple slices

Dissolve honey or fructose in cooling camomile tea. Add spices and mix well. Gradually pour in apple juice. Refrigerate till cold.

Serve over ice in 4 tall glasses. Garnish.

SERVES 4. CALORIES PER SERVING: 52
PREPARATION TIME: 5 MINUTES

Citrus Cooler

⅓ cup	fresh lemon juice
½ cup	water
	honey to taste, or 2 teaspoons fructose
3 cups	fresh orange juice
	crushed ice
garnish:	orange wedges and mint sprigs

Combine lemon juice and water. Stir in honey or fructose. Add orange juice. Pour over crushed ice in 4 tall glasses. Garnish.

SERVES 4. CALORIES PER SERVING: 102
PREPARATION TIME: 5 MINUTES

Iced Pink-Mint Tea with Lemonade

2 cups	pink-mint or pink-lemon tea (double strength)
¼ cup	fresh lemon juice
2 cups	water
	crushed ice
2-3 teaspoons	fructose or honey (optional)
garnish:	lemon wedges and mint sprigs

Cool tea. Add lemon juice and water. Stir to mix well. Pour over crushed ice in 4 tall glasses. Add fructose or honey, if desired, and mix well. Garnish.

SERVES 4. CALORIES PER SERVING: 12

PREPARATION TIME: 5 MINUTES

Hot Spiced Tea

6 cups	water
5 tea bags	orange-spice flavor
1	cinnamon stick
3	cloves
1	orange, sliced
2 tablespoons	honey

In large pot, bring water to boil. Add tea bags, cinnamon, cloves, and orange slices. Steep 10 minutes. Strain into teapot or pitcher. Add honey. Stir well and serve piping hot.

SERVES 4. CALORIES PER SERVING: 49

PREPARATION TIME: 15 MINUTES

Festive Fruit Punch

10 ounces	frozen strawberries (1 box), thawed
10 ounces	frozen raspberries (1 box), thawed
2 cups	pineapple, fresh or frozen; diced
2 ounces	brandy
2 tablespoons	fresh lemon or lime juice
1 fifth	Sauterne wine
1 23-ounce-bottle	soda water
1 fifth	Champagne
	crushed ice

Combine fruits with brandy, lemon juice, and Sauterne. Refrigerate 3-4 hours.

Just before serving, add soda water and Champagne. Add ice and serve.

SERVES 20-25. CALORIES PER SERVING: 76

PREPARATION TIME: 5 MINUTES

Spritzer

1 cup	Burgundy wine
3 tablespoons	frozen orange-juice concentrate, thawed
3 teaspoons	fresh lime juice
1½ cups	soda water
3 teaspoons	fructose
	crushed ice
garnish:	4 lime slices

Combine all ingredients. Pour over ice in 4 tall glasses. Garnish and serve.

SERVES 4. CALORIES PER SERVING: 119

PREPARATION TIME: 5 MINUTES

Sauterne Spritzer

1 cup	Sauterne wine
1 cup	cranberry juice, sugar-free
1 cup	soda water
3 tablespoons	frozen orange-juice concentrate, thawed
	crushed ice
garnish:	4 orange slices

Combine all ingredients. Pour over ice in 4 tall glasses. Garnish and serve.

SERVES 4. CALORIES PER SERVING: 113

PREPARATION TIME: 5 MINUTES

Grape Spritzer

1½ cups	grape juice
1½ cups	soda water
	crushed ice
garnish:	lime quarters

Combine all ingredients. Pour over ice in 4 tall glasses. Garnish and serve.

SERVES 4. CALORIES PER SERVING: 50

PREPARATION TIME: 5 MINUTES

Anisette Spritzer

1 cup	soda water
1 cup	Chablis wine
1 cup	pear juice or nectar
3 tablespoons	Anisette liqueur
garnish:	mint sprigs

Combine all ingredients. Pour over ice in 4 tall glasses. Garnish and serve.

SERVES 4. CALORIES PER SERVING: 180

PREPARATION TIME: 5 MINUTES

Chablis-Cassis Spritzer

1 cup	Chablis wine
1½ cups	soda water
6 tablespoons	Creme de Cassis liqueur
	crushed ice
garnish:	strawberries

Combine all ingredients. Pour over ice in 4 tall glasses. Garnish and serve.

SERVES 4. CALORIES PER SERVING: 180

PREPARATION TIME: 5 MINUTES

Pineapple Cooler

1½ cups	fresh pineapple
1 cup	apple juice (unfiltered)
1 cup	crushed ice
garnish:	pineapple slices and mint sprigs

Mix all ingredients in blender till smooth. Pour into 4 4-ounce glasses. Garnish and serve.

SERVES 4. CALORIES PER SERVING: 56

PREPARATION TIME: 5 MINUTES

Pineapple-Coconut Frappe

(PINA COLADA)

1 cup	fresh pineapple, diced
1½ cups	pineapple/coconut juice
1 cup	crushed ice
garnish:	pineapple wedges and mint sprigs

Mix all ingredients in blender till smooth. Pour into 4 4-ounce glasses. Garnish and serve.

CALORIES PER SERVING: 67

PREPARATION TIME: 5 MINUTES

Raspberry Frappe

1 cup	raspberries, fresh or sugarless frozen
1½ cups	fresh orange juice
¼ teaspoon	fructose
1 cup	crushed ice
garnish:	fruit slices, mint or raspberry leaves

Mix all ingredients in blender till smooth. Pour into 4 4-ounce glasses. Garnish and serve.

SERVES 4. CALORIES PER SERVING: 68

PREPARATION TIME: 5 MINUTES

Orange-Melon Frappe

1½ cups	fresh orange juice
1½ cups	melon
¼ teaspoon	fructose
1 cup	crushed ice
garnish:	orange slices

Mix all ingredients in blender till smooth. Pour into 4 4-ounce glasses. Garnish and serve.

SERVES 4. CALORIES PER SERVING: 61

PREPARATION TIME: 5 MINUTES

Sangria Soleil

1 ½ cups	fresh cranberry juice
2 tablespoons	fresh lime juice
2 cups	rose wine (chilled)
3 tablespoons	fructose
2 cups	soda water
garnish:	4 orange slices, twisted, or 4 thin pear slices cut lengthwise; mint sprigs

Combine all ingredients in pitcher. Pour over ice in 4 tall glasses.

Garnish and serve.

SERVES 4. CALORIES PER SERVING: 118

PREPARATION TIME: 5 MINUTES

Apple-Lime Cooler

3 cups	unfiltered apple juice
1 6-ounce can	frozen lime concentrate, thawed
½ teaspoon	ground cloves
2 cups	soda water
4 teaspoons	Grenadine
garnish:	thin lime slices

Combine all ingredients in pitcher except Grenadine. Pour over crushed ice in 4 tall glasses. To each glass, add 1 teaspoon Grenadine. Garnish and serve.

SERVES 4. CALORIES PER SERVING: 132

PREPARATION TIME: 5 MINUTES

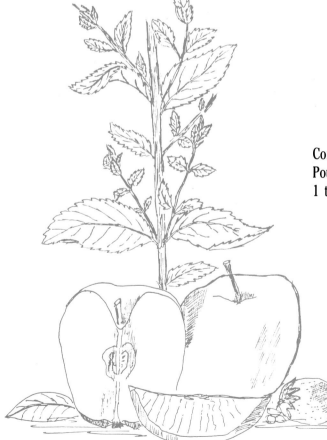

THE VIRTUE-MAKING DAY

This diet makes you feel so virtuous, so aware of your body and the fantastic beauty of its functioning.

Designed to clarify one's thinking and to cleanse one's system, the Virtue-Making Day is much loved by 'Golden Door' guests.

8:00 a.m. Grapefruit juice — 1 cup freshly squeezed juice combined with ½ cup spring water

(CALORIES PER SERVING: 60)

10:30 a.m. Almond milk — 12 almonds (freshly blanched and peeled), ¾ cup water, 3 ice cubes, and dash of vanilla extract combined in blender and liquefied till smooth. Add sprinkle of grated nutmeg.

(CALORIES PER SERVING: 86)

1:00 p.m. Gazpacho — 1 medium-size fresh tomato (peeled and chunked), ¼ large bell pepper (seeded and chunked), 2 parsley sprigs, 2 onion slices (chunked), ¼ celery stalk (chunked), and ¼ cup **Potassium Broth** (page 143) or V-8 vegetable juice combined in blender; work quickly with the pulse. Mixture should be chunky. Add ¼ large cucumber (grated).
On side, serve ⅓ ounce raw sunflower seeds.

(CALORIES PER SERVING — JUICE: 34
— SEEDS: 27)

4:00 p.m. Pineapple-cucumber juice — ¼ cup cucumber (peeled and chunked), ½ cup fresh pineapple (chunked), 2 parsley sprigs, ½ cup unfiltered apple juice, and 2 ice cubes combined in blender and liquefied.
On side, serve ⅓ ounce raw sunflower seeds.

(CALORIES PER SERVING — JUICE: 50
— SEEDS: 27)

7:00 p.m. Almond milk — <u>See at left.</u>

9:30 p.m. Carrot-apple juice — ½ cup unfiltered apple juice, ½ cup fresh carrot juice*, ½ small apple, and 2 ice cubes combined in blender and liquefied.
On side, serve ⅓ ounce raw sunflower seeds.

(CALORIES PER SERVING — JUICE: 65
— SEEDS: 27)

*To make carrot juice, liquefy ½ cup grated carrot with ½ cup water; press through a sieve.

NOTE: All liquid consumed through the day should be healthful. For example, supplement the diet with fresh lemonade, herb teas, spring water, etc. No coffee or tea.

SERVES 2. TOTAL CALORIES PER DAY — JUICE: 379
— SEEDS: <u>81</u>
460

Vegetable Soup for Liquid Diet

8 cups	Vegetable Stock (page 47) or water
1 cup	broccoli, cut into 1″ pieces
1	leek (or onion), cut into 1″ pieces
4	celery stalks, cut into 1″ pieces
1	zucchini, cut into 1″ pieces
1	carrot, cut into 1″ pieces
1 teaspoon	dried sweet basil
½ teaspoon	vegetable seasoning
garnish:	8 teaspoons sesame seeds, freshly toasted

Place all ingredients in a pot. Simmer gently, uncovered, 35 minutes, or till vegetables are tender.

Blend till smooth.

Serve piping hot, garnished with sesame seeds.

SERVES 4. CALORIES PER SERVING: 60

PREPARATION TIME: 45 MINUTES

Clear Potassium Broth

8 cups	water
4	celery stalks
8	parsley sprigs
1	carrot
1	onion (or leek)
1 teaspoon	natural kelp, granulated
1	parsnip
	sea salt, to taste (optional)

Place all ingredients in a pot. Simmer gently, uncovered, 1 hour, reducing to 5 cups.

Strain, and drink hot.

SERVES 4. CALORIES PER SERVING: 42

PREPARATION TIME: 1 HOUR 10 MINUTES

Potassium Broth

Vigorous physical exercise, particularly during warm summer months, depletes the body's potassium. A daily serving of the 'Golden Door' special Potassium Broth, made from vitamin- and mineral-rich vegetable trimmings in a tomato-puree base, provides an excellent means of maintaining potassium balance:

3 cups	vegetable trimmings (celery, carrot, parsley, zucchini, mushrooms, lettuce, spinach, etc.)
8-10	fresh tomatoes, liquefied in blender
1	onion, diced
½ teaspoon	ground sweet basil
2	bay leaves
1	garlic bud (separate cloves)
2 cups	liquid from steamed vegetables (if available), or water

Place all ingredients in stockpot; boil 20 minutes.

Strain through sieve or colander, and serve hot or cold.

If desired, next day reheat broth with fresh vegetable trimmings.

SERVES 8. CALORIES PER SERVING: 35

PREPARATION TIME: 35 MINUTES

GOLDEN DOOR MENUS

4 weeks of dinner menus for the busy cook, with the 4th and final week totally vegetarian

(a health secret we commend to you)

GOLDEN DOOR MENUS

	SUNDAY	MONDAY	TUESDAY
Hors d'Oeuvres	Seafood Hors d'Oeuvres with Sauce Raifort		Crudites for Hors d'Oeuvres with Sauce Celeriac
Soup	Vegetable Stock	Basil Soup	Vichysoisse
Salad	Two-Cabbage Slaw	Romaine and Blue Cheese	Belgian Endive
Entree	Almond Chicken	Greek Shrimp	Veal Roast
Vegetable	Tofu Cutlets with Oriental Vegetables	¾ cup cooked whole-wheat pasta	Green Beans Summer Savory
Bread			
Dessert	Carob Creme	Pears in Burgundy Wine Cassis	Strawberry Strawberries
Total Calorie Value	747	648	635

Week Number One

WEDNESDAY	THURSDAY	FRIDAY	SATURDAY
Corn Chowder	Chinese Vegetable Soup	Hot and Sour Chicken Soup	Minestrone Soup
Parsley-Carrot	Green Salad with Onion and Orange	Watercress Salad	Sprout Salad
Broccoli/Broccoli	Sesame Chicken Breast with Ginger	Sea Bass Romaine	Curried Leg of Lamb
Tomato Parmesan	Corn with Mint	Couscous	Barley Pilaf
1 slice Tecate Bread		2 sesame crackers	
Pumpkin Custard	Cold Lemon Souffle	Hot Bananas and Blueberries	Apricot Mousse
710	710	787	629

GOLDEN DOOR MENUS

	SUNDAY	MONDAY	TUESDAY
Hors d'Oeuvres	Stuffed Mushrooms Florentine		
Soup	Cold Cucumber Soup	Broccoli Soup with Sesame Seeds	Egg Soup
Salad	Grated-Beet Salad	Apple-Mushroom Salad	Tabbouleh
Entree	Lentil-Spinach Loaf	Golden Door Breast of Chicken	Baked Dill Salmon
Vegetable	Curried Carrots	Acorn Squash	Brussel Sprouts w/Sesame Seeds
Bread		2 garlic-bread sticks	
Dessert	Mocha Mousse	Banana Ice Cream	Strawberry Ice
Total Calorie Value	627	739	639

Week Number Two

WEDNESDAY	THURSDAY	FRIDAY	SATURDAY
	Oysters Rockefeller		Eggplant "Caviar"
Hot and Sour Shrimp Soup		Broth from Pot au Feu	Grapefruit Gazpacho
Cucumber Salad Nippon	Hearts of Palm Vinaigrette	Spinach Salad Mimosa	butter lettuce with Ginger Dressing
Veal Scallopini	Chicken Ratatouille	Pot au Feu	Yoshe Nabe
Stuffed Potato	Zucchini Saute		Brown Rice
		Persimmon-Walnut Whole-Wheat Bread	
Melon Balls Amaretto	Vanilla Custard	Kiwi on Snow	Baked Apples
679	739	682	590

GOLDEN DOOR MENUS

	SUNDAY	MONDAY	TUESDAY
Hors d'Oeuvres			
Soup	Chilled Lemon Soup	Vegetable Stock with Onions	Clam Vichysoisse
Salad	Tomato Oregano	Caesar Salad	Garden Salad
Entree	2 Broiled Lamb Chops	Vegetables with Pasta	Curried Chicken Breast
Vegetable	Carrots Vichy and Parsnip Whip		Steamed Onions and Spinach
Bread			
Dessert	Glazed Pineapple	Mango Creme with Ricotta	Pear Souffle
Total Calorie Value	788	536	766

Week Number Three

WEDNESDAY	THURSDAY	FRIDAY	SATURDAY
Mushroom Guacamole	Seafood Hors d'Oeuvres with Yogurt-Dill Sauce		Fresh tender raw asparagus on jicama sticks with 2 tbsp Sauce Madras
Chicken Broth	Cream of Asparagus Soup	Chinese Pea Pod Soup	
Tossed Salad w/Vegetarian Dressing Delight	Garden Salad	Green Bean-Tomato Salad	Celery-Root-and-Apple Salad
Fillet of Sole California Style, w/Grapes	Veal Roulade	Foil-Wrapped Baked Chicken	San Francisco Cioppino
Artichokes w/ Puree of Leeks		Baked Potato Romanoff	
1 slice Tecate Bread			2 whole-wheat crackers
Carob Mousse	Tofu Cheesecake	Cantaloupe Sherbet	Chocolate Souffle
588	747	666	685

GOLDEN DOOR MENUS

	SUNDAY	MONDAY	TUESDAY
Soup	Spinach-Pear Soup		Gazpacho
Salad	Leek Salad	Greek Salad	California-Style Salad
Entree	Asparagus Omelette	Eggplant Parmigiana	Tecate Tostadas
Vegetable	Yasai Itame (Stir-Fried Vegetables and Tofu)	Steamed Millet and Herbs	Vegetable Melange
Bread	2 rye thins		
Dessert	Peach Sherbet*	Blueberry Frozen Yogurt**	Peppermint-and-Rose-Hip Sherbet
Total Calorie Value	627	747	782

* see Cantaloupe Sherbet
** see Mango Frozen Yogurt

Week Number Four

WEDNESDAY	THURSDAY	FRIDAY	SATURDAY
Fresh Watercress Soup	Peanut Butter Soup	Miso Soup	Lima Bean Soup
Jerusalem Artichoke Salad	Yogurt Salad	Lifeline Salad	Leaf Salad
Zucchini-Spinach Frittata	Vegetable Pate	Herbed Vegetable Rice with braised tofu	Onion-Tomato Pie
Cheese Blintzes			Walnut-Stuffed Cabbage
	2 sesame-seed sticks	Bran-Nut Muffins	
Fresh Fruit Macedoine	Frozen Pumpkin Dessert	Apricot Creme	Mango-Lime Paradise
750	633	691	748

Index

A Permanent Diary of My Favorites

Name of Recipe	Cookbook	Page No.

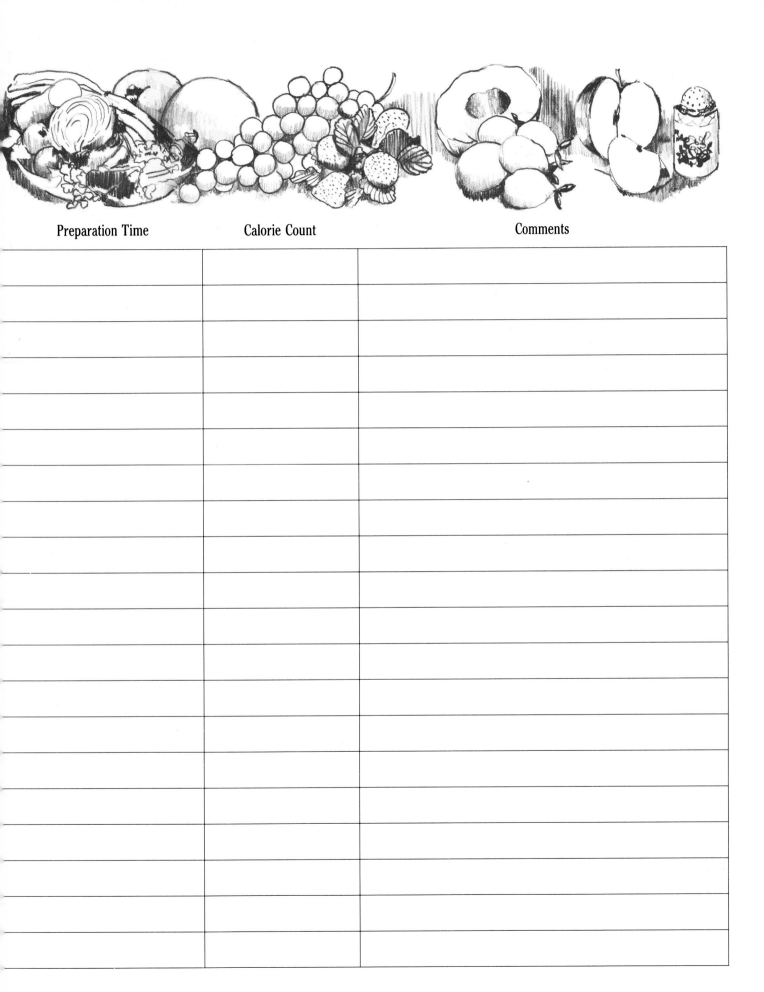

Preparation Time	Calorie Count	Comments

A Permanent Diary of My Favorites

Name of Recipe	Cookbook	Page No.

Preparation Time	Calorie Count	Comments

Conversion Chart

Substitutes to use in Baking

1 C white flour = 1 C unbleached white flour
    1 C fine whole wheat flour
    1 C pastry whole wheat flour
    ⅞ C stone ground whole wheat flour
    ⅞ C rice flour
    ⅝ C potato flour
    1½ C rye flour
    1½ C ground rolled oats

1 T fat (shortening) = 1 T oil
    2 T fat = 1½ T oil
    4 T fat = 3 T oil
    ⅓ C fat = 4 T oil
    ½ C fat = 6 T oil
    ¾ C fat = ⅔ C plus 1 T oil
    1 C fat = ½ C plus 2 T oil
    2 C fat = 1½ C oil

Adjustments in recipes usually involve using more liquid and less shortening when baking with whole grains.

    1 cake yeast = 1 T dry, granular yeast
½ t baking powder = 1 egg (for baking powder, soda substitution, experiment with more eggs added to a recipe or use yeast as leavening)
1 C bread crumbs = 1 C whole wheat bread or ½ C whole wheat bread crumbs and ½ C wheat germ

1 square bitter chocolate = 3 T carob powder plus 1 T dry milk powder or 2 T fresh milk or water

1 square semi-sweet chocolate = 4 T carob, 4 t honey
sweet chocolate = combine equal amounts of carob and date sugar, add vanilla and milk

1 C milk = 1 C soy milk
    1 C fruit juice
    1 C coconut milk (used in sauces and puddings)
    1 C coconut water

1 C sour milk or buttermilk = 1 C milk, plus 1 T lemon juice (let stand 10 minutes)
    1 C yogurt

1 C sugar = 1 C date sugar
    ¾ C maple syrup (reduce liquid 2 T)
    ¾ C honey or 1 C honey and reduce liquid ¼ C

(When using honey in a batter, mix the liquid ingredients before combining. Honey has almost twice the sweetness, that is, flavor of sugar. Use light colored honey in baking. Honey in cake, cookies, bread dough gives a chewy texture, browner color, better keeping qualities.)

salt = equal amounts of a vegetable salt or sea salt (used in bread baking).
    sesame salt (8 parts raw sesame seeds, 1 part sea salt—brown seeds, grind, mix with salt)
    powdered kelp
    Tamari style soy sauce

½ t dried or crushed herbs or spices = ⅓ t powdered
    1 T fresh chopped

⅛ t powdered ginger = 1 T raw
1 t lemon juice = ½ t vinegar
1 T coffee = 1 T coffee substitute (made from a variety of cereals, grains, chicory, figs, barley)
1 C butter = ⅞ C nut or vegetable oil
1 T margarine = 1 T butter
    1 T vegetable oil
    1½ t butter & 1½ t vegetable oil

Honey—1 cup equals 1¼ cups sugar. For baking, also decrease liquid in recipe by ¼ cup. If there is no liquid in recipe, add ¼ cup flour. Unless sour cream or sour milk is used in recipe, add a pinch of baking soda.

Molasses—1 cup unsulphured molasses equals ¾ cup sugar. In baking decrease liquid by ¼ cup for each cup of molasses, omit any baking powder and add ½ teaspoon baking soda.

Raisins—½ cup equals ½ cup cut, plumped, pitted prunes or dates.

Sour Cream—½ cup equals 3 tablespoons butter plus ⅞ cup buttermilk or yogurt.

Sour Cream—For dips, 1 cup equals 1 cup cottage cheese pureed with ¼ cup yogurt or buttermilk, or 6 ounces cream cheese plus enough milk to make 1 cup.

Sour Milk—1 cup: Place 1 tablespoon lemon juice or distilled white vinegar in the bottom of a measuring cup. Add enough milk to make 1 cup. Stir and let mixture clabber, about 10 minutes.

Onions without tears—Cut the root end of the onion off last.—Peel under cold running water. —Periodically rinse hands under cold water while chopping.

GOLDEN DOOR COOKBOOK

Order Forms

Price per copy $24.75
California residents add 6% sales tax.

━━━━━━━━━━━━━━━━━━━━━━━━━━ **ORDER FORM** ━━━━━━━━━━━━━━━━━━━━━━━━━━

Please send _____ copies of the Golden Door Cookbook to:

Name _____

Address _____

City _____ State _____ Zip _____

Enclosed is my check ☐   money order ☐   in the amount of $_____, made payable to
GOLDEN DOOR, P.O. Box 1567, Escondido, CA 92025

━━━━━━━━━━━━━━━━━━━━━━━━━━ **ORDER FORM** ━━━━━━━━━━━━━━━━━━━━━━━━━━

Please send _____ copies of the Golden Door Cookbook to:

Name _____

Address _____

City _____ State _____ Zip _____

Enclosed is my check ☐   money order ☐   in the amount of $_____, made payable to
GOLDEN DOOR, P.O. Box 1567, Escondido, CA 92025

━━━━━━━━━━━━━━━━━━━━━━━━━━ **ORDER FORM** ━━━━━━━━━━━━━━━━━━━━━━━━━━

Please send _____ copies of the Golden Door Cookbook to:

Name _____

Address _____

City _____ State _____ Zip _____

Enclosed is my check ☐   money order ☐   in the amount of $_____, made payable to
GOLDEN DOOR, P.O. Box 1567, Escondido, CA 92025

GOLDEN DOOR COOKBOOK

Order Forms

Price per copy $24.75
California residents add 6% sales tax.

━━━━━━━━━━━━━━ ORDER FORM ━━━━━━━━━━━━━━

Please send _____ copies of the Golden Door Cookbook to:

Name _____

Address _____

City _____ State _____ Zip _____

Enclosed is my check ☐ money order ☐ in the amount of $_____, made payable to
GOLDEN DOOR, P.O. Box 1567, Escondido, CA 92025

━━━━━━━━━━━━━━ ORDER FORM ━━━━━━━━━━━━━━

Please send _____ copies of the Golden Door Cookbook to:

Name _____

Address _____

City _____ State _____ Zip _____

Enclosed is my check ☐ money order ☐ in the amount of $_____, made payable to
GOLDEN DOOR, P.O. Box 1567, Escondido, CA 92025

━━━━━━━━━━━━━━ ORDER FORM ━━━━━━━━━━━━━━

Please send _____ copies of the Golden Door Cookbook to:

Name _____

Address _____

City _____ State _____ Zip _____

Enclosed is my check ☐ money order ☐ in the amount of $_____, made payable to
GOLDEN DOOR, P.O. Box 1567, Escondido, CA 92025